Statistics in Education

Statistics in Education

C. NASEEMA

SHIPRA

Rs. 1200; US$ 60.00

ISBN: 978-93-86262-47-9

First Published in 2017

Statistics in Education

Published by:

SHIPRA PUBLICATIONS
LG 18-19, Pankaj Central Market,
I.P. Ext., Patparganj, Delhi 110092, India
Ph.: +91 11 22235152/6152
Email: info@shiprapublication.com
Website: www.shiprapublication.com

Dedicated to Baba

Foreword

A special characteristic of today's era observed in the form of knowledge-society is considered as and understood to be the process of scientific inquiry, and its basic premise is contained in the process of knowledge building. It is evident that finding the basic goal of university education has been attempted only in the creation of knowledge. This is the reason why research or exploration came to emerge as a fundamental dimension of the university education. Often the main aim of all the departments of every university comes to be fixed only at the research process. Several approaches were developed in the context with reference to the various dimensions of the research process; however, a specific trend emerged in all of them. This tendency got ingrained in the research process in the form of using statistics in terms of factuality or objectivity in the process.

From this point of view, the use of statistics in research has become an important basic dimension and instrument of research students. But even though it is based on the most common mathematical formulas, statistics has emerged as a difficult subject for the students, especially those related to Applied and Social Sciences. As a part of social science, education is a rapidly developing discipline wherein statistics has begun to be used abundantly. In this context, the importance of this book *Statistics in Education*, by Professor C.Naseema, an accomplished education expert at Calicut University, pertaining to Statistics, can be understood as a solution to the needs and problems of those students.

The style of the present book provides students of statistics, especially the initial level students, with an understanding and finding solutions of their problems. Different types of examples and diagrams provided not only make the book interesting, but also strengthen the sense of learning.

The writing of this book by Prof. C. Naseema reveals her understanding of students and the creative art skills of gauging the depth of the students' needs.

I dedicate my whole hearted, heartfelt good wishes for her dynamic going on and keeping educational world well, flowered and fragrant, and request her to accept them all.

Good wishes

June 7, 2017

Dr Chand Kiran Saluja
Director
Sanskrit Promotion Foundation
Doriwalan
New Delhi-110006

Preface

The objective of this book on Statistics in Education is to introduce to students and researchers in psychology and education the concepts and applications of statistics. Standard books on the subject of statistics are available and many areas have been covered in those books. But this book covers the content with a simpler style and approach, based on the experience of classroom interaction with post-graduates and research scholars in Education. Emphasis is placed on the analysis and interpretation of data obtained from research. Students from other branches of Behavioural and Social Sciences may also find the book useful.

The writing of this type of book demands numerous compromises between a logical arrangement of material, sound pedagogy and common usage which are not always compatible. The text develops an understanding of statistical logic and procedures, the properties of statistical devices, and the significance of assumptions underlying statistical tools among the students.

Some changes, both sequential and trivial, have been made in this book. This book has been benefited greatly from many helpful criticisms offered by individuals from the field of Social Sciences. The book is appropriate for students at different levels of sophistication, and it is accessible to those with a limited mathematical background.

I hope that the topics dealt in different chapters will help to eliminate the current gap between the researchers and practitioners in education. The topics covered are organized approximately in a sequence which a student will find useful as one works through a project. I hope that readers will find it useful for their post graduate project work and further research in Education and other Social Science Disciplines.

C. Naseema

Contents

1

Statistics in Education

1.1 INTRODUCTION

Think for a moment of the thousands of complex tasks you perform each and every day and stand in awe at the marvel you represent. You are absolutely unique. No one else possesses your physical features, your intelligence, your personality, or your values. What is perhaps even more impressive is that your ensuing actions reveal a wisdom that is statistically correct on most occasions. In short, you are a finely tuned and enormously sophisticated decision making statistical instrument.

In daily living, our statistical functioning is usually informal and loosely structured. We behave statistically, even though we may be only vaguely aware of the formal laws of probability. This section will help you learn about collecting and analyzing data. As you will see, the data for behavioural scientists are the numbers and measurements collected as a result of making careful and systematic observations. In addition, it helps you learn how to make decisions or inferences based on careful analysis of the data.

There are a variety of reasons why you should learn statistics. First, not only you currently encounter statistics in your daily activities, but throughout your life. You have been and will continue to be affected by the results of research and statistical analyses. Which college or institution you attended is based on some test scores developed by psychologists. You may also have to take a personality or intelligence test to get a job. The choices of drugs and medicines available to you are based on medical research and statistical analyses. If you have children, their education may be affected by their scores on achievement or aptitude tests. Learning about statistics will help you become a more informed and aware consumer of research and statistical analyses that affect many aspects of your life.

A second reason for learning statistics is that you may be asked or required to read and interpret the results of statistical analyses. Many college courses require students to read articles in academic research journals. Evaluating published research is complicated by the fact that the different people studying the same topic may come up with diverse or even opposite conclusions. Understanding statistics and their role in the research process will help you to decide whether conclusions drawn in research articles are appropriate and justified.

Another reason for learning statistics is that it will be of use to you in your own research. College courses sometimes make students design and conduct mini-research studies; undergraduate majors might require or encourage students to do senior level theses; graduate research programmes often require master's level theses and doctoral dissertations. Learning to collect and analyze data for such assignments will help you address your own questions in an objective, systematic manner.

You have been calculating arithmetic means almost all of your life – Whether you have to find the average of your test scores in a subject or calculate the batting average of your favourite player of the women's or men's cricket team. You may need statistics. There is no reason to fear statistics. Much of what you will be learning to do, you are already doing in an informal manner in routine life.

Definition: ***Statistics is a branch of scientific methodology which deals with the collection, classification, description and interpretation of data by the conduct of surveys and experiments.*** Its purpose is to describe and draw inferences about the numerical properties of population. Population means a group or aggregate of any kind.

1.2 STAGES OF THE RESEARCH PROCESS

Much of scientific research involves asking questions. Let us examine how contemporary researchers have asked and attempted to answer a broad range of questions regarding human attitudes and behaviour. Some research questions are presented below:

- Is student's achievement is influenced by their learning performance or achievement motivation?
- Is over use of social media influence the learning in adolescents?

You could base your answers on your personal beliefs, or you could adopt the answers given to you by others. But, rather than relying on subjective beliefs and feelings, researchers test their ideas using science and the scientific method. The scientific method is a method of investigation that uses the objective and systematic collection and analysis of empirical data to test theories and hypotheses.

In general, the scientific method consists of six main steps:

1. Identifying a problem.
2. Developing research hypotheses to be tested.
3. Collecting data.
4. Analyzing the data.
5. Drawing conclusion regarding the research hypotheses, and
6. Communicating the findings of the study.

The following diagram explain the steps of research:

Identify a Problem of Study
↓
Develop a research hypotheses to be tested

↓

Identify questions or issues of interest
Review and evaluate relevant theory and research
State research hypotheses

↓

Collect data

↓

Draw a sample from population
Determine how the variables will be measured
Select a method to collect the data

↓

Analyze the data

↓

Determine descriptive statistics
Determine inferential statistics

↓

Draw conclusion regarding research hypotheses

↓

Communicate the findings of the study

Identification of the research problem is the first step of the research. First of all, the researcher has to identify the problem area and then specifically state the problem for research.

Developing Research Hypotheses to be tested

The second step of the research process is to develop research hypotheses to be tested. A research hypothesis is a statement regarding an expected or predicted relationship between variables. A variable is a property or characteristic of an object, event, or person that can take different values.

Identifying a Question or Issue to be Examined

Most research starts with a question posed by the researcher. These questions often come from the researcher's own ideas and daily observations. Although this may not seem terribly scientific, there is an advantage in using one's own experience as a starting point. People are generally much more motivated to explore a question or topic that concerns them personally. In teaching statistics, we frequently advise students developing their own research projects to study something that is of interest to them. Conducting research can be tedious, difficult, and frustrating. At various points during your research, you may ask yourself, "Why am I doing this?" Being able to provide a satisfactory answer to this question will help you overcome whatever obstacles you encounter along the way.

Reviewing and Evaluating Relevant Theories and Research

Beyond the researcher's own curiosity, research questions often arise from an examination of the theories, ideas, and research of others. A theory is a set of propositions used to describe or explain a phenomenon. The purpose of a theory is to summarize and explain specific facts using a logically consistent framework. Placing question within a theoretical framework provides guidance and structure to research.

Reviewing and evaluating existing theories and research helps the researcher decide whether it is worth the time and energy required to conduct the study. By seeing what others have done, the researcher may decide that a particular idea has already been investigated and there is no reason to duplicate earlier efforts. By doing the review, researchers are able to ensure that the studies they undertake add to and improve upon an existing body of knowledge.

Collecting Data

Once a research hypothesis has been formulated, researchers are ready to proceed to the second state in the research process: collecting data relevant to this hypothesis. This step is seen as being composed of three tasks:

i. Drawing a sample from a population,
ii. Determining how the variables will be measured, and
iii. Selecting a method by which to collect the data.

Drawing a Sample from a Population

Identify the group of participants to which the research hypothesis applies. The group to which the results of a study may be applied or generalized is called a population. A population is the total number of possible units or elements that could potentially be included in a study. For example, researchers could identify the population of interest for the first research hypothesis as "high school students".

Researchers typically try to define their populations as broadly as possibly (e.g., "high school students in Uttar Pradesh) to maximize the applications or implications of their research.

It is typically difficult to collect data from all members of a population. Imagine, for example, the time and money that would be needed to collect information from every high school student. For this reason, researchers typically draw conclusions about populations based on information collected from a sample drawn from the population. A sample is a subset or portion of a population. Samples greatly vary in terms of their targeted population and size.

Analysis of the Data

The next step of the research involves the analysis of the data. Since this book itself deals with the analysis and statistics, here only a mentioning of the purpose of analysis is made use of. There are two main purposes:

1. To organize, summarize and describe data that have been collected, and
2. To test and draw conclusions about hypotheses formulated.

These two purposes are met by calculating two main types of statistics:

a. Descriptive Statistics, and
b. Inferential Statistics

The details of these two main branches of statistics will be explained in the coming chapters.

Drawing Conclusion Regarding Hypotheses

If the statistical analysis have been completed, the next step is to interpret the result of the analysis as they relate to the hypotheses. Since the researcher do not collect data from the population, there is a possibility of some error in the prediction.

Communicating the Findings of the Study

For many years, the American psychological corporation (APA), the professional association for psychologists, has recognized the need to provide researchers guidance on how to communicate the results of their research. The increase in length of APA manual which was published in 2010 in contrast to the manual published in 1929 clearly shows the challenges faced by researchers in communicating their research in an effective and efficient manner.

1.3 WHY YOU STUDY STATISTICS IN EDUCATIONAL RESEARCH?

Perhaps the reason that many students dread taking statistics is that they do not understand why they have to take the course.

All psychologists use the scientific method to understand behaviour and mental processes. An essential aspect of any scientific work is collecting data and making decisions based on these data. As we noted previously, statistics is the process of collecting data and making decisions based on the analysis of these data. Therefore, statistics is a tool that helps you to solve complex problems and think rationally about various problems addressed in psychology.

You may object and say that your personal experiences have allowed you to learn a lot about human behaviour. If personal experiences are so valued, why should they be replaced with empirical methods and statistics? The truth is that the personal experiences have limitations for learning more about the world around us. Although personal experience may be beneficial to us in our daily lives, the procedure is haphazard at best. Personal experience is useful, but as we shall see, the empirical method is far more satisfactory in addressing specific questions.

Psychologists base their knowledge of human behaviour on empirical evidence. Any student who wishes to become a professional psychologist must be familiar with statistical procedures and research techniques in order to perform their job effectively. Even if you do not pursue a professional career as a psychologist, you will constantly be confronted with opportunities to make decisions based on empirical evidence. Your knowledge of statistical reasoning will help you to make good decisions.

If statistics is approached with positive expectations and attitudes, it can be one of the most exciting fields of study. Depending upon the purpose and use of statistics, the branch of study can be mainly divided into two categories: 1. Descriptive statistics, and 2. Inferential statistics.

1.4 DESCRIPTIVE STATISTICS

Consider a group of students in a class. We can see that there are too many scores to keep in mind at once. The names in attendance sheet will be in alphabetical order, the scores are in numerical order. In order to simplify the consideration, we can organize the scores in descending order and then find the class average. In recognizing and comparing the students' scores a teacher can make use of techniques that are part of the body of descriptive statistics. The purpose of Descriptive Statistics is to organize and to summarize observations so that they are easier to comprehend.

1.5 INFERENTIAL STATISTICS

The purpose of inferential statistics is to draw inference about conditions that exist in a population from study of a sample drawn from the population. Because of chance factors associated with drawing a sample, the outcome like any estimate is subject to error.

But, if the sample for the study has been chosen according to statistical principles, it is possible to know what margin of error is involved.

1.6 MEASUREMENT IN EDUCATION/PSYCHOLOGY

What is a Number?

Symbols denoting amounts, things that can be added, subtracted, multiplied and divided.

Numbers are used in a variety of ways to achieve different goals

1) To name or identity – Nominal
2) To represent position or order in a series – Ordinal
3) To represent quantities such as how many or how much – Interval or Ratio

Measurement

It is an act of assigning numbers to the qualitative or quantitative aspects of objects, events or constructs in a systematic, reliable and valid manner.

Scales of measurement falls under four broad categories namely:

1) Ratio or Absolute scale; 2) Interval scale; 3) Ordinal scale; and 4) Nominal scale, depending upon the attributes possessed by the set up measures like, **magnitude, equal intervals** and **absolute zero point.**

When a scale has magnitude, one instant of the attribute (variate) can be judged as greater than (>), Less than (<) or equal to (=) another instance of the attribute. For example, measurements of height, weight, family size, etc.

Equal intervals denote that the magnitude of the attribute represented by a unit of measurement on the scale is equal, regardless of these on the scale that the unit falls. For example, height.

An absolute zero point is a value that indicates, nothing at all of the attribute being measured exists. For example, intelligence.

A scale of measurement which possesses attributes like magnitude, equal intervals and absolute zero point is called a ***ratio scale or an absolute scale***. This scale is termed "ratio" because the collection of properties that it possesses allow ratio statements to be made about the attribute being measured.

An ***interval scale*** possesses the attribute of magnitude and equal intervals but not an absolute zero point. For example, temperature. An ***ordinal scale*** reflects only magnitude. ***A nominal scale*** refers to be classified items into discrete groups which do not bear any magnitude relationships to one another.

1.7 CHARACTERISTICS OF SCALES OF MEASUREMENT

To conduct a research study, the researcher must determine an appropriate way to measure the variables stated in the research hypothesis. Measurement is the assignment of categories or numbers to objects or events according to rules.

For example, to measure the variable "height," a researcher might use "number of inches from the ground in bare feet" as a form of measurement. To measure a variable such as "success in college", a student's grade point average (GPA) may be obtained from school transcripts. "Self-esteem" might be measured by having people who complete a questionnaire and, on the basis of their responses, be categorized as having either "low" or "high" self-esteem. As these examples demonstrate, the result of measurement is an assignment of a number or a category to each participant in the research study.

Nominal scale: Mutually exclusive categories differing in some qualitative aspect. For example, classification of data into groups say, group 1,2,3, or Eye colour.

The values of variables measured at the nominal level of measurement differ in category or type. The word *nominal* implies having to do with "names", such that we use first names and surnames as ways of distinguishing between people. Gender is an example of a nominal variable, in that it consists of categories or types (male and female) rather than numeric values.

Ordinal scale: This scale has the property of a nominal scale and in addition has the observations ranked in order of magnitude. For example, students ranked in order of marks according to their merit.

Variables measured at the ordinal level of measurement have values that can be placed in an order relative to the other values. Rankings (such as finishing first, second, or third in a race) and size (small, medium, large, or extra large) are familiar examples of an ordinal scale. Ordinal scales allow researchers to demonstrate that one value represents more or less of a variable than do other values; however, it is not possible to specify the precise size or amount of the difference between values. For example, although you can say that a runner who finishes "first" in a race is faster than the runner who finishes "second", but one cannot specify the exact time difference between the two runners.

Interval scale: Scale has all the properties of an ordinal scale and in addition numerical values indicate order of merit and relative distances between points along the scale. For example, Psychological measurement like Intelligence, aggressiveness, temperature in degree celsius, etc.

The values of variables measured at the interval level of measurement are equally spaced along a numeric continuum. One example of an interval variable is the Fahrenheit scale of temperature. Here, a difference of five degrees has the same meaning anywhere along the scale; for example, the difference between 45°F and

50°F is the same as the difference between 65°F and 70°F. Many variable studied in the behavioural sciences (e.g., personality characteristics or attitudes) are considered to be measured at the interval level of measurement. Interval variables not only provide more precise and specific information than do ordinal variables, but they also fulfill the requirements of the most commonly used statistical procedures.

Variables at the ratio level of measurement are identical to interval variables, with one exception: Ratio scales possess what is known as a true zero point, for which the value of zero (0) represents the complete absence of the variable. Variables that describe a physical dimension (such as height, weight, distance, and time duration) typically have a true zero point. In a research hypothesis, the researchers in this study measured the variable "test performance" by recording the number of correct answers to a test of reading comprehension. Test performance is a ratio variable because it has a true zero point, where zero would indicate the complete absence of correct answers.

Ratio scale: Scale has all the properties of an interval scale and in addition has an absolute zero point. For example, CGS and MKS scales of measurement, temperature in Kelvin scale.

One advantage of ratio measurement versus interval measurement is that ratio variables allow for a greater number of comparisons among values. Consider, for example, the value 6 for the ratio variable "inches". Not only is the difference between 4 and 6 inches the same as the difference between 6 and 8 inches (thereby involving addition and subtraction), 6 inches is also twice as long as 3 inches and half as long as 12 inches (involving multiplication and division). Multiplication and division comparisons cannot be made with interval variables. You cannot, for example, say that a temperature of 90°F is three times as much temperature as 30°F.

Variables: Observation and measurement are very essential in physical and social sciences.

The things we observe are referred as variables and any particular observation as value of the variable.

Independent → Dependent

E.g.: Effect of Sex difference (Independent ↓ Nominal) on the amount of time spent on studying Mathematics (Dependent ↓ ratio scale)

1.8 FREQUENCY DISTRIBUTION

The following are the scores obtained on an English test. Convert this into frequency distribution.

52, 28, 42, 56, 47, 78, 82, 55, 56, 41, 62, 38, 57, 55, 50, 37, 72, 65, 66, 52, 54, 62, 68, 42, 47, 39, 44, 47, 52, 48, 62, 54, 42, 48, 53, 60, 42, 56, 48, 68.

The procedure or steps in organizing a frequency distribution are the following:

1) Determine the range. (range = highest score – lowest score + 1)

$$\text{Range} = (82 - 28) + 1 = 55$$

2) Divide this by a number between 10 & 20 (the convention is that the number of class interval between 10 and 20) to estimate the appropriate size of the interval
3) List the intervals beginning at the bottom left. The lowest interval begin with a number which is a multiple of the interval size
4) Tally the frequency.
5) Summarize these under column labelled 'f".
6) Total this column and record the number of cases at the bottom as N

Class	Tally	F
80-84	I	1
75-79	I	1
70-74	I	1
65-69	IIII	4
60-64	IIII	4
55-59	~~IIII~~ II	7
50-54	~~IIII~~ I	6
45-49	~~IIII~~ I	6
40-44	~~IIII~~ I	6
35-39	III	3
30-34	–	0
25-29	I	1
		N = 40

1.9 GRAPHICAL REPRESENTATION OF FREQUENCY DISTRIBUTION

Graphical representation is used for the comparison of two or more data. Measurement of the variable is represented along the horizontal axis and the respective frequencies along the vertical line. Height of a graph should be less than the length or in the ratio 3:5.

Some Conventions for the Construction of Graphs

1) It is customary to let the horizontal axis (abscissa) represent measures of the variable under construction and the vertical axis represent the frequency.
2) The arrangement of the graph should proceed from left to right i.e., the low numbers on the horizontal axis should be on the left. Similarly, the low numbers at the ordinate should start from the bottom.
3) Select the units of representation along the axes in such a way that the ratio of height to length is roughly 3:5
4) Whenever possible the vertical scale should be so selected that a zero point falls at the intersection of the axes. When this is not possible, designate the

point of intersection as zero and make a small break in the vertical axis to represent the units of frequencies.

5) Both the horizontal and vertical axes should be appropriately labelled.
6) Assign a descriptive title which states previously what it is meant.
7) The break "∫∫" on X axis indicates that the vertical axis has been moved for convenience.

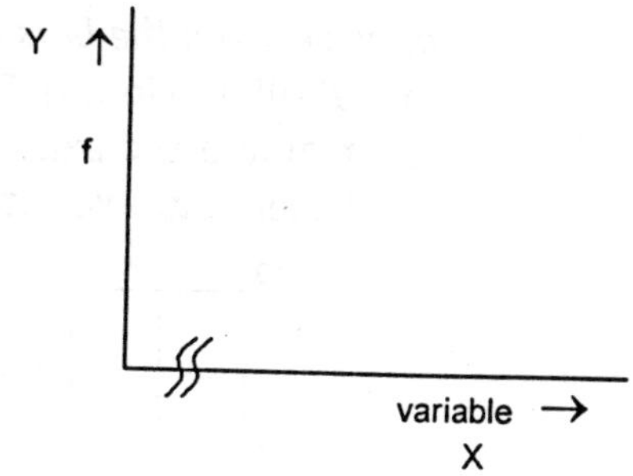

a) Histogram

For a histogram the exact class limits are marked along the horizontal axis and the frequencies along the vertical axis. Draw bars on these exact limits with area being equal to that of the respective frequencies.

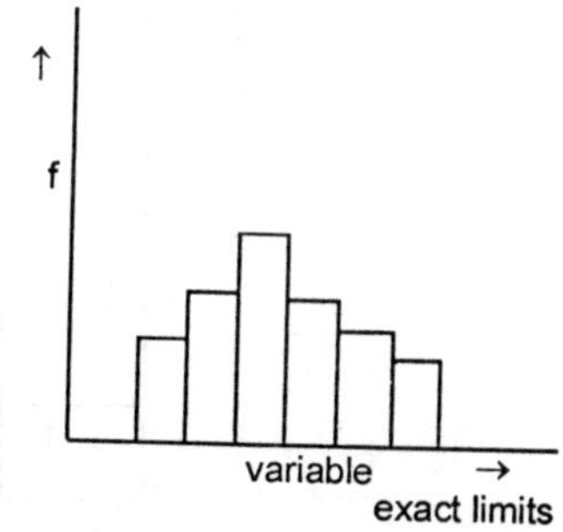

Suppose, after constructing a grouped frequency distribution of exam scores, we can draw the distribution in different ways. The histogram consists of a series of rectangles, each of which represents the scores in one of the class intervals of the tabulated distribution. The two vertical boundaries of a rectangle coincide with the real limits of the particular interval, whereas its height depends on the frequency of scores for that interval. A histogram is only a visual display of the tabulated distribution.

Results from 50 Students on a Class Examination

B: FREQUENCY AND CUMULATIVE FREQUENCY DISTRIBUTIONS

Class	*Exact limits*	*f*	*Relative f (%)*	*Cum f*	*cum %f*
96-98	95.5-98.5	1	2	50	100.0
93-95	92.5-95.5	0	0	49	98.0
90-92	89.5-92.5	2	4	49	98.0
87-89	86.5-89.5	7	14	47	94.0
84-86	83.5-86.5	10	20	40	80.0
81-83	80.5-83.5	6	12	30	60.0
78-80	77.5-80.5	8	16	24	48.0
75-77	74.5-77.5	4	8	16	32.0
72-74	71.5-74.5	3	6	12	24.0
69-71	68.5-71.5	4	8	9	18.0
66-68	65.5-68.5	3	6	5	10.0
63-65	62.5-65.5	0	0	2	4.0
60-62	59.5-62.5	2	4	2	4.0
	Total =	50	100%		

Draw bars of equal width for each interval. The height of a bar corresponds to the frequency or relative frequency in that particular interval. *There should be no gaps between the bars except for intervals in which there are no scores* (such as 63-65 and 93-95 in Figure). The edge of a bar represents both the exact upper limit for one interval and the exact lower limit for the next higher interval.

Label your axes and give your histogram a title.

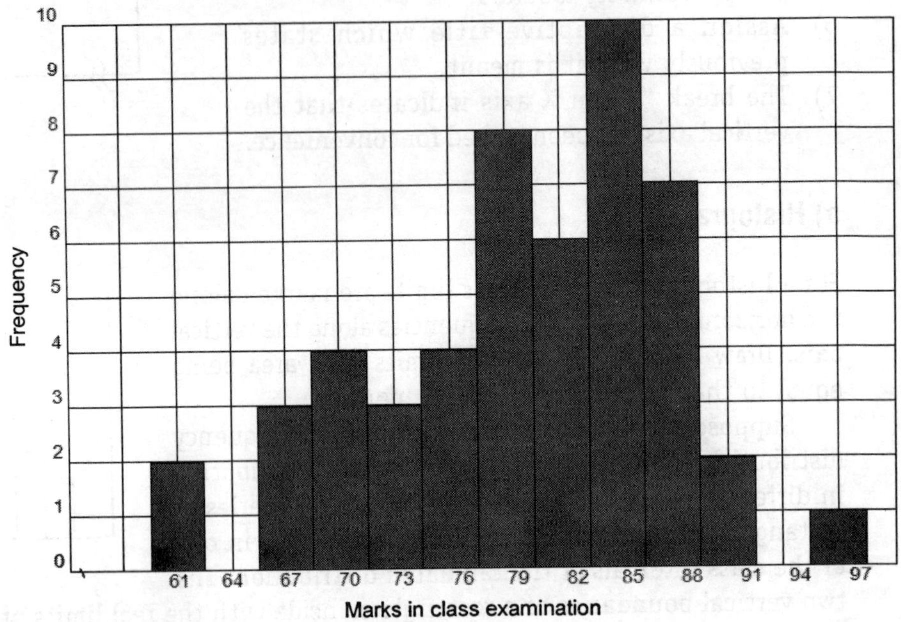

b) Frequency Polygon

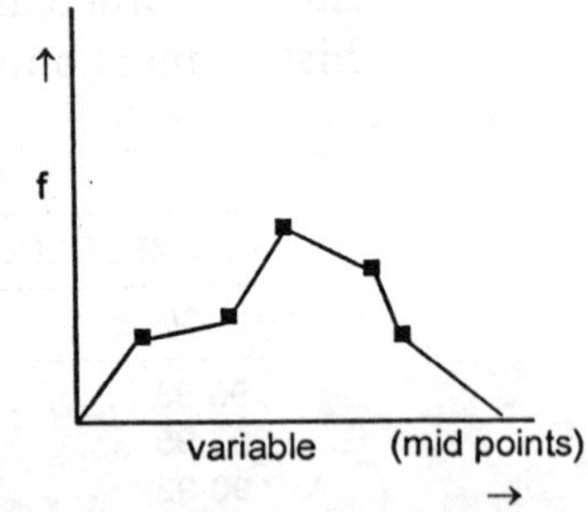

To draw a frequency polygon, the midpoints of class intervals are marked along the horizontal axis (instead of the exact limit in the histogram). The respective frequencies are plotted above the midpoint. Join these points by broken lines. The figure thus obtained is the frequency polygon.

As you can see in figure, a frequency polygon is a series of connected dots above the midpoint of each possible class interval. Each dot is at a height equal to the frequency or relative frequency of scores in that interval.

The steps in constructing a frequency polygon are summarized as follows:

Decide on a suitable scale for the horizontal and vertical axes. Label your class interval midpoints along the horizontal axis.

Place a dot above the midpoint of each class interval at a height equal to the frequency or relative of the scores in that interval. Connect the dots with straight lines.

Notice that in figure the polygon touches the horizontal axis at 64 and 94, the midpoints of the intervals 63-65 and 93-95, respectively. This indicates that there were zero scores in those intervals. Ordinarily, we bring the polygon down to the horizontal axis at both ends as well. To do so, identify the two class intervals falling immediately outside those end class intervals containing scores.

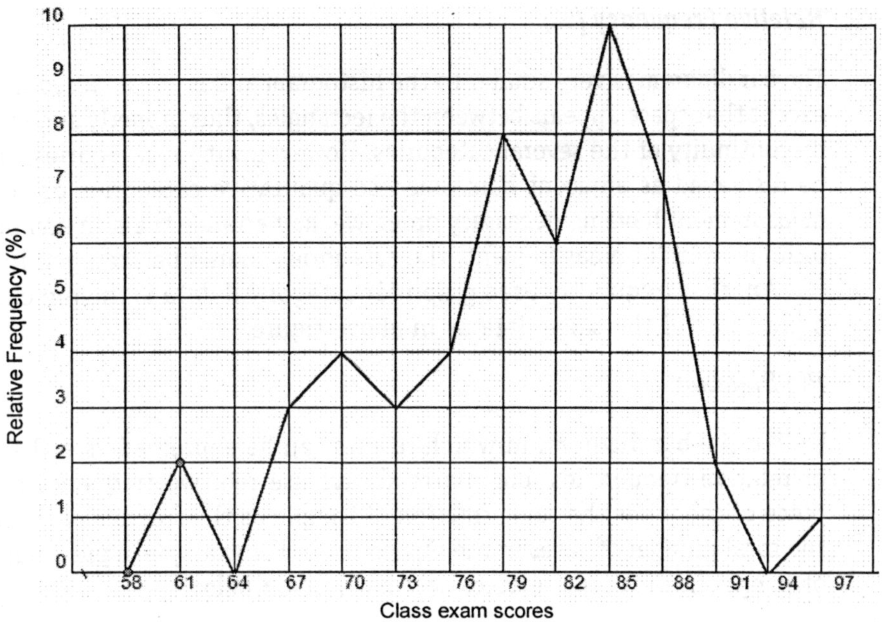

c) Bar Diagram and the Pie Chart

What should we do when graphing a distribution of categorical data? In this case, there are two widely used possibilities. Figure shows a bar diagram of the distribution of American psychologists in major employment settings. (Minium, King & Bear, 1993)

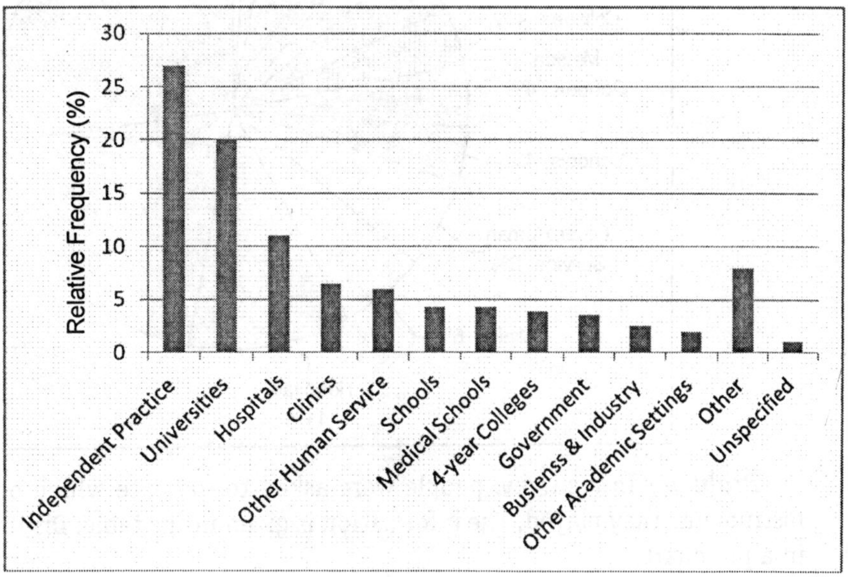

Relative Frequency (%)

The bar diagram is very similar to the histogram and is constructed in the same manner except that space appears between the rectangles, thus properly suggesting the essential discontinuity of the several categories. However, within categories, subcategories may be displayed as adjacent bars. Because qualitative categories on a nominal scale of measurement have no necessary order, we may arrange them in any order. However, for ordinal scales of measurement, the categories should be arranged in order of rank.

Another frequently used graph for categorical data is the pie chart. Figure shows a pie chart of the same data as in above figure.

Pie Diagram

Unlike the bar diagram, in which results can be expressed as either raw frequencies or relative frequencies, pie charts always use relative frequencies. The area in any piece of the pie is the same fraction of the pie as the frequency of that category is of the total number of cases in the distribution. For example, a pie diagram of percentage of people in different services sectors is given below

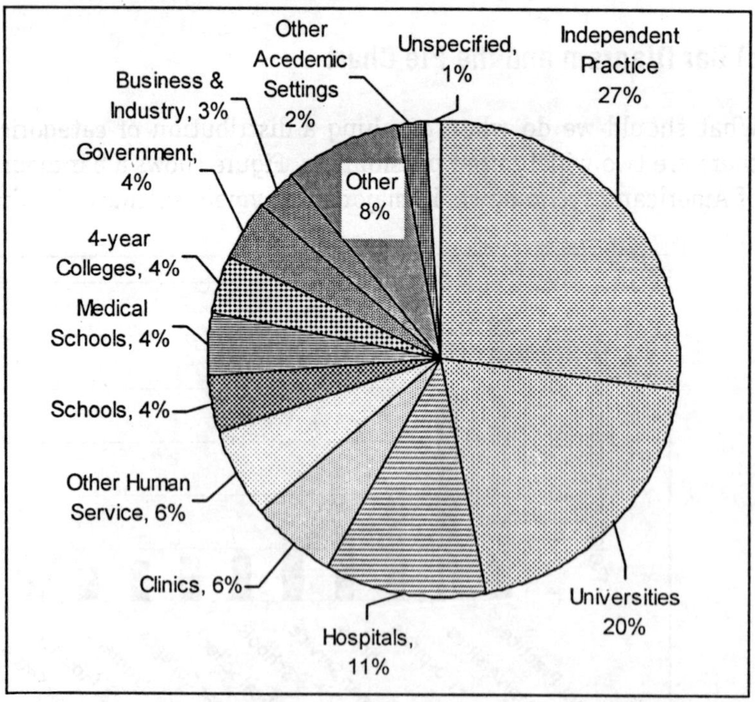

Problem: In a survey, people were asked to indicate which one of five musical instruments they played. The information is given in the table. Display the information in a pie chart.

Musical instrument

Guitar	35
Violin	10
Recorder	15
Drum	5
Keyboard	25

Guitar angle = (35/90) × 360 = 140°

Violin angle = (10/90) × 360 = 40°

Recorder angle = (15/90) × 360 = 60°

Drum angle = (5/90) × 360 = 20°

Keyboard angle = (25/90) × 360 = 100°

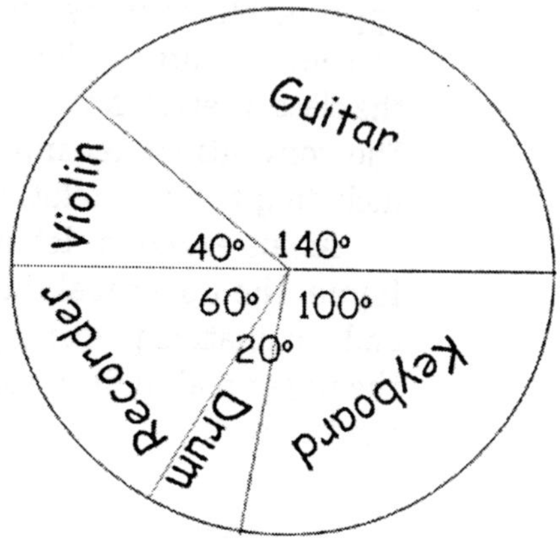

d) Cumulative frequency curve

Both the cumulative frequency and the cumulative percentage distribution may be cast in graphic form.

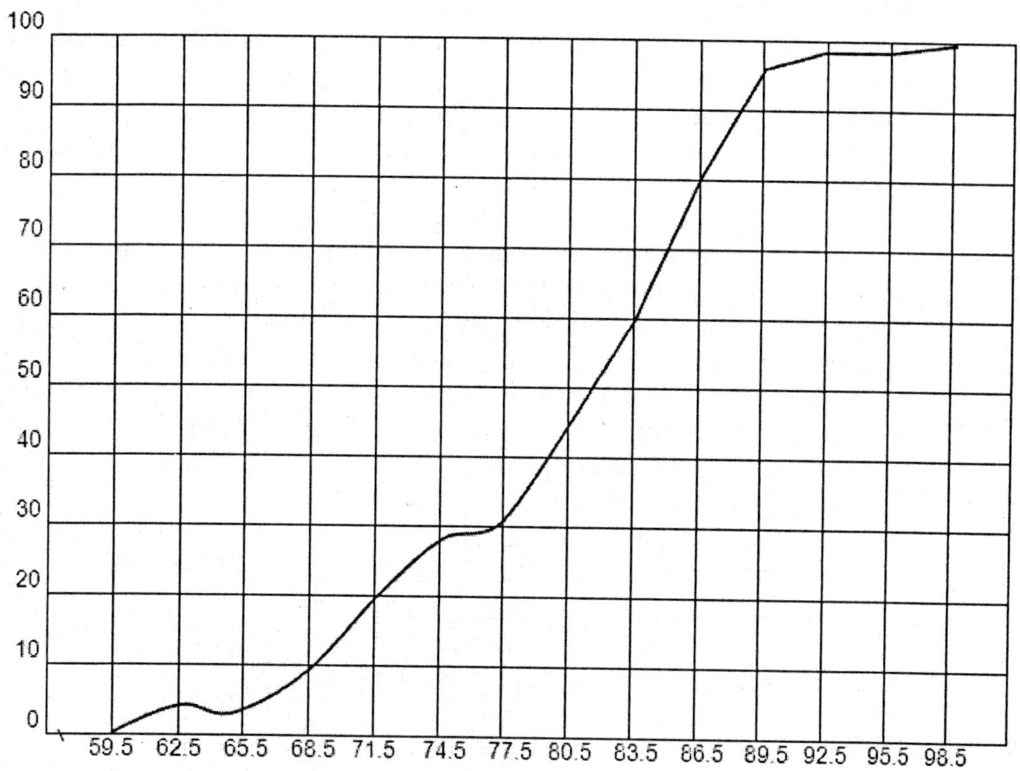

A cumulative percentage indicates the percentage of scores that lies below the upper real limit of the associated class interval. Therefore, in constructing cumulative percentage curves, the cumulative percentage is plotted at the upper real limit of the class interval. Note that this procedure differs from that for the frequency polygon. The conventions regarding construction that we discussed earlier also apply here, including the rule relating height to width.

As an example, let us refer again to the results of midterm history exam. In figure, the upper real limit for each class interval is labeled on the horizontal axis, and cumulative percentage appears on the vertical axis. We then place a point over the upper real limit of each interval corresponding to the cumulative percentage for the interval.

For example, the cumulative percentage for the interval 84-86 is 80%; therefore, we place a point at the intersection of 86.5 (the upper real limit of the interval) and 80%. We then connect the points with straight lines and bring the curve down to zero at the lower end at the upper real limit of the next adjacent class interval (in which there were zero scores).

A cumulative percentage curve never has a negative slope (that is, it never comes down). For class intervals in which there are zero scores (such as 63-65 and 93-95), the cumulative percentage curve remains horizontal. The curve shows a small rise in intervals with relatively few scores and a sharp rise in intervals with many scores. You can see this by comparing the frequency histogram or polygon of the history exam scores (figures) with the cumulative percentage curve in figure. Like the distribution of history exam scores, many distributions have most of the cases in the middle portion of the distribution. This results in a cumulative percentage curve with an S-shaped figure called an **ogive curve.**

We may determine percentile or percentile ranks from the cumulative percentage curve with nearly the same results obtained from the computational procedures. Connecting the points on the cumulative curve with straight lines is the graphic equivalent of assuming (as we did when computing) that scores are evenly spread throughout the interval. For the history exam scores illustrated in figure, for example, we can find the percentile rank of a score of 88 by locating it on the horizontal axis and then moving vertically upward until we intersect the curve. From there we read horizontally to the vertical axis and find the percentile rank to be 87. The process may be reversed as well. To find p_{50} follow the second set of dotted lines from the vertical axis to the intersection with the curve, and then descend to the horizontal axis. Thus, $P_{50} = 81$.

In a cumulative frequency distribution, the frequency are successively added. Along the abscissa, exact upper limits are marked.

Smoothening

To get an idea how the figure might look if the data were more numerous, the frequency polygon may be smoothed. For this adjusted frequencies are determined. To find adjusted or smoothed f, add frequency 'f' on the given interval and 'f' s on the two adjacent intervals.

EXERCISES

1. Generate a set of data where the mean, median and mode are the same and then create a figure for these data. Describe the shape of the distribution.
2. Prepare a frequency distribution for the following scores and draw a frequency curve and histogram of the distribution:
   52, 71, 65, 87, 90, 77, 83, 71, 82, 75, 84, 99, 70, 85, 93, 81, 72, 77, 89, 83, 55, 75, 90, 83, 78, 86, 71, 66, 60, 87, 97, 83, 95, 71

2

Measures of Central Tendency

We can proceed to a consideration of how a collection of numbers, whether arranged in the form of a frequency distribution or not, may be described. One property of a collection of numbers is ***central location,*** and several indices **or** measures may be used to describe it. The term central location means a central reference value which is usually close to the point of greatest concentration of the measurements.

Measures of this type are called measures of central tendency. Their purpose is to provide a single summary figure that best describe the central location of an entire distribution of observations. A measure of central tendency helps to simplify comparison of two or more groups tested under different conditions. There are many measures of central tendency. We will consider only three most commonly used measures in Education and behavioural sciences i.e., Mean, Median and Mode.

2.1 ARITHMETIC MEAN

The Arithmetic mean is the sum of all the scores in a distribution divided by the total number of scores. For brevity, we can call it as mean. We can use the letter 'X' to symbolize a particular set of scores. Here X include $X_1, X_2, X_3, \ldots X_n$

Therefore, $\Sigma X = X_1 + X_2 + X_3 + \ldots X_n$

The equation for finding the mean for Ungrouped data is, Mean = $\dfrac{\sum X}{N}$

where $\dfrac{\sum X}{N}$ denotes the sum of all the observations and N, the number of observations.

Problem

Find the mean of the measures 10, 12, 15, 18, 20

Mean $= 75/5 = 15$

For Grouped data, the formula for finding mean is,

Mean $= \frac{\sum fX}{N}$ where X is the midpoint of the class interval and f is the frequency of the corresponding class.

Consider the following data:

Class	f	Midpoint X	fX
80-84	1	82	82
75-79	1	77	77
70-74	1	72	72
65-69	4	67	268
60-64	4	62	248
55-59	7	57	399
50-54	6	52	312
45-49	6	47	282
40-44	6	42	252
35-39	3	37	111
30-34	0	32	0
25-29	1	27	27
	N = 40		ΣfX = 2130

Mean $= \frac{\sum fX}{N} = 2130/\ 40 = 53.3$

There is another method for calculating mean i.e., Assumed mean method

Assumed mean method

In this method, we are assuming a mean and calculate the mean according to the following formula.

Let the assumed mean be A = 62,

Then, $\overline{X} = A + i\ \frac{\sum fx'}{N}$

Where $X' = \frac{X - A}{i}$

Please see the previous frequency distribution. From the distribution,

x'	fx'
4	4
3	3
2	2
1	4
0	0
–1	–7
–2	–12
–3	–18
–4	–24
–5	–15
–6	–0
–7	–7
	Σfx' = –70

$$\text{Mean} = A + i\frac{\sum fx'}{N}$$

$= 62 + 5 \times (-70)/40$
$= 62 - 35/4$
$= 62 - 8.7$
$= 53.3$

Combined Mean of Two Groups

Consider a set of N measurements with mean $\overline{X}_1$, and another set of N_2 measurement with arithmetic mean $\overline{X}_2$, then the arithmetic mean of the N combined group can be computed by the formula,

$$\overline{X}_{comb} = \frac{N_1\overline{X}_1 + N_2\overline{X}_2}{N_1 + N_2}$$

This formula can be extended to any number of groups. Thus, when there are three groups, the formula becomes $\overline{X}_{comb} = \frac{N_1\overline{X}_1 + N_2\overline{X}_2 + N_3\overline{X}_3}{N_1 + N_2 + N_3}$

For a group of N = 50, mean is 25 and for another group with N = 40, Mean is 40

Then, Combined Mean $= \frac{50 \times 25 + 40 \times 40}{25 + 40} = \frac{2850}{65} = 43.85$

Major Properties of Arithmetic Mean

Arithmetic mean has the following properties:

1. Sum of deviation of measures taken from the mean = 0

2. Sum of squares of deviations of the measures taken from the mean is minimum i.e., it is less than the sum of squares of the deviations taken from any measurement from the data.

In the above problem, sum of squares of deviations of mean

= 16+, 4+, 0+, 4+, 16 = 40

If we take deviations from 20 or 12, and square is 0, 4, 16, 36, 64 sum = 120

So, it is always greater than the mean.

2.2 MEDIAN

It is the middle most value of a set of observations when arranged in the order of magnitude. When n is odd, median is the middle most value.

It is the $\frac{n+1}{2}$th value, when 'n' is even, median is the arithmetic mean of the two middle values.

Calculating median from a frequency distribution

Class	f	Cum. Frequency
45-49	1	76
40-44	2	75
35-39	3	73
30-34	6	70
25-29	8	64
20-24	17	56
15-19	26	39
10-14	11	13
05-09	2	2

$$\text{Median} = l + i\frac{\left(N/2 - F\right)}{f}$$ for a frequency distribution where

l = Lower limit of the median class

i = Size of the class interval

N = Size of the sample

F = Cumulative frequency corresponding to 'l'

f = Actual frequency of the median class

$l = 14.5$ $F = 13$

$i = 5$ $f = 26$ $N/2 = 76/2 = 38$

$$\text{Median} = 14.5 + \frac{(38-13)\times 5}{26}$$

$$= 14.5 + 25 \times 5/26 = 14.5 + 4.8$$
$$= \underline{19.3}$$

Example:

Find the median of the frequency distribution given below:

$$\text{Median} = l + i\frac{\left(N/2 - F\right)}{f}$$

Median is in the class, $\left(N/2\right) = 20$.

Cumulative frequency of 20 is coming in the class 70-74

Class	f	Cum f
95-99	2	40
90-94	2	38
85-89	4	36
80-84	6	32
75-79	5	26
70-74	4	21
65-69	5	17
60-64	2	12
55-59	2	10
50-54	4	8
45-49	1	4
40-44	2	3
35-39	1	1
	N = 40	

$$N = 40$$

$$\text{Median} = 69.5 + 5 \times \frac{(20-17)}{4}$$
$$= 69.5 + 5 \times 3/4$$
$$= 69.5 + 3.75 = 73.25$$

2.3 MODE

Mode is that measure which occurs most frequently. Consider the ungrouped data, 2, 6, 7, 8, 10, 11, 8, 8. Here, the mode is 8

In a frequency distribution mode is the midpoint of the class having the highest frequency. A frequency distribution, having two equal high frequencies not in the adjacent classes is called bimodal frequency distribution. Mode of a frequency distribution can be calculated by the formula.

$$\text{Mode} = l + \frac{c.f_2}{f_1 + f_2}$$

Where l = is the lower limit of the modal class
c = is the size of the class interval
f_1 = is the frequency of the class preceding to the model class
f_2 = is the frequency of the class succeeding to the model class

Mode can be calculated using another formula

$$\textbf{Mode} = 3 \textbf{ Median} - 2 \textbf{ Mean}$$

MEASURES OF DISPERSION

All researchers encounter and are interested in the variability of the data they collect. Consider some simple examples. When a teacher conducts an examination, there is variance among the grades: Some students do better than others. The teacher may be interested in why some students receive good grades whereas others struggle to pass. A researcher may want to show that a new drug is effective for the treatment of depression. She wants to find out whether people treated with the drug differ from people given a placebo. The difference between the people in the two treatment groups is another form of variability. Therefore, measures of dispersion, like measures of central tendency, are descriptive statistics that all researchers use to understand their data.

Studying the variability of data is essential to the use and interpretation of many statistics. We can see that a score by itself is meaningless and takes on meaning only when it is compared with other scores or other statistics. Consequently, if we know the mean of the distribution of a variable, we can determine whether a particular score is higher or lower than the mean. Now comes the next important question, How much higher or lower? What if the mean of the distribution is 100 and an individual's score is 105? Obviously, there is a 5-point difference and the individual's score is above the mean. Does this 5-point difference represent an exceptional difference or a trivial difference? We can answer these questions directly by examining the relative dispersion of the data.

Consider the following Figure, which shows two distributions of data. In both the cases, the mean of the distribution is 100.0 and the number of observations is the same. How should we interpret a score of 105.0 in the two distributions? In distribution A, the data are more broadly dispersed than the data in distribution B. In other words, the data in distribution A is more variable than the data in distribution B. What is the relative position of 105.0 in each of the distributions? In distribution A, the score is relatively close to the mean. That is, the percentile ranking of the score is only slightly above the mean. In distribution B, however, the same score of 105 appears to be exceptionally far from the mean and close to the most extreme score. We would expect the percentile ranking to be high in this case. Therefore, a score of 105 can be considered to be only slightly greater than the mean or much greater than the mean depending upon the overall dispersion of the data.

Distribution A

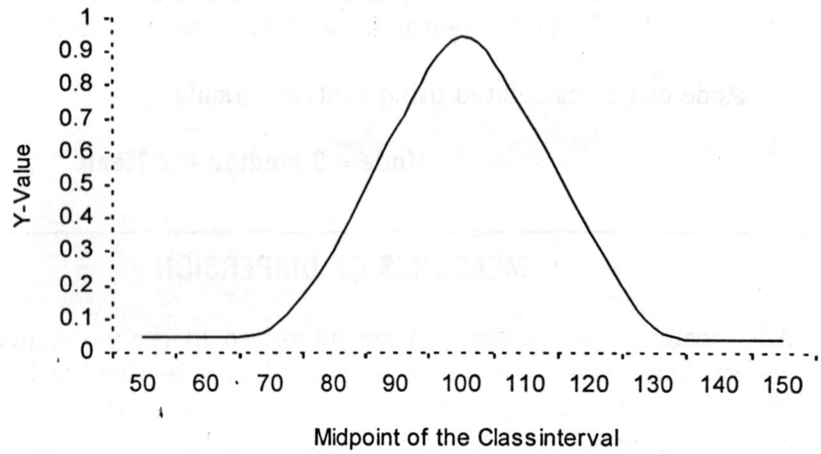

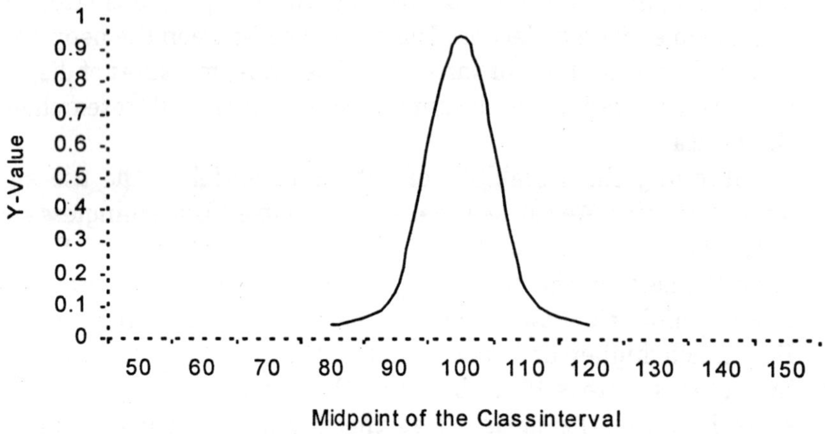

This example illustrates our need to calculate a measure of dispersion. Knowing the measure of central tendency and the measure of dispersion of the data, we can better interpret the meaning of individual scores in a set of data. In this Chapter, we will discuss four measures of dispersion or variability: the range, the semi-inter quartile range, the variance, and the standard deviation.

2.4 THE RANGE

When you calculate the various measures of central tendency, you locate a single point along the scale of scores and identify it as the mean, the median, or the mode. When your interest shifts to measures of dispersion, however, you must look for an index of variability that indicates the spread of scores around that central location.

One of the first measures of dispersion is the range. It consists simply of the scale distance between the largest and smallest scores; that is, the range is equal to the highest score minus the lowest score. Thus, if the highest score is 140 and the lowest is 30, the range is 140-30 = 110. Note that the range is a single value, not two values as is commonly reported in the media. Thus, the range is 110, not 30 to 140.

Although the range is meaningful, its usefulness is limited by its instability. Note that if there is one extreme score (an outlier) in a distribution, the dispersion of scores will appear to be large when in fact the removal of the outlier may reveal an otherwise "compact" distribution.

There are times, however, when the range merits careful consideration. For example, our preoccupation with averages can cause us to lose sight of the fact that many of the most important workaday decisions are based on considerations of dispersion rather than on measures of central tendency.

2.5 VARIANCE (s^2) AND THE STANDARD DEVIATION (s)

Before we begin to discuss these topics, we need to review some material covered in previous sections. The sum of the mean subtracted from all values of a variable is equal to zero (i.e., $\Sigma(X-\overline{X}) = 0$). When divided by N, this sum is said to be the first moment about the mean. The word "moment" is a technical term that represents the point where there is equilibrium between opposite forces. We said that the mean represents the balance point in the distribution. That is why the sum of the deviation scores is always 0; the mean is the point of equilibrium between high and low scores. The first moment about the mean describes the mean along the measurement scale. Specifically, the first moment about the mean is calculated as

$$0 = \frac{\sum\left(X-\overline{X}\right)}{N}$$

Note that the first moment about the mean always equals 0 because the mean is the point in the distribution that balances the opposing forces of large and small numbers.

If we square the deviation scores, all the numbers will become positive and larger relative to the size of the deviation. The sum of these squared deviations is known as the sum of squares, abbreviated (SS).

$$SS = \sum\left(X-\overline{X}\right)^2$$

					X				
				X	X	X			
	X	X	X	X	X	X	X	X	X
DISTANCE	-4	-3	-2	-1	0	+1	+2	+3	+4
$(\text{DISTANCE})^2$	16	9	4	1	0	1	4	9	16

$\Sigma\ (\text{DISTANCE})^2 = 60$

Before proceeding with the procedures for calculating measures of dispersion, it will be advantageous to think more about the notion of distance from a mean and the impact of squaring each deviation. The above figure illustrates a distribution of scores. It is clear that the scores farther from the mean will contribute more to the overall total when these squared deviations or distances are summed. Small deviations, when squared, increase by relatively small amounts ($2^2 = 4$, $3^2 = 9$). Numbers that are a greater distance from the mean, when squared, become much larger ($9^2 = 81$, $11^2 = 121$). This fact suggests that scores further from the mean have a greater effect on the sum of squares than scores closer to the mean.

As should be obvious, as we add more scores to the set, the sum of squares becomes larger, especially if these scores deviate from the mean. As a consequence, we cannot use the sum of squares as a direct measure of dispersion. To make a more useful measure of dispersion, we divide the sum by the total number of scores (N). In effect, we are calculating the average squared deviations. Consequently, we have a statistic that represents the average squared deviation for a set of data. This average is called the variance of a sample and is represented by s^2.

Specifically, the variance of a set of data is calculated by

$$s^2 = \frac{\sum (X - \bar{X})^2}{N}$$

and may also be represented as the sum of squares (SS) divided by N. i.e., $\frac{SS}{N}$

Statisticians also call this equation the second moment about the mean. Again, it is critical to recognize the concept of equilibrium between opposing forces. The variance averages the effects of large and small deviations from the mean. We can use this fact to our advantage because we can use the variance to help us characterize how much the typical score deviates from the mean.

Because we squared all the deviation scores before dividing by N, the variance represents the average of the sum of *squared* difference between each score and the mean. If we take the square root of the variance, we will convert the variance to a score that represents our measurement scale. The result of this transformation is called the standard deviations and is represented by s.

$$s = \sqrt{\frac{\sum \left(X - \bar{X}\right)^2}{N}}$$

Therefore, most researchers report the standard deviation because it represents the average deviation between the mean and the observed score.

Calculation of the Variance and Standard Deviation from an Array of Scores

You are now ready to apply these formulae to some examples. It encourages you to use a calculator or a computer to help you with the calculations. Our experience has been that many people are prone to make mistakes when trying to do these calculations by hand. You should also get into the habit of preparing a neat, step-by-step account of your work. As you will find, the calculations for most statistics are easy and do not require complicated mathematical procedures.

The computational equation produces the same result as the definitional equation. The only real difference is that the computational equation takes less time to perform.

Definitional equation for variance:

$$s^2 = \frac{\sum (X - \overline{X})^2}{N} \text{ and standard deviation, } s = \sqrt{\frac{\sum \left(X - \overline{X}\right)^2}{N}}$$

computational equation for standard deviation is,

$$s \text{ or } \sigma = \frac{1}{N}\sqrt{N\sum X^2 - \left(\sum X\right)^2}$$

It is the measure of the scatter or spread of the separate observations around the central tendency, especially the mean.

Homogeneous Groups

Two groups are said to be homogenous if the variability of the two groups are equal.

Standard Deviation : Definition

The standard deviation of a group of measurements is defined as the square root of the sum of squares of deviations of each observation from the mean divided by the size of the sample

$$\text{Thus, } s \text{ or } \sigma = \sqrt{\frac{\left(\sum X - \overline{X}\right)^2}{N}}$$

$$= \sqrt{\frac{\sum x^2}{N}} \text{ Where } x = X - \overline{X}$$

$$= \sqrt{\frac{\sum X^2}{N} - \frac{\left(\sum X\right)^2}{N}} = \frac{1}{N}\sqrt{N\sum X^2 - \left(\sum X\right)^2}$$

Standard Deviation of a Frequency Distribution

For a frequency distribution, the standard deviation can be calculated by the formula,

$$s \text{ or } \sigma = \frac{i}{N}\sqrt{N\sum fx'^2 - \left(\sum fx'\right)^2}$$

$$\text{Where, } x' = \frac{X - A}{i}$$

Percentile Points

The method of calculating percentiles is the same as that employed in finding the median. Percentile points are points below which lies a given percentage of cases. In general, percentile points are denoted by Pp. This implies that Pp is the Pth percentile which again denotes point below which lie P percentage of cases

Pp is calculated by the formula $Pp = l + i\,\dfrac{\left(P\dfrac{N}{100} - F\right)}{f}$

Where,

l = exact lower limit of the class in which the pth percentile lies

F = the cumulative frequency corresponding to l

f = actual frequency of the class containing the pth percentile point

N = size of the sample.

The percentile points are p_1, p_2.... Among these the percentile points lie p_{10}, p_{20}, p_{30}.... p_{90} are called deciles.

p_{25}, the 25th percentile, the point below which lie 25% of the cases of the distribution is called the first quartile of the distribution denoted by Q_1

p_{50}, the 50th percentile, the point which lie 50% of the cases of the distribution is called the second quartile and is denoted by Q_2.

p_{75}, the 75th percentile, the point below which the 75% of the cases of the distribution which is called as the 3rd quartile, Q_3.

2.6 QUARTILE DEVIATION (THE SEMI-INTERQUARTILE RANGE)

In order to overcome the instability of the range as a measure of dispersion, we sometimes use the semi-interquartile range (Q). To calculate the semi-interquartile, subtract the score at the 25th percentile (called the first quartile or Q_1) from the score at the 75th percentile (the third quartile or Q_3) and divide by 2 (*see* Figure). Then we will have a measure of the width of the semi-interquartile range on either side of the median.

If the distribution takes on the symmetrical bell-shaped form identified as a normal curve (*see* Figure), the median plus and minus the Q cuts off the middle 50% of all cases in the distribution. Thus, if the median is 70 and the Q is 10, we can conclude that 70±10 (60 to 80) includes the middle 50% of all cases. Even with markedly skewed distributions (*see* figure), the median plus and minus the Q accounts for the middle 50% of cases. Thus, 65 ± 6.5 yields 58.5 and 71.5 as the values that bracket the middle 50% of cases. For this reason, the Q is most frequently used in conjunction with the median when extreme skew rules out the use of mean and the standard deviation as measures of central tendency and variability, respectively.

$$\text{Semi-interquartile Range} = \frac{73-60}{2} = 6.5$$

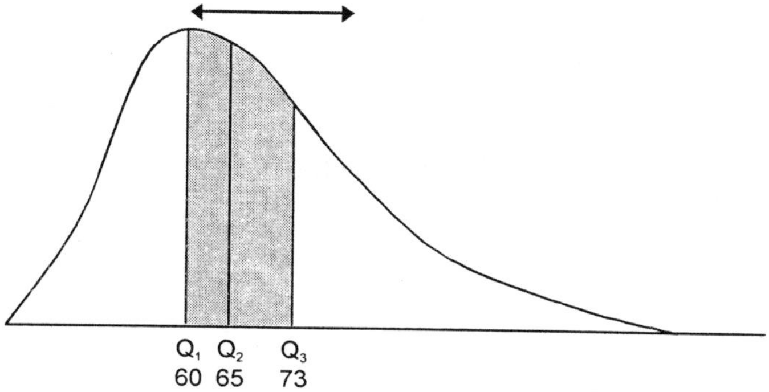

In the behavioural sciences, we find that some interval- and ratio-scaled data such as reaction time scores, heart rate measures, and income figures are usually sufficiently skewed to justify the use of the median as the measure of central tendency, and the semi-interquartile range as the index of dispersion. These measure are often used to describe ordinally scaled data as well.

Although the Q is far more meaningful than the crude range, it has two significant shortcomings: (1) Like the crude range, it does not by itself permit the precise interpretation of a score within a distribution, and (2) like the median, it does not enter into any of the higher mathematical relationships that are basic to inferential statistics. As a consequences, we need to turn our attention to the most frequently used measures of dispersion, variance and the standard deviation.

Q, the quartile deviation has been defined as half the range between Q_1 and Q_3

i.e., $$Q = \frac{Q_3 - Q_1}{2} \text{ or } \frac{P_{75} - P_{25}}{2}$$

Since in the calculation of quartile deviation, we are considering the range between the first and third quartiles only, i.e., (the middle portion of the continuum of measurements), Q is the measure of variability at the middle portion of the distribution.

Calculate Q from the following:

class	f	Cum. f
136-139	3	200
132-135	5	197
128-131	16	192
124-127	23	176
120-123	52	153
116-119	49	101
112-115	27	52
108-111	18	25
104-107	7	7
	200	

$$Q = \frac{Q_3 - Q_1}{2} \text{ or } \frac{p_{75} - p_{25}}{2}$$

$$p_{75}:- p_{75} = l + \frac{i\left(\frac{3N}{4} - F\right)}{f}$$

$$\frac{PN}{100} = 75 \times 200/100 = 150$$

$$l = 119.5 \quad F = 101 \quad f = 52 \quad i = 4$$

$$p_{75} = 119.5 + 4\frac{(150\text{-}101)}{52} = \underline{123.26}$$

$$p_{25} = l + \frac{i\left(N/4 - F\right)}{f}$$

$$\frac{PN}{100} = 25 \times 200/100 = 50$$

$$p_{25} = 111.35 + 4\ (50\text{-}25)/27 = 115.203$$

$$Q = \frac{p_{75} - p_{25}}{2} = 123.26 - 115.20/2 = \underline{4.03}$$

2.7 AVERAGE OR MEAN DEVIATION

It is the arithmetic mean of absolute deviations of all the observations from the mean. (Absolute deviations means deviations disregarding the sign). Mean deviation is calculated by:

1) In an ungrouped data, M.D = $\frac{\sum|x|}{N}$

   Where, $x = X - \overline{X}$ 52, 50, 56, 68, 65, 62, 57, 70

2) In a grouped data, frequency distribution MD = $\frac{\sum|fx|}{N}$

   where $x = X - \overline{X}$, X is the midpoint of the class intervals

Calculate Mean Deviation:

Class	f	X	$x' = \frac{X-A}{i}$	fx'	$X - \bar{X}$	fx
195-199	1	197	5	5	26	26
190-194	2	192	4	8	27	42
185-189	4	187	3	12	16	64
180-184	5	182	2	10	11	55
175-179	8	177	1	8	6	48
170-174	10	172	0	0	1	10
165-169	6	167	–1	–6	–4	–24
160-164	4	162	–2	–8	–9	–36
155-159	4	157	–3	–12	–14	–56
150-154	2	152	–4	–8	–19	–38
145-149	3	147	–5	–15	–24	–72
140-144	1	142	–6	–6	–29	–29
	N = 50			Σfx'=-12		$\sum \lvert fx \rvert = 500$

$$\text{Mean} = A + \frac{i\sum fx'}{N}$$

$$= 172 + \frac{5 \times -12}{50} = 170.8 = 171$$

$$\text{MD} = \frac{\sum \lvert fx \rvert}{N} = 500/50 = 10$$

Combined Standard Deviation

Consider a set of N_1 measures having standard deviation σ_1 and N_2 measures with standard deviation σ_2 and so on.

$$s_{Comb} = \frac{\sqrt{N_1\left(\sigma_1^2 + d_1^2\right) + N_2\left(\sigma_2^2 + d_2^2\right) + \ldots\ldots\ldots\ldots}}{N_1 + N_2 + \ldots\ldots\ldots\ldots}$$

Where $d_1 = \bar{X}_1 - \bar{X}_{comb}$

$d_2 = \bar{X}_2 - \bar{X}_{comb}$

Mean, standard deviation and size of three groups A, B and C are given below: Compute the mean and standard deviation of the three groups combined, which group is more consistent?

Group	X	σ	N
A	82	10	25
B	86	12	35
C	88	16	20

$$\overline{X}_{comb} = (x-\bar{x})^2$$

$d_1 = X_1 - \overline{X}_{comb} = 82 - 85.25 = -3.25$

$d_2 = X_2 - \overline{X}_{comb} = 86 - 85.25 = 0.75$

$d_3 = X_3 - \overline{X}_{comb} = 88\text{-}85.25 = 2.75$

$$\sigma_{comb} = \frac{\sqrt{N_1\left(\sigma_1^2 + d_1^2\right) + N_2\left(\sigma_2^2 + d_2^2\right) + \ldots\ldots\ldots}}{N_1 + N_2 + \ldots\ldots\ldots\ldots}$$

$$= \frac{\sqrt{25\times(100+3.252)+35(122+0.752+20(162+2.752))}}{80} = \underline{\underline{12.794}}$$

Effect upon mean and σ when a constant is added:

Consider the following scores:

X	$X-\overline{X}$	$(X-\overline{X})^2$
9	2	4
8	1	1
7	0	0
6	−1	1
5	−2	4
ΣX = 7		$\Sigma x^2 = 10$

$$\sigma = \sqrt{\frac{10}{5}} = \sqrt{2}$$

Adding 5 to each value,

X	$X-\overline{X}$	x^2
14	2	4
13	1	1
12	0	0
11	−1	1
10	−2	4
M = 12		$\Sigma x^2 = 10$

$$\sigma = \sqrt{\frac{10}{5}} = \sqrt{2}$$

It can be seen that mean is added by 5 units and σ is not affected

Effect upon $\bar{x}$ and σ on multiplication:

Multiply each score by 10.

X	$X_1 = X \times 10$	x	x^2
9	90	20	400
8	80	10	100
7	70	0	0
6	60	-10	100
5	50	-20	400
			$\sigma_1 = \sqrt{2} \times 10$
$\overline{X} = 7$	$\overline{X}_1 = 70$		

$\overline{X}_1 = 70$; i.e., 10×7 and $\sigma_1 = \sqrt{2} \times 10$

When each measure is added by the same constant $\overline{X}$ becomes $\overline{X}$ + constant and σ is unchanged. When each measure is multiplied by a constant, $\overline{X}$ and σ are multiplied by the same constant.

When to Use Various Measures of Central Tendencies

Mean

1) When most of the measures are distributed around a central point.
2) When other measures like SD, MD, correlation, etc. involving mean are to be computed.
3) When a measure of central tendency of greatest stability is needed.

Median

1) When the exact midpoint of distribution is needed.
2) When there are extreme scores which would affect the mean.

Mode

1) When a quick and approximate measure of central tendency is needed.
2) When the measure of central tendency should be the most typical value.

When to Use Measures of Variability

***Range*:** When the data are too scattered, when a type of extreme scores or of a total spread is wanted.

QD: 1) When median is used as the measure of central tendency.
2) When there are extreme scores which would affect the standard deviation disproportionately.

3) When the measure at the middle of the distribution is wanted.

AD: 1) When it is devised to get all the deviations from the mean
2) When there are extreme scores which may influence SD

SD: 1) When the statistic having the greatest stability is needed
2) When extreme deviation should exercise a proportionately greater effect on the variability
3) When coefficient of correlation and other statistics are subsequently to be computed.

2.8 PERCENTILE RANKS (GARRETT, 1961)

Consider the following frequency distribution. We have to calculate the percentile ranks.

Class	f	F
195-199	1	50
190-194	2	49
185-189	4	47
180-184	5	43
175-179	8	38
170-174	10	30
165-169	6	20
160-164	4	14
155-159	4	10
150-154	2	6
145-149	3	4
140-144	1	1

Calculation of percentile rank of score – 163

The score 163 lies in the interval 160 – 164. i.e., 159.5 – 164.5. From the given data we can see that up to the score 159.5. (the exact lower limit of the interval containing the score 163) the cumulative frequency is 10.

The interval 159.5 – 164.5 has 5 units of interval and 4 scores are distributed in this interval. Then one unit of interval when converted into score gives us. $4/5$

= 0.8 distance

The score 163 is 3.5 units distance from 159.5. These 3.5 units of interval equals 3.5 × 0.8 score distance. Thus, on the whole the number of scores below 163 is (10 + 3.5 × 0.8). This figure is for the given sample size of N = 50. When this is converted into a percentage.

The percentile rank of 163 $= \frac{(10+3.5\times0.8)}{50}\times100 = 25.6 = 26$

Question: Calculate the percentile rank of 171, 188 and 156.

Percentile rank of 171 (PR)
It lies in the interval 170 – 174

$$PR = \frac{(20+2\times1.5)}{50}\times100 = 46$$

PR of 188: It is in the interval 185-189

$$PR = \frac{(43+3.5\times0.8)}{50}\times100 = 91.6 = 92$$

PR of 156: It is in the interval 155 – 159

$$\frac{(6+1.5\times0.8)}{50}\times100 = 14.4 = 14$$

$$PR = \frac{F+(\text{given score}-l)f/i}{N}\times100$$

F → Cum. Frequency up to lower limit of the class interval
l → lower limit   i → class interval
f → frequency of the interval containing the given score
N → number (size)
PR of upper limit = Cum. freq. F × 100/N

Calculating PRs from ordered data

Ordinary ranks can be converted into percentile ranks using the formula,

$$PR = 100 - \frac{(100R-50)}{N}$$

Where R is the rank position

20 children are put in order of merits for scores on an achievement test. Compute the PR of each child

For 1: $PR = 100 - \frac{100\times1-50}{20} = 100 - 2.5 = 97.5$

For 2: $PR = 100 - \frac{100\times2-50}{20} = 92.5$

For 3: $PR = 100 - \frac{100\times3-50}{20} = 87.5$

For 4: $PR = 100 - \frac{100 \times 4 - 50}{20} = 82.5$

For 5: $PR = 100 - \frac{100 \times 5 - 50}{20} = 77.5$

For 6: $PR = 100 - \frac{100 \times 6 - 50}{20} = 72.5$

For 7: $PR = 100 - \frac{100 \times 7 - 50}{20} = 67.5$

For 8: $PR = 100 - \frac{100 \times 8 - 50}{20} = 62.5$

For 9: $PR = 100 - \frac{100 \times 9 - 50}{20} = 57.5$

For 10: $PR = 100 - \frac{100 \times 10 - 50}{20} = 52.5$

For 11: $PR = 100 - \frac{100 \times 11 - 50}{20} = 47.5$

For 12: $PR = 100 - \frac{100 \times 12 - 50}{20} = 42.5$

For 13: $PR = 100 - \frac{100 \times 13 - 50}{20} = 37.5$

For 14: $PR = 100 - \frac{100 \times 14 - 50}{20} = 32.5$

For 15: $PR = 100 - \frac{100 \times 15 - 50}{20} = 27.5$

For 16: $PR = 100 - \frac{100 \times 16 - 50}{20} = 22.5$

For 17: $PR = 100 - \frac{100 \times 17 - 50}{20} = 17.5$

For 18: $PR = 100 - \frac{100 \times 18 - 50}{20} = 12.5$

For 19: $PR = 100 - \frac{100 \times 19 - 50}{20} = 7.5$

For 20: $PR = 100 - \frac{100 \times 20 - 50}{20} = 2.5$

2.9 DERIVED SCORES

Why derived scores?

A raw score, by itself is unpredictable. So, we need a frame of reference to decide whether a given score indicates a good performance or a poor one. Suppose, a student says, "I got a score of 86" where the class mean was 56 and score range was from 23 to 60. His answer indicates that his performance is very near to the best in the class. The raw score became interpretable by relating it to a measure of central tendency and a measure of variability.

The solution to the problem of making scores meaningful involves providing an adequate frame of reference. A derived score relates the position of a raw score either to the other scores in the same distribution or to the distribution of raw scores obtained by a representative group. The advantage of derived score is that they provide a standard frame of reference within which the meaning of a score can be better understood.

1. Standard Scores

For a variable X if a set of measures are given then their mean will be denoted by $\overline{X}$ and Standard deviation by σ or s. Then $X - \overline{X}$ are called deviation scores. When these deviation scores are divided by the standard deviation of X, we get Standard scores.

They are denoted by z and also called σ – scores. Thus $z = X - \overline{X}/\sigma$

The mean and SD of these standard scores will be 0 and 1 respectively.

Convert the following scores into z values

X	$X-\overline{X}$	$(X-\overline{X})^2$	$z = \frac{X-\overline{X}}{\sigma}$	$(z-\overline{z})^2$
70	14	196	1.668	2.782
60	4	16	0.476	0.226
50	–6	36	–0.715	0.5112
54	–2	4	–0.238	0.566
46	–10	100	–1.192	1.420
		332		**4.9975**

$$\overline{X} = 56;\ \sigma = \sqrt{\frac{\sum(X-\overline{X})^2)}{N}} = \sqrt{\frac{352}{5}} = 8.39$$

$$\text{Mean of } z = \frac{-0.001}{5} = 0 \text{ and SD, } \sigma = \sqrt{\frac{4.9975}{5}} = \sqrt{\frac{5}{5}} = 1$$

i.e., the mean and SD of standard scores are 0 and 1

Another important property of the standard scores is that they all preserve the shape of the original distribution of raw scores.

2. T –Scores

Standard scores with a mean of 50 and a standard deviation of 10 are called as T Scores.

i.e., **T = 10 z+ 50**

If z = 0.0 (the mean), then T = 50 + (10 × 0.0) = 50

3. Stanine Scores

Stanine (STAndard NINE) is a method of scaling test scores on a nine-point standard scale with a mean of five and a standard deviation of two. The underlying basis for obtaining stanines is that a normal distribution is divided into nine intervals, each of which has a width of 0.5 standard deviations excluding the first and last, which are just the remainder (the tails of the distribution). The mean lies at the centre of the fifth interval.

Difference between z-score, T-scores and Stanine scores:

- As you know, z-scores are expressed via decimal numbers (e.g., z = 1.40) that can be positive or negative
- T-scores are expressed via 2-digit whole numbers (e.g. T = 64) that are always positive numbers.
- Stanine scores are simpler, for they are expressed as 1-digit whole numbers.
- A stanine score can be any number between 1 and 9 (inclusive). Typically, a person is said to be "average" (i.e., near the mean) if his / her stanine score is 4, 5, or 6.
- Stanine scores of 7 or 8 are usually interpreted as indicating "above average" performance.
- Stanine score of 9 is normally considered to reflect "outstanding" performance, for that's the highest score one can get.

The first of the two new things to know about stanine scores is the percentage of people who will receive any given stanine.

4% - in stanine 1
7% - in stanine 2
12% - in stanine 3
17% - in stanine 4
20% - in stanine 5
17% - in stanine 6
12% - in stanine 7
7% - in stanine 8 and
4% - in stanine 9.

The second thing to know about stanines concerns the "boundary lines" (on the baseline under the normal curve) between adjacent stanines. All stanines except the upper and lower ones have a "width" (on the baseline under the curve) equal to one-half of a standard deviation.

EXERCISES

1. Calculate the Mean for each of the following data:
   a) 1,1,2,3,3
   b) 75,23,48,60,98,65,8,12,39
   c) 12,10,9,11,9,15,10,9,8,13,9,10
2. Calculate Mean, Median and Mode of the following scores:
   a) 9,14,17,23
   b) 5,16,14,8,15,11,13,9,12,19,13,10,17
   c) 27,19,14,25,19,22,26,23
3. Calculate standard deviation of the above scores.

REFERENCES

1. Ferguson, G.A (1971). *Statistical Analysis in Psychology and Education* (3rd Edn.). Tokyo: Mc Graw Hill.
2. Hays, W.L (1988). *Statistics* (4th Ed). New York: Holt, Rinehart &Winston.
3. Garrett, H. E & Woodworth, R.S. (1961). *Statistics in Psychology and Education*. New York: Vakils, Feffer and Simon Ltd.
4. Springer, K (2010). *Educational Research – A contextual approach*. Chennai: John Wiley & Sons, Inc.
5. Tokunaga, H.T (2016). *Fundamental Statistics for the Social and Behavioural Sciences*. New Delhi: Sage.

3

Normal Distribution

3.1 WHAT ARE NORMAL DISTRIBUTIONS?

Evaluating a score relative to the other scores in a population may require an understanding of a specific type of distribution known as a normal distribution, defined as a distribution based on a population of an infinite number of scores calculated from a mathematical formula. Note that a normal distribution differs from the types of distributions discussed earlier in this book (what we have referred to as frequency distributions) in that scores in a normal distribution are generated from a mathematical formula rather than data collected from research participants. An example of a normal distribution is illustrated in Fig 1.

There are four distinguishing features of normal distributions. First, because they consist of an infinite number of scores generated from mathematical formulas, the left and right ends of normal distributions continue to infinity (symbolized by the Greek symbol ∞) and do not touch the horizontal (X) axis. The ends, or tails as they are sometimes called, of normal distributions do not touch the X-axis because to do so would signify the end of the distribution (a score with a frequency f of zero). Second, in terms of their shape, normal distributions are uni-modal and symmetric and are often referred to as "bell-shaped". The symmetrical nature of normal distributions implies that if you were to fold middle, the left and right halves of the distribution would exactly match one another. Third, in terms of central tendency, because normal distributions are based on a population of scores, the mean of normal distribution is the population mean μ. Finally, in terms of variability, the standard deviation of a normal distribution is the population standard deviation σ.

3.2 WHY ARE NORMAL DISTRIBUTIONS IMPORTANT?

Normal distributions differ from frequency distributions in that frequency distributions are constructed using data collected from samples, whereas normal distributions consist of an infinite number of score generated by mathematical formulas. Because data collected by researchers often do not closely resemble the smooth, curved shape of a normal distribution, you may wonder why normal distributions are the basis of statistical techniques designed to analyze collected data. The answer to this question is threefold.

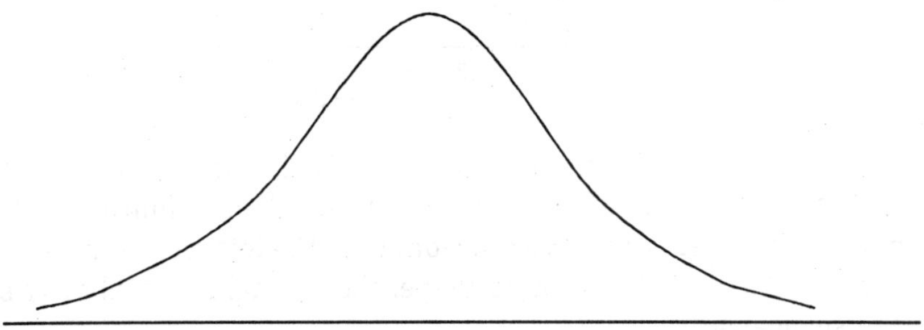

Example of a Normal Distribution

First, normal distributions are used because many variables (e.g., height or weight) are generally believed by researchers to be normally distributed in the population. Therefore, researchers apply the characteristics of normal distributions to data collected from samples, particularly when the sample is large. The discovery that such variables are not normally distributed in a particular sample is typically attributed to limitations in how the data were collected. For example, findings that a variable is not normally distributed commonly result from samples that are relatively small or not representative of the entire population.

A second reason for using normal distributions, related to the first, is that many statistical procedures designed to test research hypotheses are based mathematically on the assumption that variables are normally distributed. This assumption reinforces the importance of examining the distribution of data collected from samples to assess the degree to which it resembles a normal distribution.

Last, because normal distributions are based on mathematical formulae, it is possible to determine the proportion of the distribution associated with any score. For example, because a normal distribution is symmetric, exactly 50% of the distribution is located below the mean and 50% is located above the mean.

3.3 THE STANDARD NORMAL DISTRIBUTION

To avoid confusion resulting from using normal distributions with different units of measurement, researchers rely on a single normal distribution that can be applied to any normally distributed variable, regardless of how the variable has been measured. This distribution is known as the standard normal distribution, which is a normal distribution measured in standard deviation units with a mean equal to 0 and a standard deviation equal to 1. Figure below is a visual illustration of the standard normal distribution.

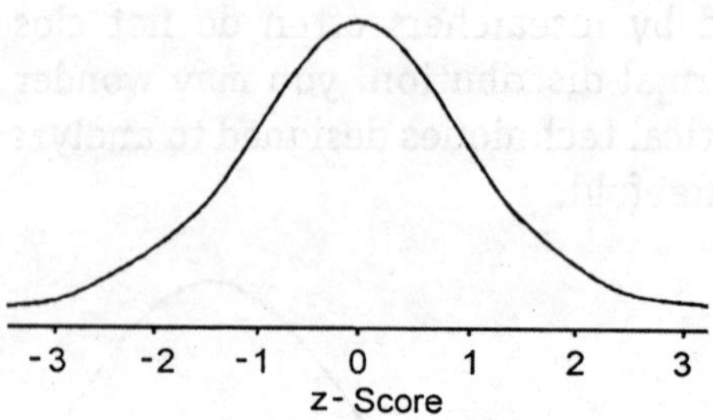

In describing the standard normal distribution, it is important to understand that it shares many of the features of normal distributions. There are an infinite number of scores in this distribution, with the left and right tails never touching the horizontal axis. In terms of its shape, the standard normal distribution is uni modal and symmetric.

However, the standard normal distribution is distinguished from other normal distributions in three important ways. First, scores for the standard normal distribution, known as z-scores, are measured in standard deviation units, which is the number of standard deviations from the mean. This is in contrast to other normal distributions, where measurements are a function of how each particular variable is measured. Second, the mean of the standard normal distribution is equal to zero, in contrast to other normal distributions, which have the population mean . Third, in terms of variability, the standard deviation of the standard normal distribution is equal to 1 rather than the population standard deviation σ.

Properties of Standard Normal Distribution

1. The normal probability distribution or simply, normal curve is expressed by the equation.

$$y = \frac{N}{\sigma\sqrt{2\pi}} e^{\frac{-x^2}{2\sigma^2}}$$

This equation when written in standard score form as

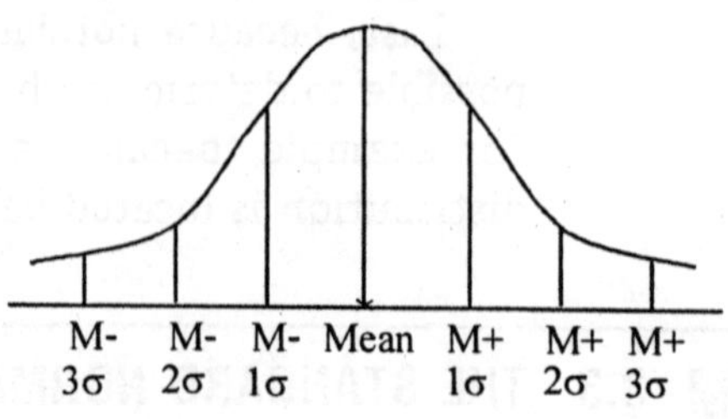

$$y = \frac{N}{\sigma\sqrt{2\pi}} e^{\frac{-z^2}{2}}$$

Where X stands for the given variable and Y, respective frequencies

2. The normal distribution is symmetrical about the ordinate at $X = \overline{X}$ and appears as a smooth curve. Since the ordinate at $X = \overline{X}$ divides the curve into two equal parts the mean, median, and mode will coincide at one point
3. For a normal distribution, Skewness = 0 and Kurtosis = 0.263
4. The curve is asymptotic i.e. the curve extends to infinity on either side of the mean.
5. The curve will be maximum at the ordinate $X = \overline{X}$ and hence the maximum ordinate is given by $Y = \frac{1}{\sqrt{2\pi}} = 0.3989$
6. The curve has points of inflection at $X = \overline{X} \pm \sigma$ (turning points)
7. The total area under the curve has considered as N. For practical purposes this area is treated as 1.
8. 68.26 % of the total area under the normal curve lies between $\overline{X} - \sigma$ and $\overline{X} + \sigma$
9. 95.44% i.e. ~95% of the total area under the normal curve lies between $\overline{X} - 2\sigma$ and $\overline{X} + 2\sigma$.
10. 99.7% of the total area under the normal curve lies between $\overline{X} - 3\sigma$ and $\overline{X} + 3\sigma$.
11. Quartile deviation of a normal distribution is $\frac{2}{3}\sigma = 0.6745\sigma$
12. Mean deviation $= 4\frac{\sigma}{5}$

3.4 APPLICATIONS OF THE NORMAL PROBABILITY CURVE

I. Find the height of the ordinate of the normal curve at the following z values

−2.15, −1.53, +0.07, +0.99, +2.76

The height of the ordinate from the table of 'areas and the ordinates' of the normal curve is as presented below (See Appendix IA).

The height at z = +2.15 = 0.0395. Since the curve is symmetrical, the height of the ordinate at z = -2.15 = 0.0395

height of the ordinate at -1.53 is 0.1238
height of the ordinate at +0.07 is 0.3980
height of the ordinate at +0.99 is 0.2444
height of the ordinate at +2.76 is 0.0088

II. Consider a normally distributed variable with $\overline{X} = 50$ s = 10 For N = 200. Find the height of the ordinate at the following value of X 25, 87, 49, 57, 63

1) $z = \frac{X - \overline{X}}{\sigma} = \frac{25 - 50}{10} = -2.5$

2) $z = \frac{35 - 50}{10} = -1.5$

3) $z = \dfrac{49-50}{10} = -0.1$

4) $z = \dfrac{57-50}{10} = -0.7$

5) $z = \dfrac{63-50}{10} = 1.3$

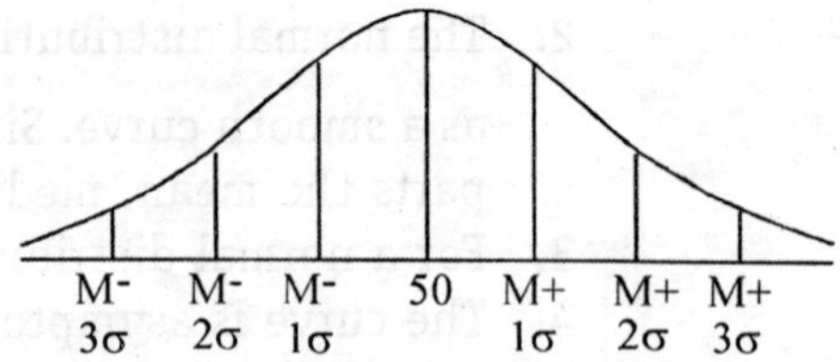

1) At z = 2.15, height of the ordinate = 0.715
   when N = 200, height of the ordinate at z = -2.15 = 0.0175 x 200 = 3.5
2) At z = -1.5, height of ordinate = 0.1295
   when N = 200, height of the ordinate at z = 0.1295 x 200 = 25.9
3) At X = 49, z = -0.1, height of the ordinate = 0.2420
   when N = 200, height of ordinate = 200 x 0.2420 = 48.4
4) At X = 57, z = 0.7, height of ordinate = 0.3123
   when N = 200, height of ordinate = 200 x 0.3123 = 62.46
5) At X = 63, z = 1.3 height of ordinate = 0.1714
   when N = 200, height of ordinate = 200 x 0.1714 = 34.28

III. Find the proportion of the area of the normal curve

a) Between mean and z = 1.49
b) Between mean and z = 1.26
c) To the right of z = 0.25
d) To the right of z = 1.50
e) To the left of z = -1.26
f) To the left of z = 0.95
g) Between z = ± 0.50
h) Between z = -0.75 & z = 1.50
i) Between z = 1.00 and z = 1.96
j) Between z = 1.00 and z = 1.01

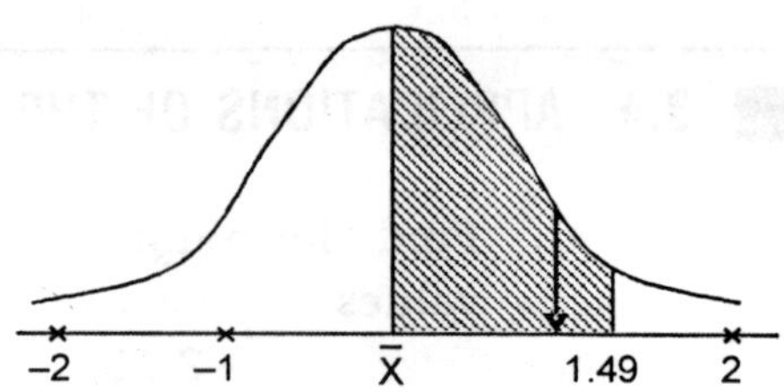

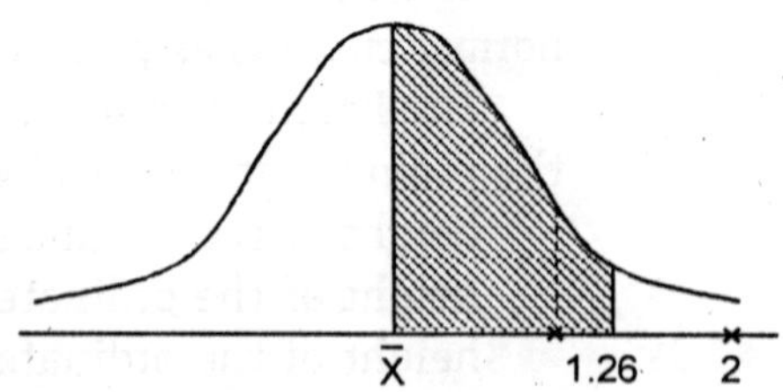

Answer: Refer Appendix IB

a) Up to z = 1.49 (i.e. between z = 0 and z = 1.49) the area = 0.4319
b) Area between mean and z = 1.26 = 0.3962
c) To the right of 0.25 means the area between 3 and 0.25 i.e., ½ of total area-area of 0.25 = 0.5– 0.0987 = 0.4013
d) To the right of z = 1.50 0.5 - 0.4332 = 0.0668
e) To the left of z = -1.26 = 0.5-0.3962 = 0.1038
f) To the left of z = 0.95 0.5+0.3790 = 0.8289
g) Between z = +0.50 = 2 x 0.1915 = 0.3830
h) Between z = -0.75 and z = 1.5 = 0.2734 + 0.4332 = 0.7066
i) Between z = 1.00 and z = 1.96
   area of z = 1.96 – area of 1.00 = 0.4750 – 0.3413 = 0.1337

j) Between z = 1.00 and z = 1.01
area of z = 1.01 – area of 1.00 = 0.3438 – 0.3413 = 0.0025

IV. Given a distribution of scores with a mean of 12 and standard deviation of 4. Assuming normality,

a) What per cent of the cases fall between 8 and 16.
b) What per cent of the cases lie above score 18.
c) Below score 6.

$\overline{X} = 12; \sigma = 4$

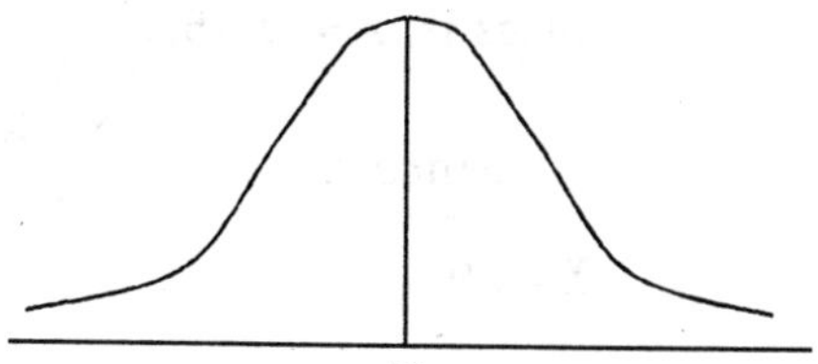

a) $\frac{X-\overline{X}}{\sigma}$

for 8, $\frac{8-12}{4} = -1 = z$

for 16, $\frac{16-12}{4} = 1 = z$

area between –1 and +1 = 0.3413 × 2 = 0.6826, i.e., 68.26% of the cases falls between 8 and 16

b) For X = 18 $z = \frac{8-12}{4} = 1.5$. Area above z = 1.5 is 0.5– 0.4332 = 0.0668,

0.68% of the cases above 18.

c) For X = 6, $z = \frac{6-12}{4} = -1.5$. Area below -1.5 is, 0.5 – 0.4332 = 0.0668 i.e.,

6.68 % of cases are below score 6.

V. Given $\overline{X} = 80$ and $\sigma = 16$, and N = 510, what per cent of the scores in this distribution fall above a score of 110 assuming a normal distribution $z = \frac{110-80}{16} =$ 1.875 N = 510

Area above 1.875 = 0.5 – 0.4693 = 0.0307,

When N = 510, Per cent of scores fall above the score 110 = 0.0307 × 510 = 15.657 = 1565.7

Area = 0.5 – 0.4696 = 0.0304 For N = 510, area = 15.504

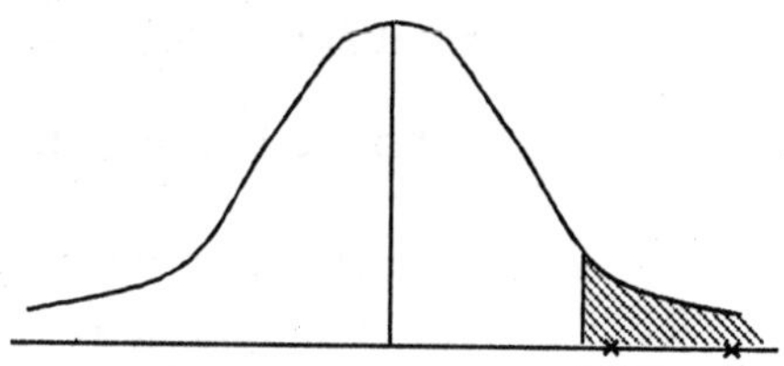

VI. Given a distribution of scores with $\overline{X}$ – 16 and σ – 4. If we assume normality, what links will include the middle 75 % of the cases.

From the table area of 37.5 % or 0.375 corresponding to z = 1.15 so z = 1.15

$$Z = \frac{X-\overline{X}}{\sigma}; \; 1.15 = \frac{X-16}{4} = 20.6$$

The middle 75% of the cases means 37.5% cases on either sides of the curve from the ordinate at z = 0. Therefore limits that will include the middle 75% of the cases means, the limit having the area between z = 0, and covering the area 37.5%. Using the table, we can see the z value corresponding to the area 0.3750 is z = 1.15

Since the curve is symmetrical, the lower limit containing the left 37.5% of the cases is, z = -1.15.

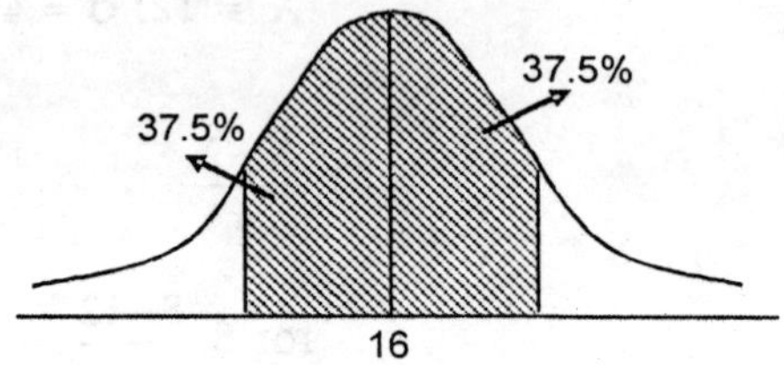

Since $z = Z = \frac{X-\overline{X}}{\sigma}$ i.e., $1.15 = \frac{X-16}{4}$

X = 20.6

For z = -1.15, $-1.15 = \frac{X-16}{4}$ X = 11.4

So the area of 75% of cases lies between scores 20.6 and 11.4

VII. The scores of an intelligent test were found to be distributed normally. If the mean and standard deviation of distribution were 40 and 8 respectively. Find

a) the limits that will include middle 50% of the cases
b) the limits that will include highest 20% of the cases
c) the limits that will include lowest 15% of cases

a) z corresponds 25% or 0.25 is z = 0.675

So limits are z = .0.675 and z = -0.675

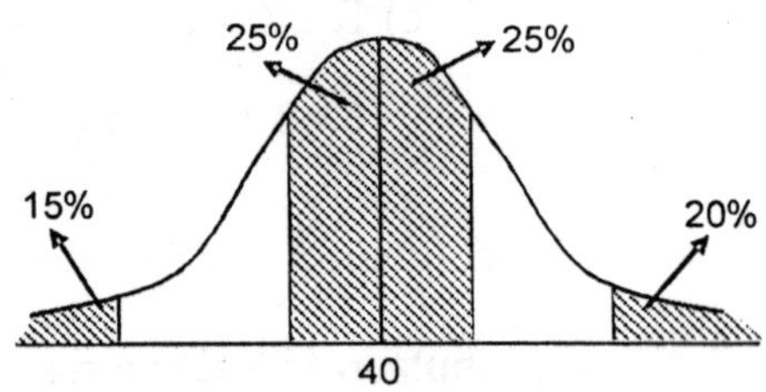

The score for z = 0.675, $0.075 = \frac{X-40}{8}$

X = 45.4

for z = -0.675, X = 34.6

So the limits are 34.6 & 45.4

b) Highest 20% means, 0.5 – 0.2 = 0.3

z = 0.845 $0.845 = \frac{X-40}{8}$ i.e., X = 46.76

For z = 0.5, X = (3 x 8) +40 = = 64 i.e., between 46.76 and 64

c) Lowest 15% means, 0.5 – 0.15 = 0.35

For area 0.35, z = -1.4

$-1.4 = \frac{X-40}{8}$; X = 31.68 for z = -3, X = 16 so the limits are 16 & 31.68

VIII. A teacher decides to fail 25% of the students in a class. Examination marks are roughly distributed with a mean of 72 and a SD of 6. What marks should a student get to pass?

Area = 0.5 − 0.25 = 0.25

z corresponds to 0.25 = 0.675 $\frac{X - \overline{X}}{\sigma}$ =

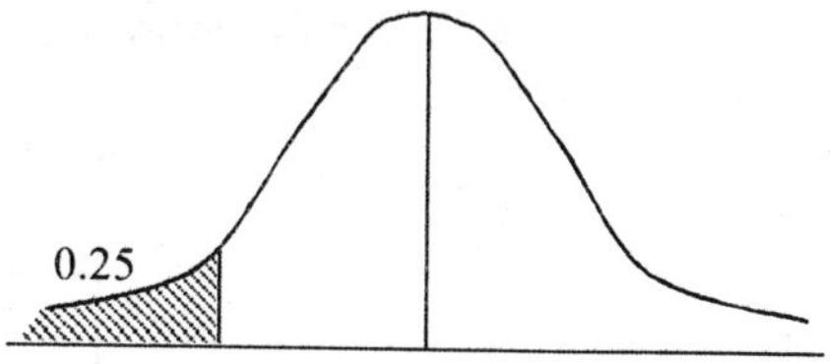

$0.675 = \frac{X - 72}{6}$, X = 67.95 ≈ 68

[The minimum mark required for a pass is the z corresponding to which first 25% denotes for a fail]

So, minimum marks required for a pass is 68

IX. Scores on a particular physical test are normally distributed with a mean of 50 and a standard deviation of 10. The decision is made to use a letter grade system A.B, C, D, E with the proportion. 0.10, 0.20, 0.40, 0.20 and 0.10 in the five grades respectively. Find the score intervals for the five letter grades.

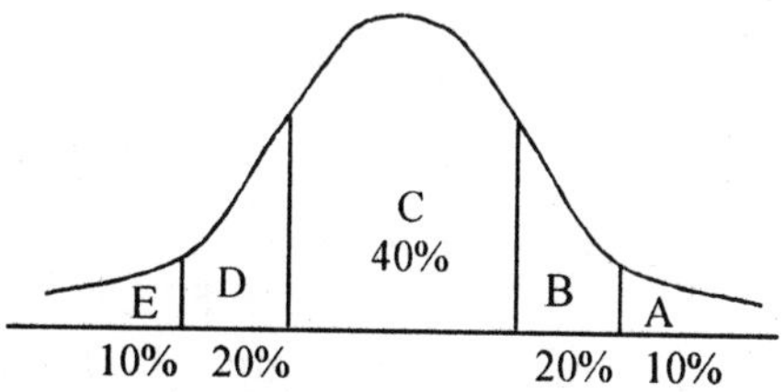

Intervals for A: 0.5-0.1 = 0.4 z = 1.285

$\frac{X - 50}{10} = 1.285$; X = 62.85

$\frac{X - 50}{10} = 3$ X = 80

Therefore, the interval for grade A is 62.85 to 80

Interval for B: area of B = 0.5 − 0.3 = 0.2

z = 0.525 $0.525 = \frac{X - 50}{10}$ X = 55.25

Therefore, the interval for grade B is 55.25 to 62.85

Interval for C: Interval for C is 50 to 55.25 and 50 to 44.75 i.e. 44.75 to 55.25

Interval for D: z of -0.2 is, $-0.525 = \frac{X - 50}{10}$ X = 44.75

Therefore, interval for D grade is from 44.75 to 37.15

Interval for E: z = -1.285 $\frac{X - 50}{10}$ or X = 37.15

$-3 = \frac{X - 50}{10}$ or X = 20

Therefore, interval for E is 20 to 37.15

X. The following are data for test scores for two age groups

	11 year group	**14 year group**
$\overline{X}$	48	56
S	8	12
N	500	800

Assuming normality, estimate how many of the 11 year old do better than the average 14 year old and how many of the 14 year old do worse than the average 11 year old.

a) 11 year olds do better than the average 14 year old means, 11 year olds do better than the score 56

z score equation of 56 is: $z = \dfrac{X-\overline{X}}{\sigma} = \dfrac{56-48}{8} = 1$

Area corresponding to the z value 1 is 0.3413. So the area above the z value i is 0.5 – 0.3413 = 0.1587

Therefore 15.87% of the cases lies above the score 56. When N = 500, the number of 11 year group = 500 × 0.1587 = 79.35

b) 14 year olds do worse than the average 11 year old means, 14 year olds do worse than the score 48.

z score corresponding to 48 is, z = 48 – 56 ÷ 12 = –0.666

Area corresponding to z = –0.666 is, 0.2486

Therefore area below the z value 0.666 is, 0.5 – 0.2454 = 0.2514. When N = 800, the number of 14 year group children below score 48 is, 0.2546 x 800 = 201.12

So 201.12 of the 14 year pupils lie below the score 48.

XI. A normal distribution has the mean 95. Find its standard deviation if 20% of the area under the curve lies to the right of 103.4.

X = – 95, z corresponding to 0.3 is z = 0.84

But $z = \dfrac{X-\overline{X}}{\sigma}$ $0.84 = \dfrac{103.4-95}{\sigma} = \dfrac{8.4}{\sigma}$

Given the area under the curve to the right of the score 103.4 is 20%. Therefore the area under the curve from the mean (z = 0) to the score 103.4 will be 30%. From the table of areas and ordinates the z – score up to which the area is 30% from the mean is, z = 0.84. Thus, z = 0.84 and the score 103.4 are the same.

z = 0.84 means, $\dfrac{X-\overline{X}}{\sigma} = 0.84$ substituting the values of X and $\overline{X}$, we get

$$\frac{103.4-95}{\sigma} = 0.84 \text{ or s} = 10$$

XII. Given the distribution of the scores made on a logical memory test by 300 boys and 250 girls. The boys mean score is 21.49 with a s of 3.63. Girls mean score is 23.68 and s is 5.12. The median of boys is 21.41. Median of girls is 23.66. What per cent of the boys exceed the median of the girl's distribution?

	Boys	Girls
N	300	250
M	21.49	23.68
σ	3.63	5.12
Mdn	21.41	23.66

We have to calculate the area of the curve above the rawscore X = 23.66 which is the median of the girl's scores. So z value corresponding to X = 23.66 is, $\overline{X}$ of boys = 21.49s of boys = 3.63 $z = \frac{X-\overline{X}}{\sigma} = \frac{23.66-21.49}{3.63} = 0.5978$

Area of the curve up to z = 0.5978 is from the tables, 0.2258. The area above the z score 0.5978 is equal to 0.5 – 0.2258 = 0.2742. But N = 300. Therefore the percentage of the boys exceeding the mean score of girls is, 0.2742 x 300 = 82.26. So 82 boys out of 300 lies above the score 23.66.

XIII. In a normal distribution with mean 45, and (– 10, at what percentile rank does a score of 58 fall? Also find 23rd percentile.

We have to find out the number of cases lies below the score 58. i.e., the area under the curve from mean to score 58 and + 0.5

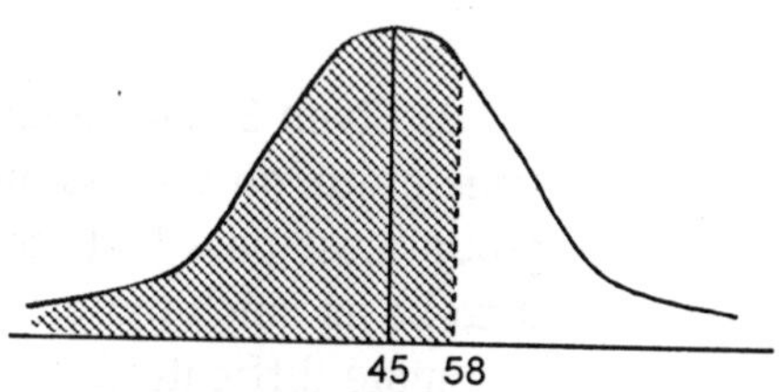

z value corresponding to 58 = $\frac{58-45}{10} = 1.3$

Area from z = 0 to z = 1.3 = 0.4032. So the total area up to z = 4.3 is, 0.4032 + 0.5 = 0.9032

The percentage of cases lies below z = 1.3 is 90.32 = 90%. So the percentile rank is 90.32

Find 23rd percentile: To find the 23rd percentile, z corresponds to area 0.23 is, the 23rd percentile mean the point below which lie 23% of the cases. The area of the curve up to the 23% is 0.5 – 0.23 = 0.27. z value corresponding to area 0.27 is -0.74

$$\frac{X-\overline{X}}{\sigma} = \frac{X-45}{10} = -0.74 \text{ or } X = 37.6$$

So the 23rd percentile = 37.6

To determine the relative difficulty of test questions, problems and other test items, properties of normal curve can be used. For example,

Given a test question solved by 10% of a large unselected group. A second problem solved by 20% of the same group and a third problem solved by 30%. If we assume the capacity measured by the test problems to be distributed normally, what is the relative difficulty of questions 1, 2, and 3?

The first item has been solved by 10% of the group. Since the capacity measured by the test problem is assumed to be distributed normally, this 10% is the extreme right 10% under a normal distribution. Therefore, the difficulty value of this item will be the lower limit of this extreme right 10%. From the table, the lower limit we can see that such lower limit is $-z = 1.28$. i.e., the lower limit is at a distance 1.286 from the mean and hence we can say the difficulty value of the item or 1.28s.

The second item has been solved by 20% of the same group. Therefore, the difficulty value of this item will be the lower limit of the extreme 20% group. From the table, this lower limit is, $z = 0.84$. i.e., this point is 0.846 distance from the mean and the difficulty value of the test item is 0.846.

The third item has been solved by 30% of the group. Therefore, the difficulty value of this item will be the lower limit of the extreme 30% group. From the table, this lower limit is $z = 0.52$ i.e., the point is 0.526 distance from the mean and hence the difficulty value of the item is 0.526.

Relative difficulty 1) $1.28\,\sigma$ } 0.44

2) $0.84\,\sigma$ } 0.32

3) $6.52\,\sigma$

2) Given 3 test items 1, 2 and 3 panel by 50% , 40%, and 30% respectively of a large group on the assumption of normality of distribution, what percentage of this group must pass test item 4 in order for it to be as much more difficult than 3 or 2 is more difficult than 1.

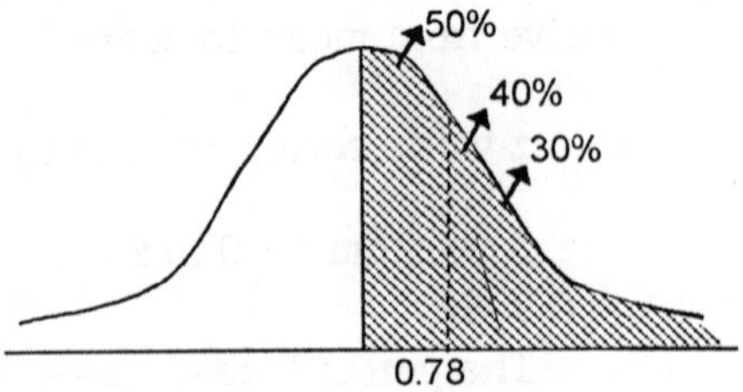

For the Ist , 50% of the group has passed. So $z = 0$

For the 2nd item, 40% z value is, $z = 0.255$. The difficulty level is 0.2556

For the 3rd item, 30% z value is, $z = 0.525$. The difficulty level is 0.5256

1 – 0 } 0.255s

2 – 0.255s } 0.270s

3 – 0.525s

2 is 0.255 σ more difficult than 1, so 4th item is 0.255 σ more difficult than 3.
So difficulty value of 4th item is, = 0.525 σ + 0.255 σ = 0.780 σ from the mean
The area corresponding to the z value z = 0.780 is, 0.2823
The area passed by 20% is, 0.5 – 0.2823 = 0.2177
Therefore 21.77% of the students passed the 4th item

Note:	1.	50%	z = 0
	2.	40%	z = 0.25
	3.	30%	z = 0.52

Looking to the above values, since item 2 is 0.25 σ further along the difficulty scale, than item 1, it is clear that item 4 must be 0.25 σ above item 3 if it is to be much farther than item z as item 2 is farther than item 2.

Therefore, item 4 must have a difficulty value 0.52 σ + 0.25 σ away from the mean. i.e., 0.77 σ distance away from the mean, which is represented by z = 0.77.

The pass percentage of item 4 means the number of cases i.e., the area under the curve from z = 0.77 onwards. From the table, this area is 0.5–area from z = 0 to z = 0.77. i.e. 0.5 – 0.280 = 0.2177. Hence, the required pass percentage of the item 4 is, 21.77%.

3.5 SKEWNESS

It refers to the symmetry or asymmetry of the frequency distribution. A frequency distribution or curve is said to be symmetrical if at the highest point of a curve, we draw a curve to the X-axis, then this line of separation splits the curve into two equal halves.

If a distribution is asymmetrical and the larger frequencies tend to be concentrated toward the low end of the variable and smaller frequencies toward the high and, it is said to be positively skewed or skewed to the right. If the opposite poles i.e., if the larger frequencies being concentrated towards the high end of the variable and the smaller frequencies toward the low end, the distribution is said to be negatively skewed or skewed to the left.

Skewness can be calculated by the formula

1) $\text{Skewness} = 3\frac{(\text{Mean} - \text{Median})}{\text{SD}}$

In a positively skewed distribution the mean lies to the right of the median and mode represents the point of highest frequency. Therefore, the points of mean, median and mode in a positively skewed distribution will be as given in the figure below.

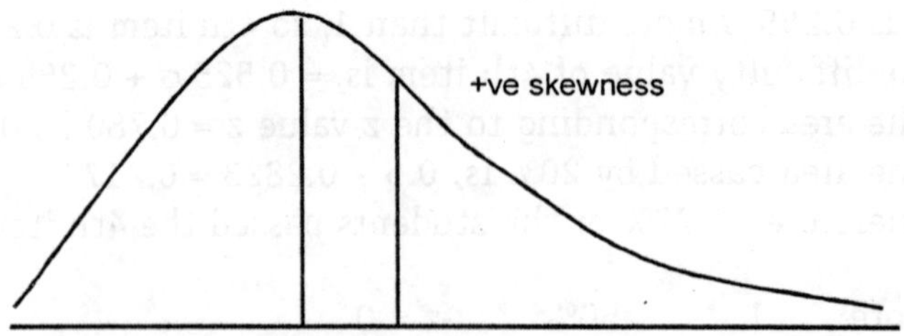

In a negatively skewed distribution, mean lies to the left of the median and since mode represents the highest point of frequency, the position of mean, median and mode will be as in the figure given below.

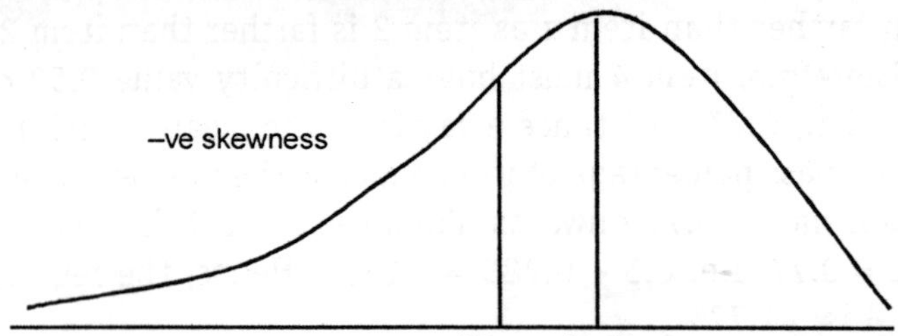

3.6 KURTOSIS

It refers to the flatness or peakedness of one distribution in relation to another. It is conventional to speak of a distribution as leptokurtic if it is more peaked than a particular type of distribution known as the normal distribution (mesokurtic) and platy kurtic if it is less peaked. This means that a mesokurtic or normal distribution falls between a leptokurtic and platykurtic distribution.

$$\text{Ku} = \frac{Q}{D} = \frac{P_{75} - P_{25}}{2(P_{90} - P_{10})}$$

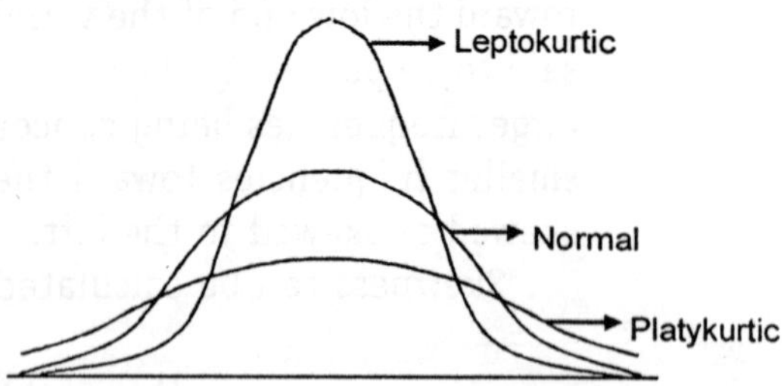

where Ku is the range between 90th and 10th percentile.

Thus, the formula $\text{Ku} = \dfrac{P_{75} - P_{25}}{2(P_{90} - P_{10})}$

For a normal distribution, the value Ku = 0.263

If Ku > 0.263 → platykurtic

If Ku < 0.263 → leptokurtic

3.7 INTRODUCTION TO THE t-DISTRIBUTION

The t-statistic is used to test the difference between a sample mean and a population mean when an unknown population standard deviation is estimated with the standard deviation of a sample. The distribution of t-statistics is known as the Student t-distribution, defined as the distribution of value of the t-statistic based on an infinite number of samples of size N randomly drawn from the population. The Student t-distribution was developed by W.S. Gosset, who wrote under the pen name "Student".

t-distributions are theoretical symmetrical distributions with a mean of zero and a standard deviation that becomes smaller when degrees of freedom increases.

Characteristics

The Student t-distribution is a theoretical distribution that is created in a similar manner to the sampling distribution of the mean. Using the unique vulnerability study to illustrate this distribution, imagine that the average estimated age of death in the population is 80. We draw a random sample from the population, calculate the mean estimate age of death for the sample, and transform the sample mean into a t-statistic.

The student t-distribution shares many of the characteristics of the standard normal distribution. For example, in terms of modality, looking at the center of the distribution in the above figure, we see that the mean of the Student t-distribution is equal to 0. Another similarity to the standard normal distribution is that the Student t-distribution is symmetrical, with an infinite number of values in both tails of the distribution. However, unlike the standard normal distribution, there is not just one t-distribution but instead a family of t-distributions: different distribution of t-statistics for each sample size. Because t-statistics involve estimating the population from a sample, and this estimate is a function of the size of the sample, it makes sense that there will be a different distribution of t-statistics for different sample sizes.

3.8 COMPARISON OF NORMAL DISTRIBUTION AND STUDENTS' T-DISTRIBUTION

When N is less than 30, 's' will under estimate 'σ'. The famous biologist William Gossett resolved the problem of small sample sizes. In such cases the scores will follow students' t-distribution.

Example of the Student t-Distribution

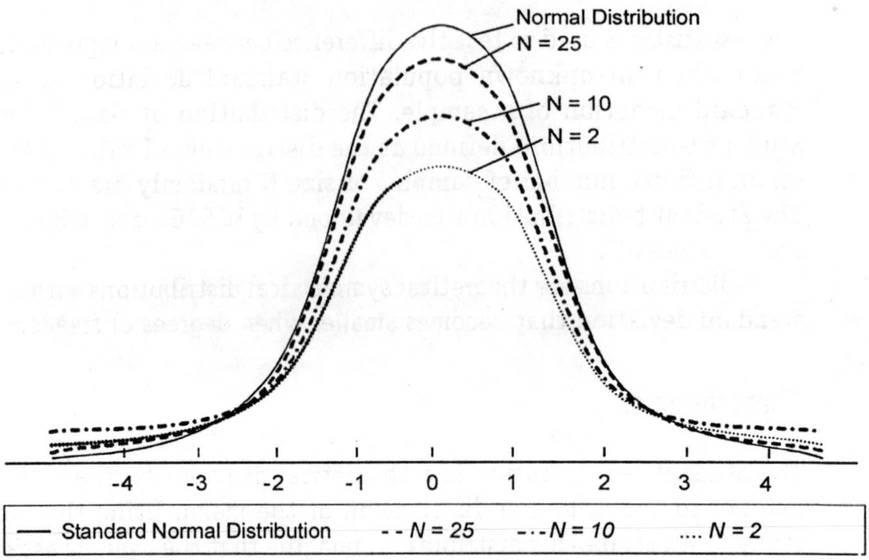

The three dashed lines in figure represent the t-distribution for three sample sizes: N = 2, N = 10, and N = 25; the solid line in this figure is the standard normal distribution. As we see, as the sample size increases, the more the t-distribution approximates the standard normal distribution. This is because the larger the sample, the more the sample resembles the population; the more a distribution of statistics based on the sample (i.e., the t-distribution) resembles a distribution of statistics based on a population (i.e., the standard normal distribution).

Similarities with Normal distribution

1) Both are sampling distributions – one for large sample, other for small sample.
2) Both distributions are symmetrical and bell-shaped.
3) Both have a mean of 0.

3.9 DEGREES OF FREEDOM

It refers to the number of observations that are free to vary after we have placed certain restrictions on the data. Imagine that we have a sample with four numbers 18, 23, 27, 32. The sum is 100 and the mean is 25. If we subtract the mean from each score, the sum of the deviation must equal zero $\sum(X_i - \overline{X}) = 0$.

Let four numbers were drawn at random from a population and are independent of each other because the selection of one number had no influence on the selection of another. i.e., each observation is free to assume any value in the population.

The deviation scores are not independent. Current definition of means requires the sum of the deviation scores to equal 0. Therefore, the mean restricts the freedom of potential values the deviation scores can take.

In the above example, we must impose the restriction that the deviations are based on the mean, the values of only three deviations are free to vary. As soon as 3 deviations are known, the 4th is determined by the fact that its addition to the other deviation scores must sum to 0. i.e., the fourth score is restricted by the definition of mean.

In general, if we have placed a single restriction, df is N-1.

In the example, N-1 = 3.

EXERCISES

1. What proportion of the cases of a normal distribution will fall: 1) to the left of $z = 0$, 2) to the right of $z = 0$, 3) to the right of $z = +1.00$, 4) to the left of $z = 1.00$
2. Determine the proportion of cases falling under the normal curve to the left of $z = -1.96$ + to the cases to the right of $z = 1.96$.
3. If the mean of a normal distribution is 43, σ–2, with how many SDs of the mean would you accept almost all of the cases to fall?
   What score values correspond to these points?
4. In a normal distribution with mean – 50 and σ – 8, what score is likely to fall at the 95th percentile
5. a. In a normal distribution, determine P_{25}, P_{46} and P81 is σ units.
   b. What are the percentile ranks of scores at -1.23б, -0.50 s, 0.84 s
6. In a certain achievement test, the 7th grade mean is 28.00 and б – 4.80 and 8th grade mean is 31.06 and S.D is 4.00. What % of the 7th grade is above the mean of the 8th grade.
   What % of the 8th grade is below the mean of the 7th grade.
7. Assume that the distribution of grades in a class of 500 freshmen is normal with M = 72 and б –10. The instructor wants to give letter grades as follows. 10% A's, 30% B's, 40% C's, 15% D's, and 5% E's. Compute to the closest score the divisions between A's and B's, B's and C's; C's and D's; D's and E's.

4 Correlation

Determining the degree of correlation and prediction is important in many areas of psychology and education. For example, to establish the reliability of a test, we would want to know to what extent initial performance correlate with performance on the same test at a subsequent time. The test would be useless if it yielded scores that fluctuate widely over time.

4.1 CORRELATION–AN INDICATION OF DIRECTION

The scatter diagram between two variables not only shows the direction of the relationship between two variables, but also a look at the direction of the relationship. A scatter plot provides an initial indication of whether scores on one variable are related to scores on another variable. The purpose of this section is to introduce the concept of correlation, which may be defined as a mutual or reciprocal relationship between two variables such that systematic changes in the values of one variable are accompanied by systematic changes in the values of another variables.

The relationship between variables can be described along three aspects: nature of the relationship, direction of the relationship, and strength of the relationship.

4.2 NATURE OF THE RELATIONSHIP

The nature of the relationship between variables pertains to the manner in which changes in scores on one variable correspond to changes in scores on another variable. The nature of the relationship between two variables may take on different forms. For example, a linear relationship is a relationship between variables that is appropriately represented by a straight line, such that increases or decreases in scores for one variable are associated with corresponding increases or decreases scores for another variable.

Figure 2 also illustrates a linear relationship between two variables. It is considered a linear relationship because the data in the scatter plot are located close to a line that has been generated to represent the relationship. Note that the line is tilted at an angle, meaning it is not parallel to either the X- or the Y-axis. The angle of the line indicates that changes in one variable are associated with changes in the other variable, which, as you will recall, is the definition of correlation.

In linear relationship, the relation between two variables may either positive or negative.

Coefficient of correlation extends from -1 through 0 to +1.

r = +1 indicate Perfect positive correlation

r = - 1 indicate Perfect negative correlation

r = 0 indicate No correlation

It is also possible for the nature of the relationship between two variables not to be linear. A nonlinear relationship is a relationship between variables that is not appropriately represented by a straight line. For example, how many hours of sleep do you need each night to be at your best? One hour? Fourteen hours? For most of us, the answer lies somewhere between these two extremes, such that too little sleep makes one inattentive but too much sleep makes one lethargic. A proposed non-linear relationship between "number of hours of sleep" and "attentiveness" is represented in Figure 2

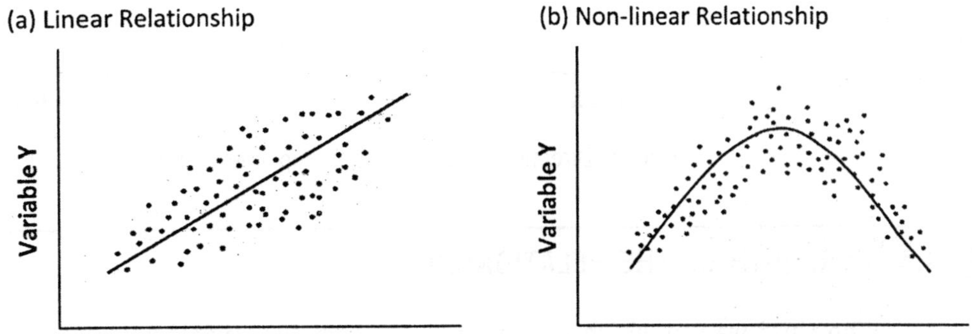

Figure 1: Nature of the Relationship Between Two Variables

Although nonlinear relationships certainly do exist, linear relationships are more common. For this reason, the correlational statistical procedures discussed later in this chapter assume that the relationship between two variables is linear in nature.

4.3 DIRECTION OF THE RELATIONSHIP

The second aspect of the relationship between variables refers to the direction in which changes in one variable are associated with changes in another. A positive relationship is a relationship in which increases in the scores for one variable are associated with increases in the scores of another variable. The scatter plot in Figure2 is an example of a positive relationship. Note that the world "positive" is not used to evaluate the relationship – it indicates the direction of the relationship rather than its value or goodness.

A negative relationship, on the other hand, is a relationship which increases in the scores for one variable are associated with decreases in the scores of another variable. Consistent with the use of the word "positive" or the word "negative" does not imply that the relationship is somehow "worse" or "less desirable" than a "positive relationship". In a negative relationship, such as the one depicted in Figure 4, the scores on two variables are in opposite directions.

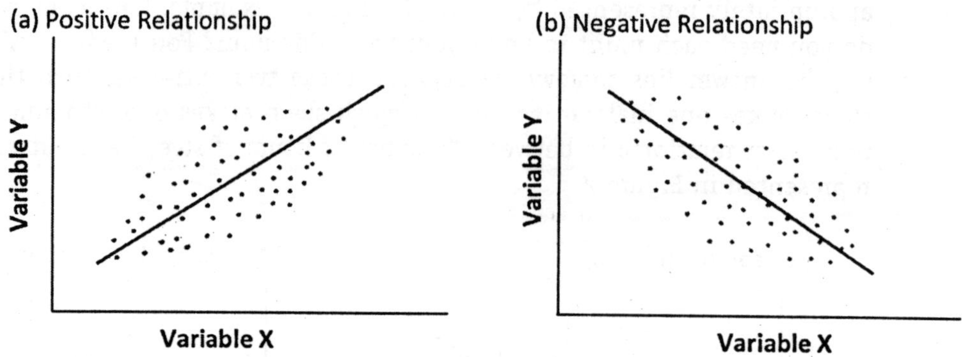

Figure 2: Direction of the Relationship Between Two Variables

4.4 STRENGTH OF THE RELATIONSHIP

The third way in which the relationship between variables may be described is in terms of its strength. The strength of a relationship is the extent to which scores on one variable are associated with scores on another variable. The scatter plot in Figure 2 illustrates what is known as a "perfect" relationship, which is a relationship in which each score for one variable is associated with one and only one score for the other variable. All of the data in a perfect relationship fall exactly on the line.

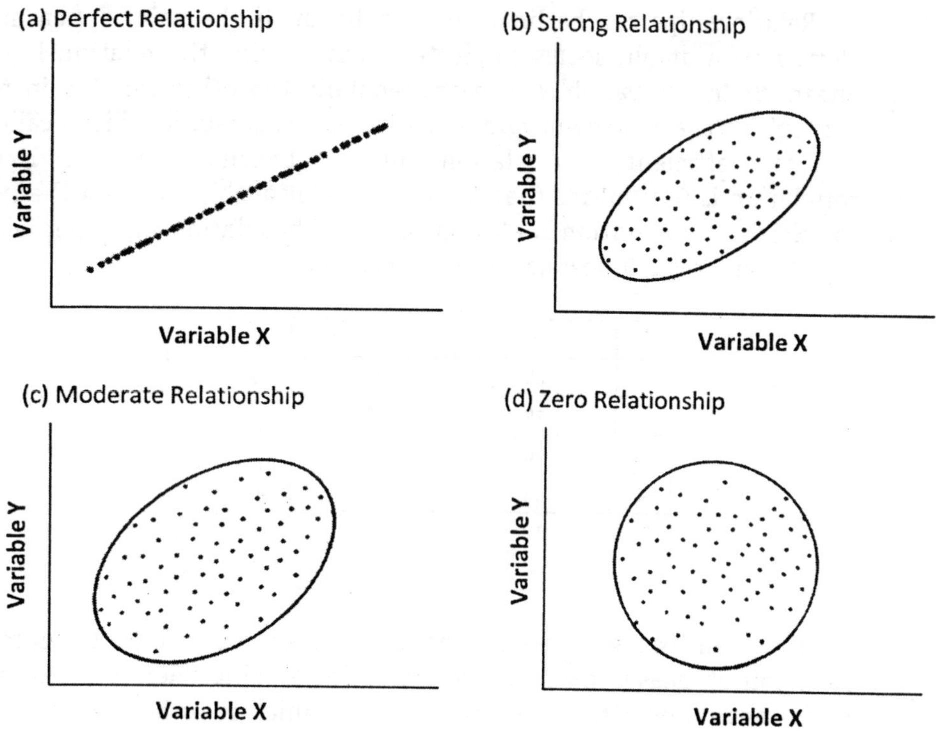

Figure 3: Strength of the Relationship Between Two Variables

As you probably suspect, perfect relationships are the incredibly rare exception rather than the rule. The scatter plot in Figure2 represents what may be referred to as a "strong" relationship, which is a relationship in which a score on one variable is associated with a relatively small range of scores on another variable. If we were to encapsulate all of the points in this scatter plot, it would assume a narrow elliptical shape. When there is a strong relationship between two variables, knowing the scores on one variable allows us to predict the score on the other variable within a small range.

4.5 PEARSON'S PRODUCT-MOMENT COEFFICIENT OF CORRELATION

Correlation is an index of the degree of relationship between two variables. By relationship means pattern of consistent variation in the two variables. There are two types of variations as explained above:

1) When one variable increases so also the other, it indicates a positive linear relationship. When one variable decreases so also the other variable, such type of variation is called positive relationship between the two variables.
2) When one variable increases and the other decreases, it is called negative relationship.

Relationships can be linear or curvilinear. If the pair of measurements when plotted on a graph, seems to cluster around a line the relationship is said to be linear. While one variable increases regularly the other variable increases up to a particular stage and then begin to decrease, such a relationship is called curvilinear.

The coefficient of correlation will be between – 1 and +1. If coefficient of correlation is 0, it means that there is no relationship between the two variable. If coefficient of correlation is +1, it means that the relationship is perfect and positive. e.g., Consider the following set of measurements.

	X	Y
1.	20	10
2.	19	9
3.	16	8
4.	14	7
5.	12	6
6.	10	5

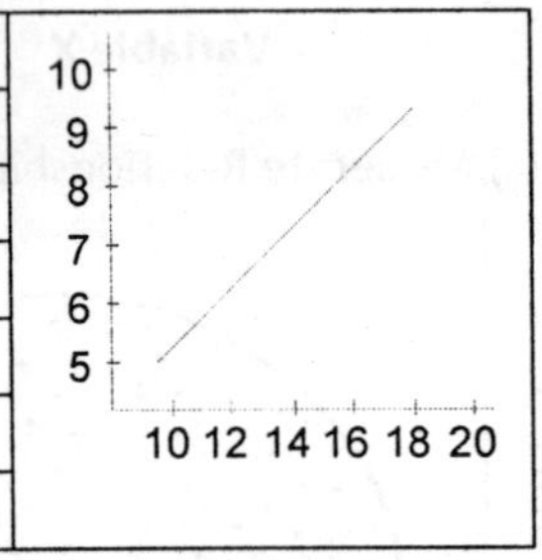

Here pairs of measurements for two variables X and Y are given for six subjects. Each pair of measurement can be plotted as a point when represented graphically. (It is conventional to denote the variable which is to be predicted along Y-axis). These six pair of measurements when represented graphically will be as in figure.

In this example, we can see that for every two units of increase in the X-variable, there is a corresponding one unit of increases in the Y-variable and hence the measures when plotted extends from lower left of the graph to the upper right, such relationship is a good example of perfect positive relationship represented by r = +1.

Consider another set of measurements.

	X	Y
1.	20	10
2.	19	9
3.	16	8
4.	14	7
5.	12	6
6.	10	5

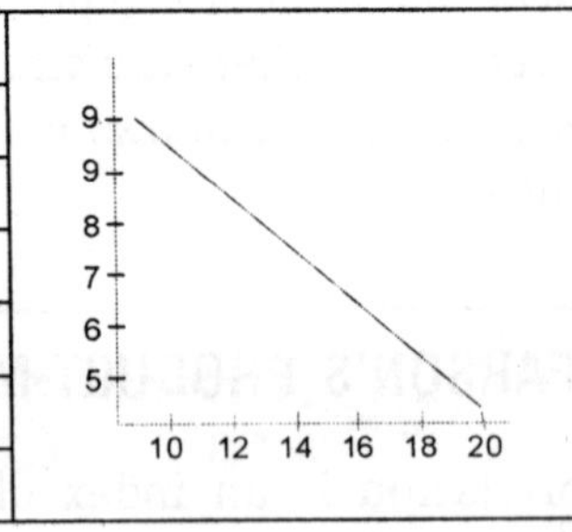

In the example, for every one unit of increases in the X-variable there in a corresponding decrease of one unit in the Y-variable and hence when these measures plotted graphically, will extend from upper left to lower right of figure. Such relationship is an example of perfect negative relationship represented by r = -1.

A standard coefficient of correlation used to calculate linear correlation is the Pearson's Product moment coefficient of correlation. When calculated for a population it is denoted by r_{xy} and if calculated from a sample, it is denoted by r_{xy}. The Pearson

Correlation Coefficient, represented by the symbol r, is a statistic that measures the linear relationship between two continuous variables measured at the interval and/ or ratio level of measurement. The Pearson r is designed to measured the three previously mentioned aspects of a relationship mentioned earlier: nature, direction, and strength.

First, in terms of the nature of the relationship, the Pearson r assesses the degree of linear relationship between two variables. It assumes that the relationship may be represented by a straight line, such that increases (or decreases) in one variable correspond to increases (or decreases) in the other variable. Second, the sign (+ or –) of a Pearson correlation coefficient indicates the direction of the relationship, with the possible values for the Pearson r being either positive or negative.

Between the two maximum values of -1.00 and 1.00, the specific value of the Pearson r represents the strength of the relationship. For example, a correlation with the value of 0.35 represents a stronger relationship than a correlation of 0.29, a weaker relationship than a correlation of -0.46 and the same strength as a correlation of -0.35. The midpoint of the range of possible values of the Pearson r is zero, which implies the complete absence of a relationship between the two variables.

If we have to find the relationship between X and Y from a sample, the symbol will be r_{xy} and the formula is $r_{xy} = \frac{1}{N}\frac{\sum xy}{\sigma_x \sigma_y}$ where x stands for deviation of X, i.e., $X - \overline{X}$ and y stands for $Y - \overline{Y}$ and σ_x and σ_y denotes standard deviation of X and Y respectively. The formula when represented in standard score form will be

$$r_{xy} = \frac{1}{N}\sum z_x z_y$$

where $z_x = \frac{X - \overline{X}}{\sigma_x}$ and $z_y = \frac{Y - \overline{Y}}{\sigma_y}$.

Problem 1: Compute the coefficient of correlation for following data:

X	Y	$x = X - \overline{X}$	$y = Y - \overline{Y}$	xy
12	7	5	–1.5	–7.5
10	3	3	–5.5	–16.5
9	8	2	–0.5	–1.0
8	5	1	–3.5	–3.5
7	7	0	–1.5	0
7	12	0	.5	0
6	10	–1	1.5	–1.5
5	9	–2	0.5	–1.0
4	13	–3	4.5	13.5
2	11	–5	2.5	–12.5
				–57.0

$\overline{X} = 7 \qquad \overline{Y} = 8.5$

$$r_{xy} = \frac{1}{N}\frac{\sum xy}{\sigma_x \sigma_y} \qquad \sigma_x = \sqrt{\frac{\sum(X-\overline{X})^2}{N}}$$

$$\sigma_x = \sqrt{\frac{\sum(X-\overline{X})^2}{N}}$$

$$= \sqrt{\frac{78}{10}} = \underline{2.793}$$

$$\sigma_y = \sqrt{\frac{\sum(Y-\overline{Y})^2}{N}}$$

$$= \sqrt{\frac{88.5}{10}} = \underline{2.975}$$

$$r_{xy} = \frac{1}{10} \times \frac{-57}{2.793 \times 2.995}$$

$$= -0.6859$$

Problem 2: Calculate the coefficient of correlation for the data below:

X	Y	x	y	xy
13	7	6	0.5	–3.0
12	11	5	4.5	22.5
10	3	3	–3.5	–10.5
8	7	1	0.5	0.5
7	2	0	–4.5	0
6	12	–1	5.5	–5.5
6	6	–1	–0.5	0.5
4	2	–3	–4.5	13.5
3	9	–4	2.5	–10.0
1	6	–6	–0.5	3.0
70	65			17

$\overline{X} = 7 \qquad \overline{Y} = 6.5$

$$\sigma_x = \sqrt{\frac{\sum(X-\overline{X})^2}{N}} = \sqrt{\frac{134}{10}} = \underline{3.66}$$

$$\sigma_y = \sqrt{\frac{\sum(Y-\overline{Y})^2}{N}} = \underline{3.324}$$

$$r_{xy} = \frac{1}{N}\frac{\sum xy}{\sigma_x \sigma_y}$$

$$r_{xy} = \frac{1}{10} \times \frac{17}{3.66 \times 3.324} = \underline{0.1397}$$

Compute coefficient of correlation using standard score form

X	Y	x	y	$z_x = \frac{x}{\sigma_x}$	$z_y = \frac{y}{\sigma_y}$	$z_x z_y$
13	7	6	0.5	1.64	0.15	0.25
12	11	5	4.5	1.37	1.35	1.85
10	3	3	–3.5	0.82	–1.05	–0.86
8	7	1	0.5	0.27	0.15	0.04
7	2	0	–4.5	0	–1.35	0
6	12	–1	5.5	–0.27	1.65	–0.45
6	6	–1	–0.5	–0.27	–0.15	0.86
4	2	–3	–4.5	–0.82	–1.35	1.11
3	9	–4	2.5	–1.09	0.75	–0.82
1	6	–6	–0.5	–1.64	0.15	–0.25
						1.73

$\sigma_x = 3.66 \qquad \sigma_y = 3.324$

$$r_{xy} = \frac{1}{N}\sum z_x z_y$$

$$= \frac{1}{10} \times 1.73$$

$$= \underline{0.173}$$

Machine formula for calculating r

$$r_{xy} = \frac{N\sum XY - \sum X \sum Y}{\sqrt{\left[N\sum X^2 - \left(\sum X\right)^2\right]\left[N\sum Y^2 - \left(\sum Y\right)^2\right]}}$$

is the machine formula for calculating correlation from raw measurements.

Problem 1: Calculate r_{xy} for the data given below using Machine formula.

X	Y	XY	X^2	Y^2
13	11	143	169	121
12	14	168	144	196
10	11	110	100	121
10	7	70	100	49
8	9	72	64	81
6	11	66	36	121
6	3	18	36	9
5	7	35	25	49
3	6	18	9	36
2	1	2	4	1
75	80	702	687	**784**

$$r_{xy} = \frac{[10 \times 702 - 75 \times 80]}{\sqrt{\left[10 \times 687 - (75)^2\right]\left[10 \times 784 - (80)^2\right]}}$$

$$= \frac{1020}{\sqrt{1245 \times 1440}}$$

$$= \frac{1020}{1338.9548}$$

$$r_{xy} = \underline{0.76178}$$

Problem 2: Calculate r_{xy} for the data given below using Machine formula.

X	Y	XY	X²	Y²
13	7	91	169	49
12	11	132	144	121
10	3	30	100	9
8	7	56	64	49
7	2	14	49	4
6	12	72	36	144
6	6	36	36	36
4	2	8	16	4
3	9	27	9	81
1	6	6	1	36
70	**65**	**472**	**624**	**533**

$$r_{xy} = \frac{[10 \times 472 - 70 \times 65]}{\sqrt{\left[10 \times 624 - (70)^2\right]\left[10 \times 533 - (65)^2\right]}}$$

$$= \frac{170}{\sqrt{1340 \times 1105}}$$

$$= \frac{170}{1216.84}$$

$$r_{xy} = \underline{0.1397}$$

Coefficient of Correlation in Terms of Deviation Scores is

$$r_{xy} = \frac{\sum xy}{\sqrt{\sum x^2 \times \sum y^2}}$$

An example of calculation of r_{xy} using deviation score formula is given below:

Compute 'r' for the following data:

X	Y	X	y	xy	X²	y²
13	11	5.5	3	16.5	30.25	9
12	14	4.5	6	27.0	20.25	36
10	11	2.5	3	7.5	6.25	9
10	7	2.5	–1	–2.5	6.25	1
8	9	0.5	1	0.5	0.25	1
6	11	–1.5	3	–4.5	2.25	9
6	3	–1.5	—	7.5	2.25	25
5	7	–2.5	–1	2.5	6.25	1
3	6	–4.5	–2	9.0	20.25	4
2	1	–5.5	–7	38.5	30.25	49
75	**80**			**102**	**124.5**	**144**

$$\overline{X} = 7.5 \qquad \overline{Y} = 8.0$$

$$r_{xy} = \frac{\sum xy}{\sqrt{\sum x^2 \times \sum y^2}} \qquad \sigma_x = \sqrt{\frac{\sum\left(X-\overline{X}\right)^2}{N}}$$

$$= \frac{104}{\sqrt{124.5 \times 144}}$$

$$r = \underline{-\ 0.7617}$$

Coefficient of Correlation by the difference formula

$$r_{xy} = \frac{\sum x^2 + \sum y^2 - \sum d^2}{2\sqrt{\sum x^2 \sum y^2}}$$

Where d = x – y

$$\Sigma x^2 = \sum X^2 - \frac{1}{N}\left(\sum X\right)^2$$

i.e.,

$$\Sigma x^2 = \sum\left(X-\overline{X}\right)^2 = \sum\left(X^2 - 2X\overline{X} + \overline{X}^2\right)$$

$$= \sum X^2 - 2\sum X\overline{X} + \sum\left(\overline{X}\right)^2$$

$$= \sum X^2 - 2N\overline{X}.\overline{X} + N\overline{X}^2$$

$$= \sum X^2 - N\overline{X}^2$$

$$= \sum X^2 - N.\left(\frac{\sum X}{N}\right)^2$$

$$\Sigma X^2 = \sum X^2 - \left(\frac{\sum X}{N}\right)^2$$

Similarly, $\sum y^2 = \sum Y^2 - \frac{1}{N}(\sum Y)^2$

D = X–Y so $d^2 = \sum D^2 - \frac{(\sum D)^2}{N}$

$\sum x^2$, $\sum y^2$ and $\sum d^2$ can be calculated from the raw score using the formulae above.

$$\sum x^2 = \sum x^2 - \frac{1}{N}(\sum x)^2$$

$$\sum y^2 = \sum y^2 - \frac{1}{N}(\sum y)^2$$

$\sum d^2 = \sum D^2 - \frac{1}{N}(\sum D)^2$ — where D = X – Y

Problem 1: Compute coefficient of correlation r_{xy} by the Different method

X	Y	X^2	Y^2	D	$(X-Y)^2 = D^2$
13	7	169	49	6	36
12	11	144	121	1	1
10	3	100	9	7	49
8	7	64	49	1	1
7	2	49	4	5	25
6	12	36	144	–6	36
6	6	36	36	0	0
4	2	16	4	2	4
3	9	9	81	–6	36
1	6	1	36	–5	25
ΣX = 70	ΣX = 65	624	533	5	213

$$r_{xy} = \frac{\sum x^2 + \sum y^2 - \sum d^2}{2\sqrt{\sum x^2 \sum y^2}}$$

$$\sum x^2 = \sum X^2 - \frac{1}{N}(X)^2$$

$$= 624 - \frac{1}{10}(70)^2$$

$$= \underline{134}$$

$$\sum y^2 = \sum Y^2 - \frac{1}{N}\left(\sum Y\right)^2$$

$$= 533 - \frac{1}{10}(65)^2$$

$$= \underline{110.5}$$

$$\sum d^2 = \sum D^2 - \frac{1}{N}\left(\sum D\right)^2$$

$$= 213 - \frac{1}{10}(5)^2$$

$$= \underline{210.5}$$

$$r_{xy} = \frac{\sum x^2 + \sum y^2 - \sum d^2}{2\sqrt{\sum x^2 \sum y^2}}$$

$$= \frac{134 + 110.5 - 210.5}{2 \times 121.68}$$

$$r_{xy} = \underline{0.1397}$$

Problem 2: Compute coefficient of correlation by difference method

X	Y
22	11
8	5
19	6
32	8
13	2
24	5
22	4
35	1
18	7
13	10
53	23
15	9
34	18
15	2
27	4

X	Y	X^2	Y^2	D	D^2
22	11	484	121	11	121
8	5	64	25	3	9
19	6	361	36	13	169
32	8	1024	64	24	576
13	2	169	4	11	121
24	5	576	25	19	361
22	4	484	16	18	324
35	1	1225	1	34	1156
18	7	324	49	11	121
13	10	169	100	3	9
53	23	2809	529	30	900
15	9	225	81	6	36
34	18	1156	324	16	256
15	2	225	4	13	169
27	4	729	16	23	529
350	115	10024	1395	235	4857

$$\sum x^2 = \sum X^2 - \frac{1}{N}\left(\sum X\right)^2$$

$$= 10024 - \frac{1}{15} \times (350)^2$$

$$= \underline{1857.33}$$

$$\sum y^2 = \sum Y^2 - \frac{1}{N}\left(\sum Y\right)^2$$

$$= 1395 - \frac{1}{15}(115)^2$$

$$= \underline{513.33}$$

$$\sum d^2 = \sum D^2 - \left(\frac{\sum D}{N}\right)^2$$

$$= 4857 - \frac{1}{15}(235)^2$$

$$= \underline{1175.33}$$

$$r_{xy} = \frac{\sum x^2 + \sum y^2 - \sum d^2}{2\sqrt{\sum x^2 \sum y^2}}$$

$$= \frac{1857.33 + 513.33 - 1175.33}{2\sqrt{1857.33 \times 513.33}}$$

$$= \underline{0.61208}$$

4.6 BIVARIANT FREQUENCY DISTRIBUTION

Question: Prepare a bi variant frequency distribution for measurements given in the case of two variables for 40 subjects.

X	Y	X	Y	X	Y
28	11	22	36	14	20
8	5	44	32	21	20
19	6	72	46	25	6
32	8	25	47	2	37
13	2	30	49	15	28
24	5	38	53	34	46
22	4	54	51	37	46
35	1	37	50	38	41
18	7	61	45	22	5
13	10	56	48	18	58
53	23	42	25	40	21
15	9	30	48	12	28
34	18	42	28	31	30
15	2	28	39		
27	29	27	23		
24	40	16	12		

For preparing a bivariant frequency distribution, Draw a scatter diagram as in the following figure. Mark tallies corresponding to each pair of the scores as indicated in the figure.

Tallies in the cell represent cell frequencies. Count the cell frequencies corresponding to each class interval and check the correctness of marking with the total frequencies.

X→ \ ←Y	60-64	55-59	50-54	45-49	40-44	35-39	30-34	25-29	20-24	15-19	10-14	5-9	0-4	45(N)
f		1	3	8	2	3	2	5	5	1	3	8	4	45(N)
70-74				/										1
65-69														0
60-64				/										1
55-59				/										1
50-54			/						/					2
45-49														0
40-44							/	//	/					4
35-39			//	/	/								/	5
30-34				///			/			/		/		6
25-29				/		/		/	/		/	/		6
20-24					/	/			/			//	/	6
15-19		/						/			/	///	/	7
10-14								/	/		/		/	4
5-9												/		1
0-4						/								1

Correlation Table or Scattergram

The formula for calculating coefficient of correlation of a bivariant frequency distribution is, $r_{xy} = \dfrac{N\sum fx'y' - \sum fx'.\sum fy'}{\sqrt{\left[N\sum fx'^2 (\sum fx')^2\right]\left[N\sum fy'^2 (\sum fy')^2\right]}}$

where $x' = \dfrac{X-A}{i}$ and $y' = \dfrac{Y-A}{i}$ where A is the assumed mean of the corresponding distribution.

The above table illustrates the steps for preparing a bivariant frequency table for calculation of 'r'. Examples are illustrated below.

1) Compute $\overline{X}$, $\overline{Y}$, σ_x, σ_y and r from the following data:

	85-89	90-94	95-99	100-104	105-109	110-114	fy	y'	fy'	fy'^{2}	Σfx'y'
50-59			*[2] 1^{-2}	1	[26] 13	[4] 1	16	2	32	64	28
40-49		-[8] 4	[-3] 3	21	[1] 1	[2] 1	30	1	30	30	-8
30-39	1	8	20	4	2	1	36	0	0	0	0
20-29	[3] 1	[38] 19	[4] 4	4	[7] 1		29	-1	-29	29	44
10-19	[42] 7	[4] 1	[2] 1				9	-2	-18	36	48
fx	9	32	29	30	17	3	120		15	159	112
x'	-3	-2	-1	0	1	2					
fx'	-27	-64	-29	0	17	6	-97				
fx'^{2}	81	128	29	0	17	12	267				
Σfx'y'	45	34	1	0	26	6	112				

* Number inside the box indicate the product of x' and y', multiplied by the cell frequency i.e., fx'y' of each cell.

$$r_{xy} = \frac{N\sum fx'y' - \sum fx'.\sum fy'}{\sqrt{\left[N\sum fx'^2 - (\sum fx')^2\right]\left[N\sum fy'^2 - (\sum fy')^2\right]}}$$

$$= \frac{120\times 112 - 97\times 15}{\sqrt{\left[120\times 267 - (97)^2\right]\left[120\times 159 - (15)^2\right]}}$$

$$= \frac{120\times 112 - 97\times 15}{150.436\times 137.31}$$

r_{xy} = **0.7254**

$$\overline{X} = A + \frac{i\sum fx'}{N} = 102 + \frac{5\times -97}{120} = \underline{97.96}$$

$$\overline{Y} = A + \frac{i\sum fx'}{N} = 34.5 + \frac{10\times 15}{1.20} = \underline{35.75}$$

$$\sigma_x = \frac{i}{N}\sqrt{N\sum fx'^2 - \left(\sum fx'\right)^2}$$

$$= \frac{5}{120}\sqrt{120 \times 267 - (97)^2}$$

$$= \mathbf{6.268}$$

$$\sigma_y = \frac{10}{120}\sqrt{120 \times 159 - (15)^2}$$

$$= \mathbf{11.44}$$

$\overline{X} = 97.96$

$\overline{Y} = 35.75$

$\sigma_x = 6.268$

$\sigma_y = 11.44$

$r_{xy} = \underline{0.7254}$

2) Calculate 'r' for the following distribution:

Y/X → ↓	15-17	18-20	21-23	24-26	27-29	30-32	33-35	36-38	fy	y'	fy'	fy'²	Σfx'y'
42-47					3	18)6	24)4	18)2	15	3	45	135	60
36-41				-2)1	3	16)8	28)7	12)2	21	2	42	84	54
30-35			-4)2	-5)5	9	4)4	6)3	3)1	24	1	24	24	4
24-29		1	2	7	7	6	4	1	28	0	0	0	0
18-23		6)2	12)6	3)3	2	-1)1	-2)1		15	-1	-15	15	18
12-17		30)5	32)8	14)4	6	-4)2			25	-2	-50	100	72
6-11	*48) 4	18)2	6)1	3)1	1				9	-3	-27	81	76
0-5	32)2	60)5	16)2	2)1					10	-4	-40	160	112
fx	6	15	21	22	31	27	19	6	**150**		**-21**	**599**	395
x'	-4	-3	-2	-1	0	1	2	3					
fx'	-24	-45	-42	-22	0	27	38	18	**-30**				
fx'²	96	135	84	22	0	27	76	54	**494**				
Σfx'y'	80	114	62	17	0	33	56	33	**395**				

* number inside the bracket indicate the value of fx'y' for each cell.

$$r_{xy} = \frac{N\sum fx'y' - \sum fx'.\sum fy'}{\sqrt{\left[N\sum fx'^2 - \left(\sum fx'\right)^2\right]\left[N\sum fy'^2 - \left(\sum fy'\right)^2\right]}}$$

$$= \frac{150 \times 395 - (-30 \times -21)}{\sqrt{\left[150 \times 494 - (-30)^2\right]\left[150 \times 599 - (-21)^2\right]}}$$

$r_{xy} = \mathbf{0.725}$

4.7 INTERPRETATION OF PEARSON'S r

Pearson's r can be interpreted in different ways:

1) Testing the significance of 'r' as ,
   $r = 1.96/\sqrt{N}$ for 0.05 level and
   $r = 2.58/\sqrt{N}$ for 0.01 level
2) Verbally interpreting the strength of correlation as follows (Garrett,1979):
   'r ' from ± 0.00 to ± 0.20 indicate negligible relationship
   'r ' from ± 2.00 to ± 0.40 indicate low relationship
   'r ' from ± 0.40 to ± 0.70 indicate substantial relationship
   'r ' from ± 0.70 to ± 1.00 indicate high to very high relationship
3) Finding the 0.95 or 0.99 confidence intervals for 'r' to determine the corresponding population values.
   It can be worked out using the formulae,
   $r \pm 1.96\ (1\text{-}r^2) / \sqrt{N}$ or $r \pm 2.58\ (1\text{-}r^2) / \sqrt{N}$
4) Determining the percentage overlap and interpreting this as a measure of association between the variables.

Jacob Cohen (1988) provided the following guidelines for interpreting values of the Pearson r in terms of its strength:

	Pearson r	
Strength of Relationship•	Negative	Positive
Weak	-.10 to -.30	.10 to .30
Moderate	-.30 to -.50	.30 to .50
Strong	-.50 to -1.00	.50 to 1.00

According to these guidelines, a relationship between two variables in a set of data is considered "weak" if the relationship has a calculated value of the Pearson r between 0.10 and 0.30 (ignoring the ± sign). A relationship is considered "moderate" if r is between 0.30 and 0.50 and "strong" if r exceeds ± 0.50.

It is critical to keep in mind that the above guidelines are designed to aid in the interpretation of a calculated value of r, they do not take into account critical factors such as the size of the sample or whether the relationship is statistically significant.

4.8 SPEARMAN'S COEFFICIENT OF CORRELATION-ρ

Variables in a research study may be measured at one of four levels of measurement: nominal, ordinal, interval, or ratio. Imagine a situation in which the goal is to correlate two variables measured at the ordinal level of measurement. The values of ordinal variables can be placed in an order relative to the other values, but the values are not assumed to be equally spaced. In ordinal variables, one value represents more or less of a variable than do other values, but it is not possible to specify the precise size or amount of the difference between values.

Ranked Variables

A common form of ordinal data is ranks. A rank is defined as a relative position in a graded or evaluated group. The numeric value for a ranked variable reflects a relative location within an order. Note that ranks are ordinal variables in that although you can say that a runner who finished "fourth" ran faster than the runner who finished "fifth", you cannot specify the exact difference between the times of the two runners.

There are perhaps two primary situations in which ranked variables may be employed in a study. The first situation is one in which the collected data themselves consist of ranks.

The Spearman rank-order correlation is a statistic measuring the relationship between two variables measured at the ordinal level of measurement, named after the British psychologist Charles Spearman in 1904.

When samples are small and when the given data does not satisfy the conditions for using Pearson's Coefficient, Spearman's r can be used.

$$\rho = 1 - \frac{6\sum D^2}{N\left(N^2-1\right)}$$

Where D is the difference between Ranks, R_1 and R_2

R_1 and R_2 are the rank orders, Rank the measures as 1, 2, 3... by giving 1 to the most high value. When the measures are repeating there will be tie among ranks. For example, if the 2nd and 3rd numbers to be selected are of the same value, then we can assign a rank of 2+3/2=2.5 each to each number.

Then, for the next higher value, give the rank of 4. Then 5, 6 and so on.

If it is in 5th rank, take $\frac{5+6}{2} = 5.5$ to each one.

If it is repeating 3 times, take $\frac{5+6+7}{3} = 6$ to each one. Then take the next lower one as the number (next) which is not considered in the repeating cases.

Problem:

X	Y	$D = R_1 - R_2$	D^2
1	6	–5	25
2	3	–1	1
3	7	–4	16
4	2	2	4
5	1	4	16
6	8	–2	4
7	4	3	9
8	9	–1	1
9	5	4	16
10	10	0	0
			$\Sigma D^2=92$

$$\rho = 1 - \frac{6\sum D^2}{N\left(N^2-1\right)}$$

$$= 1 - \frac{6\times 92}{10\left(10^2-1\right)} = \mathbf{0.442}$$

Spearman's ρ with tied ranks :

Creativity score	Cartoon score	R_1	R_2	D	D^2
47	75	11	8	3	9
71	79	4	6	2	4
52	85	9	5	4	16
48	50	10	14	4	16
35	49	14.5	15	0.5	0.25
35	59	14.5	12	2.5	6.25
41	75	12.5	8	4.5	20.25
82	91	1	3	2	4
72	102	3	1	2	4
56	87	7	4	3	9
59	70	6	10	4	16
73	92	2	2	0	0
60	54	5	13	8	64
55	75	8	8	0	0
41	68	12.5	11	1.5	2.25
			$\Sigma D^2 = 171.0$		

$$\rho = 1 - \frac{6\sum D^2}{N\left(N^2-1\right)}$$

$$= 1- [6\times171/15\times224] = 0.69$$

EXERCISES

1. Calculate Pearson coefficient of correlation for each of the following sets of data:

   a) X: 15 10 8 23
      Y: 24 8 15 21

   b) X: 3 6 7 1 5 8 5
      y: 1 8 1 8 7 2 1

   c) X : 17 23 9 15 12 20 19 10 14 8
      Y: 41 11 17 32 23 46 20 37 13 39

2. Find Rank correlation of the following scores.
   X: 185 203 188 195 176 174 158 197 176 138 126 160 151 185 185
   Y: 110 98 118 104 112 124 119 95 94 97 110 94 126 120 118
   In Y the two smallest scores i.e., 94 are highest and are ranked as 1.5 each.

5

Regression

We may concern with estimating or predicting one variable from knowledge of another. This is the prediction. i.e., problems of predicting one variable from knowledge of another are usually referred to as regression problems. We are dealing with linear regression. It is assumed that a straight line is an appropriate model for describing the relation between two variables the equation for a straight line:

The general equation for any straight line is given by

$$Y = a + b\,X$$

where a is a constant. It is the distance on the Y axis (Y-intercept) from the origin to the point where the line meets the Y-axis and b is the slope of the line. The slope describes the rate of increase in Y with increase in X. If a and b are known, the location of the line is uniquely fixed. For any given value of X, we can compute a corresponding value of Y.

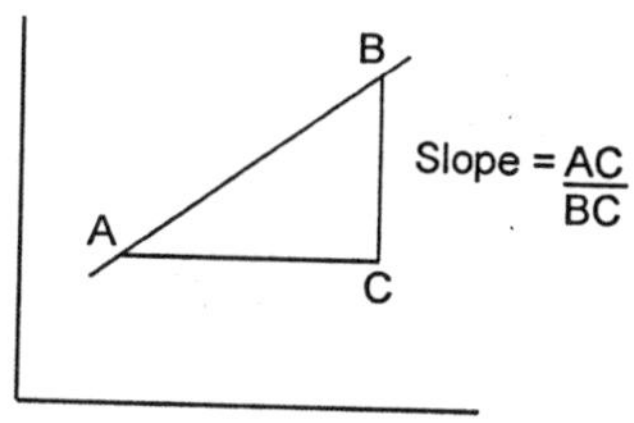

Regression Line of Y on X

Any set of paired observations may be plotted on a graph paper, each pair of observation being represented by a point. Then we can fix a straight line to this set of points by the method of least squares (states that the sum of squares of deviations from the points to the line is a minimum).

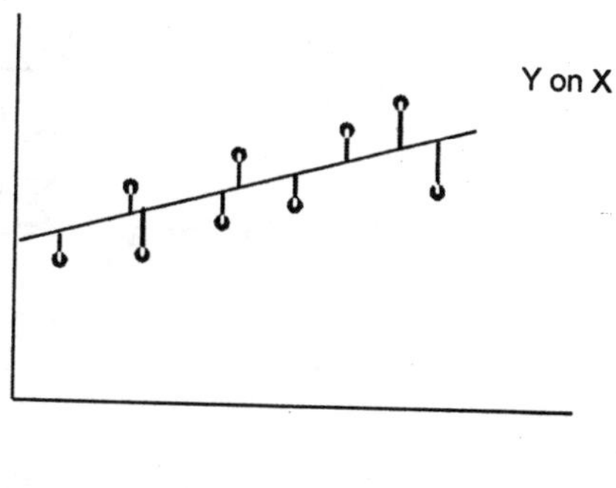

If our interest is in predicting Y from X, the method of least squares locates the line in a position such that the sum of squares of distances from the points to the line taken parallel to the Y axis is a minimum. This line is known as the regression line of Y on X.

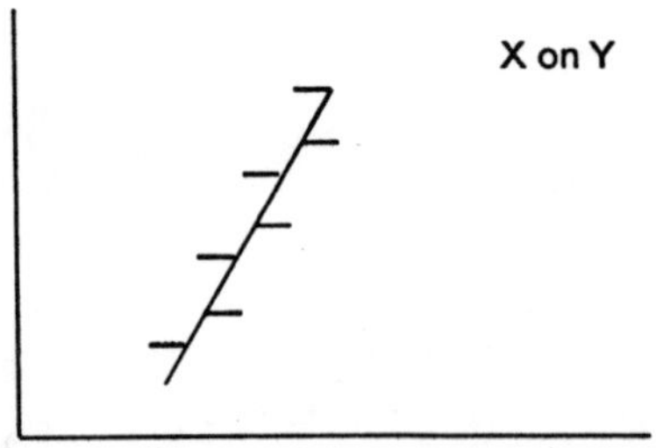

If our interest is predicting X from Y, the method of least square locates the line in a position such that the sum of squares of distances from the points to the line taken parellel to the X axis is a minimum. This line is known as regression line of X on Y.

For a bivariate frequency distribution, the two regression lines will be as in the figure. When the correlation is perfect, the two regression lines coincides through out their lengths. The higher the correlation, the closer they be in one direction. All regression lines intersect at a point representing means of X and Y.

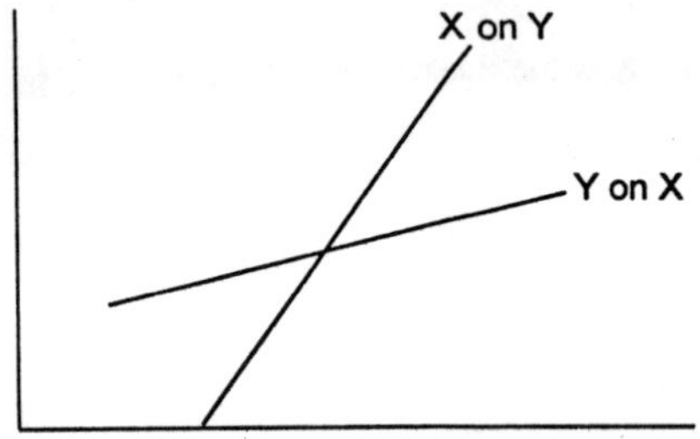

5.1 REGRESSION EQUATIONS AND REGRESSION COEFFICIENTS

Equation for a straight line is, $Y = a + bX$

Equation for the regression line of Y on X is

$$Y' = a_{yx} + b_{yx} X$$ where ,

Y'= estimated value of Y

$$\text{Slope, } b_{yx} = \frac{N\sum XY - \sum X \sum Y}{N\sum X^2}$$

$$\text{Y-intercept } a_{yx} = \frac{\sum Y - b_{yx}\sum X}{N}$$

Equation for the regression line of X on Y is,

$$X' = a_{xy} + b_{xy} Y$$

X' = estimated value of X.

$$\text{Slope } b_{xy} = \frac{N\sum XY - \sum X \sum Y}{N\sum Y^2}$$ and

$$\text{X - intercept } a_{xy} = \frac{\sum X - b_{xy}\sum Y}{N}$$

Examples:

(1) Calculate the two equations of the regression lines from the given data:

X : 118 99 118 121 123 98 131 121 108 111

Y : 66 50 73 69 72 54 74 70 65 62

Ans: Y′ = 0.7074 X −15.679 and X′= 1.22514 Y + 34.55

(2) Calculate the estimated value of Y for the given value of X

We have, Y′ = 0.71 X − 15.68 . Substituting for each value of X, Y′ will be: 68.1, 54.6, 68.1, 70.2, 71.6, 53.9, 77.3, 70.2, 61 and 63.13

(3) Calculate predicted value of X for the given value of Y.

We have, X′= 1.22514 Y + 34.55

Estimated values of X will be: 115.01, 95.55, 123.6, 118.7, 122.4, 100.4, 124.8, 119.95, 113.8 and110.19

4) Consider the following observations: **X: 1 2 3 4 5**
Y: 2 1 3 5 4

a) Obtain the regression line for predicting values of Y from a knowledge of X
b) Obtain Y′ the predicted values of Y.

Ans: (a) b_{yx} = 0.80, a_{yx} = 0.60 Y′ = 0.80 X + 0.60
(b) 1.4, 2.2, 3.00, 3.8, 4.6

(3) X : 1 5 6 6 2
Y : 2 4 5 3 1

Compute

1) the correlation between X and Y
2) the slope of the regression line for predicting X from a knowledge of Y
3) the slope of regression line for predicting Y from a knowledge of X
4) the regression equation for predicting a raw score on X from a raw score on Y.

Ans. (1) r_{xy} = 0.809 (2) 1.2
(3) 0.5455 (4) X′ = 1.2 Y + 0.4

5.2 RELATION OF REGRESSION TO CORRELATION

When there is perfect relationship between variables, the two regression lines coincide. When this is not so, the two regression lines have an angular separation. i.e., when the degree of relationship between the variables decreases, the angular separation increases. Thus, we can see that a relationship exist between r and the slopes of the two regression lines.

1) $b_{yx} = r \frac{\sigma y}{\sigma x}$

2) $b_{xy} = r \frac{\sigma x}{\sigma y}$

From equation (1) & (2), $b_{yx} b_{xy} = r^2$ or $r = \sqrt{b_{yx} b_{xy}}$.

The regression coefficient 'a' is a constant that we must add in order to ensure that the mean of the predicted values will be equal to the mean of the observed values. We have, the equations for regression lines,

$$Y' = b_{yx} X + a_{yx} \quad \text{... (1)}$$

$$X' = b_{xy} Y + a_{xy} \quad \text{... (2)}$$

$$a_{yx} = \frac{\sum Y - b_{yx} \sum X}{N} = \overline{Y} - \overline{X}\, b_{yx}$$

Similarly, $a_{xy} = \frac{\sum X - b_{xy} \sum Y}{N} = \overline{X} - \overline{Y}\, b_{yx}$. Substituting for the slopes in equation (2) & (3),

$$Y' = r\left(\frac{\sigma y}{\sigma x}\right) X + \overline{Y} - (\overline{X})\, r \frac{\sigma y}{\sigma x}$$

$$Y' = r\left(\frac{\sigma y}{\sigma x}\right)(X - \overline{X}) + \overline{Y}$$

Similarly, $$X' = r\left(\frac{\sigma x}{\sigma y}\right)(Y - \overline{Y}) + \overline{X}$$

These two equations are known as **equations in the deviation score form.**

Example:

From the data $\overline{X} = 40.3$, $\overline{Y} = 12.5$, $\sigma x = 12.6$, $\sigma y = 3.6$ and $r_{xy} = 0.60$. Find the regression equations for predicting Y from X and X from Y.

The regression equation for predicting Y from X is,

$$Y' = r\left(\frac{\sigma y}{\sigma x}\right)(X - \overline{X}) + \overline{Y}$$

$$Y' = 0.60 \times 3.6/12.6(X - 40.3) + 12.5$$

$$= 0.1714(X - 40.3) + 12.5$$

The regression equation for predicting X from Y is,

$$X' = r\left(\frac{\sigma_x}{\sigma_y}\right)\left(Y - \overline{Y}\right) + \overline{X}$$

$$X' = 0.60 \times 12.6/3.6(Y-12.5)+40.3$$

$$X' = 2.1\ (Y - 12.5) + 40.3$$

If the measurements are represented in standard score form, the coefficient of correlation can be calculated by, $r = \frac{1}{N}\sum z_x z_y$

Regression equation with standard measures are,

$$z_y' = r.z_x \text{ and } z_x' = r.z_y$$

where z'_x and z'_y stands for the predicted or estimated standard scores. Here, both the regression lines have the same slope and is equal to r, coefficient of correlation between the variables.

5.3 STANDARD ERROR OF ESTIMATE

The difference between an observed value and a predicted value is an error of estimate. From the regression equations, Y-Y' is an error of estimate of Y and X-X' that of X. Perfect prediction is possible when error of estimate is zero. Hence, variance of error of estimate or standard error of estimate is taken as a measure of the accuracy of estimate.

The variance of error of estimate in predicting Y from X is, *(variance means square of standard deviation)*

$$S_{y.x}^2 = \sigma_{y.x}^2 = \sum\frac{(Y-Y')^2}{N-1}$$

∴ Standard error of estimate of Y, when X is given is,

$$S_{y.x} = \sigma_{y.x} = \sqrt{\frac{\sum(Y-Y')^2}{N-1}}$$

Secondly, standard error of estimate of X when Y is given

$$S_{x.y} = \sigma_{x.y} = \sqrt{\frac{\sum(X-X')^2}{N-1}}$$

Error of estimate in terms of r is,

$\sigma_{y.x} = \sigma_y\sqrt{1-r^2}$ When $r = 0$, $\sigma_{y.x} = \sigma_y$, and there is no meaning for prediction.

$\sigma_{x.y} = \sigma_x\sqrt{1-r^2}$ when $r = 1$, $\sigma_{y.x} = \sigma_{x.y} = 0$

Example:

(1) Given the following data for two tests:

History (X)	English (Y)
$M_x = 75$	$M_y = 70$
$\sigma x = 6$	$\sigma y = 8.00$
$r_{xy} = 0.72$	

a) Work out the regression equations in score form

b) Predict the probable grade in English of a student whose history mark is 65. Find the standard error of estimate of this prediction.

c) If r_{xy} had been 0.84 (σ's and M's are same) what is the standard error of estimate?

Answers: a) $Y' = 0.96\,X - 2.00$; $X' = 0.54\,Y + 37.2$

b) $Y' = 0.96\,X - 2.00 = 60.4$ $S_{y.x} = \sigma y\sqrt{1-r^2} = 8\sqrt{1-(0.72)^2} = 5.55$

c) $Sy.x = 8\sqrt{1-(0.84)^2} = 4.34$

EXERCISES

1. Standard scores on variables X for four individuals are -2.0, -1.68, 0.18 and 1.16 respectively. If $r_{xy} = 0.5$, what are the estimated standard scores on Y?
2. What is the standard error in estimating standard scores on Y from standard scores on X?

   $Sy.x = \sigma y\sqrt{1-r^2}$. Here a set of standard scores are given. Their mean = 0, standard deviation = 1 always.

   $r = 0.5$ $\therefore S_{y.x} = 1\sqrt{1-0.5^2} = 0.866$
3. A variance $Sy^2 = 400$ and $r_{xy} = 0.5$. What is the variance of error of estimation in predicting Y from X?
   Given , $Sy^2 = 400$ $r_{xy} = 0.5$. We have to find $S_{y.x}$.
   We can see that, $Sy = 20$;

   $S_{y.x.} = 20\sqrt{1-(0.72)^2} = 17.32$
   $S_{y.x^2} = 17.32^2 \approx 300$
4. Explain the term correlation and regression. Set up the regression equation a) for Y on X and b) X on Y for the following data:

X:	6	9	12	15	18
Y:	18	10	24	20	28

   b) Given the following data on two tests:

	Maths (X)	Reading (Y)
	Mean = 50	Mean = 60
	SD = 10.00	S.D. = 8
		r = 0.05

   Work out reqression equations in score form and also predict the probable

6

Multiple Regression Theory and Analysis

We are now ready to extend regression theory and analysis to more than one independent variable. In this Chapter, two independent variables are considered. The advantage in separating the discussion of two and three or more variables lies in the relatively simple ideas and calculations with only two independent variables. With three or more variables, complexities of conceptualization and calculation arise that can impede understanding. The study of regression analysis with two variables should give us a firm foundation for understanding the *k*- variable case.

6.1 BASIC IDEAS

The basic equation of simple linear regression was given by

$$Y' = a + bX \quad \ldots (1)$$

Where Y' = Predicted *Y* (raw) scores of Y.

a = Y- intercept and is a constant

b = regression coefficient or weight

and *X* = raw scores of an independent variable.

The equation means that knowing the values of the constants *a* and *b*, we can predict *Y* from X.

The idea can be extended to any number of independent variables or *X's*:

$$Y' = a + b_1X_1 + b_2X_2 + \ldots + b_kX_k \quad \ldots (2)$$

where b_1, b_2, ..., b_k are regression coefficients associated with the independent variables X_1, X_2, ... X_k. Here we predict *Y* from X using *a* and the *b*'s.

The Principle of Least Squares

In simple regression, the calculation of *a* and *b* is easy. In all regression problems, simple and multiple, the *principle of least squares* is used. In any prediction of one variable from other variables there are errors of prediction. All scientific data are fallible. The data of the behavioural sciences are considerably more fallible than most data of the natural sciences. This really means that errors of prediction are larger and more conspicuous in analysis. In a word, error variance is larger. The principle of least squares tells us, in effect, to so analyze the data that the squared errors of prediction are minimized.

For any group of *N* individuals, there are *N* predictions, Y_i' (*i* runs from 1 through *N*). That is, we want to predict, from the *X*'s we have, the *X*'s observed, the *Y* scores of all the individuals. In doing so, we will be more or less in error. The principle of least squares tells us to calculate the predicted *Y's* so that the squared errors of prediction are a minimum. In other words, we want to minimize $\Sigma(Y_i - Y_i')^2$, where *i* = 1, 2, ..., *N, Yi* = the set of observed dependent variables scores, and Y_i' = the predicted dependent variable scores.

It is not necessary to discuss the least squares principle mathematically and in detail. It is sufficient for the purpose at hand if we get a firm intuitive grasp of the principle. The idea is to calculate *a*, the intercept constant, and *b*, the regression coefficient, to satisfy the principle.

The following formula can be used to calculate *a*:

$$a = \overline{Y} - b\overline{X} \qquad \text{... (3)}$$

The constant calculated with this formula helps to reduce errors of prediction. In multiple regression the formula for *a* is merely an extension of formula (3):

$$a = \overline{Y} - b\overline{X}_1 \cdots - b_k \overline{X}_k \qquad \text{... (4)}$$

This formula will take on more meaning later when the data of a problem are analyzed.

One of the main calculation problems of multiple regression is to solve equation (2) for the *b's*, the regression coefficients. With only two independent variables, the problem is not difficult.

With more than two *X's*, however, it is considerably more difficult. We will first take a fictitious problem with two independent variables, going through all the calculations. Second, we will interpret as much of the analysis as we are able to at this point. It is important to point out before going further that the principles and interpretations discussed with two independent variables apply to problems with more than two independent variables.

6.2 EXAMPLE WITH TWO INDEPENDENT VARIABLES (Kerlinger & Pedhazur, 1973)

Suppose we have reading achievement, verbal aptitude, and achievement motivation scores on 20 eighth-grade pupils. (There will, of course, usually be many more than 20 subjects.) We want to calculate the regression of Y, reading achievement, on *both* verbal aptitude and achievement motivation. We already know that since the correlation between verbal aptitude and reading achievement from verbal aptitude rather well. We wonder, however, whether we can substantially improve the prediction if we know something of the pupils' achievement motivation.

Calculation of Basic Statistics

Suppose the measures obtained for the 20 pupils are those given in Table.

In order to do a complete regression analysis, a number of statistics must be calculated. The sums, means, and sum of squares of raw scores on the three sets of scores are given in three lines directly below the table. In addition, however, we will need other statistics: the deviation sums of square of the three variables, their deviation cross products, and their standard deviations.

Table 1: Fictitious Example: Reading Achievement (Y), Verbal Aptitude ($X1$), and Achievement Motivation ($X2$) Scores *

Y	X_1	X_2	Y'	$Y - Y' = d$
2	2	4	3.0305	−1.0305
1	2	4	3.0305	− 2.0305
1	1	4	2.3534	−1.3534
1	1	3	1.9600	−.9600
5	3	6	4.4944	.5056
4	4	6	5.1715	−1.1715
7	5	3	4.6684	2.3316
6	5	4	5.0618	.9382
7	7	3	6.0226	.9774
8	6	3	5.3455	2.6545
3	4	5	4.7781	−1.7781
3	3	5	4.1010	−1.1010
6	6	9	7.7059	−1.7059
6	6	8	7.3125	−1.3125
10	8	6	7.8799	2.1201
9	9	7	8.9504	.0496
6	10	5	8.8407	−2.8407
6	9	5	8.1636	−2.1636
9	4	7	5.5649	3.4351
10	4	7	5.5649	4.4351
Σ: 110	99	104		
M: 5.50	4.95	5.20		
Σ^2: 770.	625.	600.		$\Sigma d^2 = 81.6091$

*Kerlinger & Pedhazur, 1973

They are calculated below:

$$\sum y^2 = \sum Y^2 = \frac{(\sum Y)}{N} = 770 - \frac{(110)^2}{20} = 770 - 605 = 165.00$$

$$\sum x_1^2 = \sum x_1^2 = \frac{(\sum X_1)^2}{N} = 625 - \frac{(99)^2}{20} = 625 - 490.05 = 134.95$$

$$\sum x_2^2 = \sum X_2^2 = \frac{(\sum X_2)^2}{N} = 600 - \frac{(104)^2}{20} = 600 - 540.80 = 59.20$$

$$\sum x_1 y = \sum X_1 Y = \frac{(\sum X_1)(\sum Y)}{N} = 645 - \frac{(99)(110)}{20} = 645 - 54.50 = 100.50$$

$$\sum x_2 y = \sum X_2 Y = \frac{(\sum X_2)(\sum Y)}{N} = 611 - \frac{(104)(110)}{20} = 611 - 572 = 39.00$$

$$\sum x_1 x_2 = \sum X_1 X_2 = \frac{(\sum X_1)(\sum X_2)}{N} = 530 - \frac{(99)(104)}{20} = 538 - 514.80 = 23.20$$

$$S_y = \sqrt{\frac{\sum y^2}{N-1}} = \sqrt{\frac{165}{20-1}} = \sqrt{8.6842} = 2.9469$$

$$S_{x_1} = \sqrt{\frac{\sum x_1^2}{N-1}} = \sqrt{\frac{134.95}{20-1}} = \sqrt{7.1026} = 2.6651$$

$$S_{x_2} = \sqrt{\frac{\sum x_2^2}{N-1}} = \sqrt{\frac{59.20}{20-1}} = \sqrt{3.1158} = 1.7652$$

These statistics are staples of multivariate analysis and are almost always calculated by computer programmes. The results of the calculations are given for visual convenience in Table 2. Since the correlations between the variable will be needed later, they are inserted below as the principal diagonal of the matrix (0.6735, 0.3946, and 0.2596).

There is more than one way to calculate the essential statistics of multiple regression analysis. Here, we can concentrate on calculations that use sums of squares. Sums of squares have the virtues of being additive and intuitively comprehensible. In addition, they spring directly from the data. Their use also enables us to keep our discussion closely related to analysis of variance procedures and calculations.

Reasons for the Calculations

Before proceeding with the calculations we need to review why we are doing all this. First, we want to fill in the constants of the prediction equation, $Y' = a + b_1X_1 + B_2X_2$. That is, we have to calculate a and b_1 and b_2 so that we can use the X's of individuals and predict the Y's. This means, in our example, that if we have scores of individuals on verbal aptitude and achievement motivation, we can easily insert them into the equation and obtain predicted *Y*'s, predicted reading achievement scores.

Table 2: Deviation Sums of Squares and Cross Products, Correlation Coefficients, and Standard Deviations of current problem*

	Y	X_1	X_2
y	165.00	100.50	39.00
X_1	0.6735	134.95	23.20
X_2	0.3946	0.2596	59.20
s	2.9469	2.6651	1.7652

Kerlinger & Pedhazur, 1973.

Second, we want to know the proportion of the variance that the regression equation "accounts for". i.e., to know how much of the total variance of *Y*, reading achievement, is due to the regression of *Y* on the *X*'s, on verbal aptitude and achievement motivation, or the relation between a linear combination of the independent variables and the dependent variable. Third, we need to know the relative importance of the different *X*'s in making the predictions to *Y*. We need to know, in this case, the relative importance of X_1 and X_2, verbal aptitude and achievement motivation, in the prediction equation. The regression weights, b_1 and b_2, will answer this question in part, although we will see later that there are other more accurate and readily interpretable measures for this purpose. The question will also be answered by certain calculations of sums of squares and R^2's.

Finally, we will be able to say whether the regression of *Y* on the *X*'s, the relation between *Y* and the 'best' linear combination of the *X*'s, is statistically significant.

Calculation of the Regression Statistics

The calculation of the *b*'s of the regression equation is done rather mechanically with formulas for two *X* variables. They are

$$b_1 = \frac{\left(\sum x\frac{2}{2}\right)\left(\sum x_1 y\right)-\left(\sum x_1 x_2\right)\left(\sum x_2 y\right)}{\left(\sum x_1^2\right)\left(\sum x_2^2\right)-\left(\sum x_1 x_2\right)^2}$$

$$b_2 = \frac{\left(\sum x\frac{2}{1}\right)\left(\sum x_1 y\right)-\left(\sum x_1 x_2\right)\left(\sum x_1 y\right)}{\left(\sum x_1^2\right)\left(\sum x_2^2\right)-\left(\sum x_1 x_2\right)^2} \quad \ldots (5)$$

Taking the appropriate values from Table 1 and substituting them in the formulas, we calculate the *b*'s:

$$b_1 = \frac{(59.20)\ (100.50)-(23.20)(39.00)}{(134.95)(59.20)-(23.20)^2} = \frac{5949.60-904.80}{7989.04-538.24} = \frac{5044.80}{7450.80} = 0.6771$$

$$b_2 = \frac{(134.95)\ (39)-(23.20)(100.50)}{(134.95)(59.20)-(23.20)^2} = \frac{5263.05-2331.60}{7989.04-538.24} = \frac{2931.45}{7450.80} = 0.3934$$

Now, calculate *a*. The formula for two independent variables, a special case of formula (4) is

$$a = \overline{Y} - b_1\overline{X}_1 - b_2\overline{X}_2$$

Substituting the appropriate values yields

$$a = 5.50 - (0.6771)\ (4.95) - (0.3934)\ (5.20) = 0.1027$$

The whole regression equation can now be written with the calculated values of *a* and the *b*'s:

$$Y' = 0.1027 + 0.6771X_1 + 0.3934X_2$$

As examples of the use of the equation in prediction, calculate the predicted *Y*'s for the fifth and the twentieth subjects of Table 1.

$$Y_5' = 0.1027 + (0.6771)(3) + (0.3934)(6) = 4.4944$$
$$Y_{20}' = 0.1027 + (0.6771)(4) + (0.3934)(7) = 5.5649$$

The *obtained* *Y*'s are: $Y_5 = 5$ and $Y_{20} = 10$. The deviations of the predicted scores from the obtained scores, or d= $Y - Y'$, are

$$d_5 = 5 - 4.4944 = 0.5056$$
$$d_{20} = 10 - 5.5649 = 4.4351$$

One deviation is quite small and the other quite large. In fact, these are the smallest and largest deviations in the set of 20 deviations. The predicted *Y's* and the deviations or residuals, *d*, are given in the last two columns of Table 1. About half the *d*'s are positive and about half negative, and most of them are relatively small. This is as it should be, of course. The *a* and the *b*'s of the regression equation, recall, were calculated to satisfy the least squares principle, that is, to minimize the *d*'s, or errors of prediction – rather, to minimize the squares of the errors of prediction.

If we square each of the residuals or *d*'s and add them, we obtain $\Sigma d^2 = 81.6091$. In short, the deviation or residual sum of squares expresses that portion of the total *Y* sum of squares, Σy^2, that is not due to the regression. Actually, as we will soon see, there is no need to go through these involved calculations. The deviation or residual sum of squares can be calculated much more readily. We went through the lengthy calculations to show clearly what this sum of squares is.

The regression sum of squares is calculated with the following general formula:

$$ss_{reg} = b_1 \Sigma x_1 y + \ldots + b_k \Sigma X_k y \qquad \ldots (6)$$

where k = the number of X or independent variables. In the case of two X variables, k = 2, the formula reduces to

$$ss_{reg} = b_1 \Sigma x_1 y + \ldots + b_2 \Sigma x_2 y \qquad \ldots (7)$$

Taking the b values calculated earlier and finding the deviation sums of cross products from Table 2, we substitute in (7):

$$SS_{xy} = (0.6771)\,(100.50) + (0.3934)\,(39.00) = 83.3912$$

This is that portion of the total sum of squares of Y, or Σy^2, that is due to the regression of Y on the two X's. Note that the total sum of squares of Y is 165.00. (from Table 2). If the regression sum of squares is added to the residual sum of squares, the sum equals the total sum of squares of Y. We write this equation again with a new number and then substitute our calculated values:

$$ss_t = ss_{reg} + ss_{res} \qquad \ldots (8)$$

$$ss_t = 83.3912 + 81.6091 = 165.0003$$

This is of course the same value given in Table 2, within errors of rounding.

The Coefficient of Multiple Correlation and its Square

One of the most valuable statistics of multiple regression is the coefficient of multiple correlation, R. The square of this coefficient, R^2, is even more valuable for reasons to be given presently. The calculation of R^2 is simple. One formula that is particularly useful and easily interpreted is

$$R^2 = \frac{SS_{res}}{SS_t} \qquad \ldots (9)$$

The square root of R^2, of course, gives R. Substituting the sums of squares calculated above, we obtain

$$R^2 = \frac{83.3912}{165.0000} = 0.5054$$

$$R = \sqrt{0.5054} = 0.7109$$

R is the product – moment correlation of the predicted Y's, Y_i', which are of course linear combinations of the X's, and the obtained Y's.

$$R^2 = \frac{(\Sigma yy')^2}{\Sigma y^2 \ \Sigma y'^2} \quad \text{... (10)}$$

$$R = \frac{\Sigma yy'}{\sqrt{\Sigma y^2 \ \Sigma y'^2}} \quad \text{... (11)}$$

The values of equation (10) can be calculated from Y and Y' columns of Table 1. We already have $\Sigma y^2 = 165$. The comparable value of $\Sigma y'^2$ is calculated:

$$\Sigma y'^2 = \Sigma Y'^2 - \frac{(\Sigma Y')^2}{N} = 688.3969 - \frac{(110)}{20} = 83.3969$$

The sum of the deviation cross product is

$$\Sigma yy'^2 = \Sigma YY' - \frac{(\Sigma Y)(\Sigma Y')}{N} = 688.3939 - \frac{(110)(110)}{20} = 83.3939$$

(The difference of 0.003 in the two sums of squares is due to errors or rounding. Actually, $\Sigma y'^2$ must equal $\Sigma yy'$. We will use calculated values as they are, however, since it makes no difference in *R2* calculation.) Substituting in equation (10), R2 is obtained:

$$R^2 = \frac{(83.3939)^2}{(83.3969)(165.)} = \frac{6954.5426}{13,760.4885} = 0.5054$$

and

$$R = \sqrt{0.5054} = 0.7109$$

Finally, we calculate the *F* ratio, first repeating the formula given in Chapter 2:

$$F = \frac{R^2 / k}{(1 - R^2)/(N - k - 1)} \quad \text{... (12)}$$

Where k = the number of independent variables.

$$F = \frac{0.5054/2}{(1 - 0.5054)/(20 - 2 - 1)} = \frac{0.2527}{0.0291} = 8.684$$

We can, of course, calculate *F* using the appropriate sums of squares. The formula is

$$F = \frac{SS_{reg} / df_{reg}}{SS_{res} / df_{res}} \quad \text{... (13)}$$

The degrees of freedom associated with SS_{reg} is k = 2, the number of independent variables. The degrees of freedom associated with SS_{res} is N – k – 1 = 17. Therefore,

$$F = \frac{83.3912/2}{81.6091/17} = \frac{41.6956}{4.8005} = 8.686$$

This agrees with F calculated using R^2 (within rounding error). It is significant at the .01 level.

6.3 REGRESSION GRAPH

To help solidity understanding of the problem and its analysis, and especially to show graphically the nature of regression, the predicted and observed Y values can be graphed as in Figure 1.

Y', the predicted Y values – which, remember, where really calculated from X_1 and X_2 – and Y, the observed Y values, are plotted. Y' is the abscissa and Y the ordinate. This is the same kind of plot we would use if we were plotting the graph of a simple two-variable correlation and regression problem. The difference is that the present independent variable, is a regression composite of X_1 and X_2 instead of a single X.

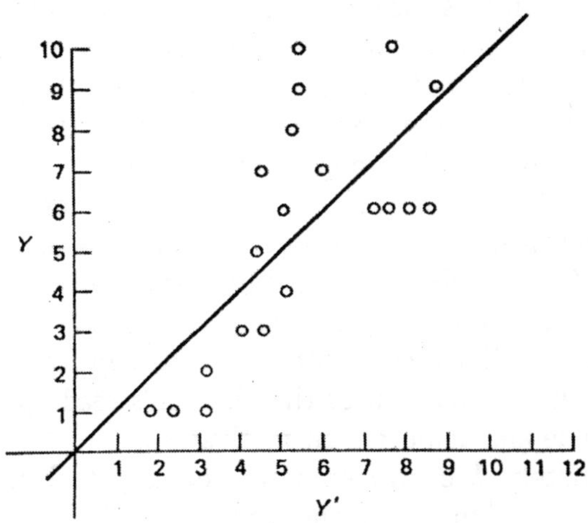

Figure 1

$R_{y.12}$ = 7.1, a fairly substantial correlation. We would expect the plotted points of Y and Y' to lie fairly close to the regression line. They do. $R_{y.12}$ = 7.1 expresses symbolically and quantitatively what the plot expresses graphically. To the extent that the points lie near the regression line (which, remember, is ruled in by drawing a straight line through a, the intercept constant, plotted on the Y axis, and the point where the two means, $\bar{Y}'$ = 5.50 and $\bar{Y}$ = 5.50, meet), the magnitude of *R* is high. If all the plotted points were on the regression line, then R = 1.00. If the points are scattered on the graph at random, then *R* will be close to zero. In other words, we can interpret the graph of *Y'* and *Y* much as we interpret an ordinary graph.

Interpretation of the Analysis

A great deal of space has been taken and detailed calculations made to try to clarify the basic business of multiple regression analysis. Even so, the calculations are incomplete; a good deal more analysis is still not only possible but desirable, especially if we are able to interpret certain highly significant studies published recently. We must pause, however, to interpret what has been done.

The *F* ratio tells us that the regression of *Y* on X_1 and X_2 is statistically significant. The probability of an *F* ratio this large occurring by chance is less than .01 (it is actually about .003). This means that the relation between *Y* and a linear least squares combination of X_1 and X_2 could probably not have occurred by chance. It tells us little or nothing about the magnitude of the relation. If the F ratio were not statistically significant, on the other hand, we would not consider the magnitude of the relation.

The measures *R* and R^2, especially the latter, tell us explicitly about the magnitude of the relation. In this case, $R^2 = 0.51$, which means that approximately 51 per cent of the variance of *Y* is accounted for by X_1 and X_2 in combination. (R^2 is called the *coefficient of determination*.) R = 0.71 can be interpreted much like an ordinary coefficient of correlation, except that values of R range from 0 to 1.00 unlike r, which ranges from -1.00 through 0 to +1.00.

Returning to the substance of the original research problem, recall that *Y* = reading achievement, X_1= verbal aptitude, and X_2 = achievement motivation. $R^2 = .51$ – and F = 8.686, which says that R^2 is statistically significant – means that of the total variance of the reading achievement of the 20 children studied, 51 per cent is accounted for by a linear *combination* of verbal aptitude and achievement motivation. In other words, a good deal of the children's reading achievement is explained by verbal aptitude and achievement motivation.

Unfortunately, *b* coefficients are not easy to interpret in multiple regression analysis. So, as not to deflect the reader from the main thrust of our discussion, we will only interpret *b*'s rather roughly. Later, we will give a more precise and correct analysis and interpretation.

It was said that a single b coefficient in the equation *Y'* = a + b*X* indicated that as *X* changes one unit *Y* changes *b* units. The regression coefficient *b* is called the slope. We say that the slope of the regression line is at the rate of *b* units of *Y* for one unit of *X*. If the regression equation were,

$Y = 4 + 0.50X$, b = 0.50, and it would mean that as X changes one unit, Y changes half a unit. In multiple regression, on the other hand, the interpretation plot thickens because we have more than one b. In general, if the scales of values of X_1 and X_2 are the same or about the same, for example, all 20 values in each case range from 1 to 10, as ours do, then the *b*'s are weights that show roughly the relative importance of the difference variables in predicting *Y*. This is seen by merely studying the regression equation with the values of the *b*'s calculated earlier:

$$Y' = 0.1026 + 0.6771\, X_1 + 0.3934\, X_2$$

X_1, verbal aptitude, is weighted more heavily than X_2, achievement motivation. But the situation is more complex than it seems and the statement may not be true in all cases.

Additional Regression Calculations (Kerlinger & Pedhazur, 1973)

Even though X_2 does not add significantly to the prediction, we pull together our summary regression analyses in Tables 3, 4, and 5. In table 3, we present 20 obtained *Y* scores and the predicted *Y* and deviation scores, Y′ and d = *Y* – Y′, for the two regressions, *Y* on X_1 and *Y* on X_1 and X_2. The obtained scores, Y, are given in the first column. The *Y* scores predicted from the regression of *Y* on X_1 alone, Y_1', are given in the second column. The deviations from regression, d_1, are listed in the third column. In the fourth and fifth columns, the *Y* scores predicted on the basis of X_1 and X_2, and the accompanying deviation scores, d_{12}, are listed.

The last three rows of the table give the sums (S) and the sums of squares (*ss*) of the five columns. The equations for the regressions of *Y* on X_1 alone and *Y* on X_1 and X_2 are

$$Y_1' = 1.8137 + 0.7447\, X_1 \qquad \text{... (14)}$$

$$Y_{12}' = 0.1027 + 0.6771\, X_1 + 0.3934\, X_2 \qquad \text{... (15)}$$

The values of equation (14) were calculated as follows (*see* Table 1 for the means and Table 2 for the sums of squares and cross products):

$$b_1 = \frac{\Sigma x_1 y}{\Sigma x_1^2} = \frac{100.50}{134.95} = 0.7447$$

$$a = \overline{Y} - b_1 \overline{X}_1 = 5.50 - (.7447)(4.95) = 1.8137$$

To calculate the 20 predicted *Y* scores, simply enter the X_1 values of Table 3 in equation (14). For example, Y_1' and Y_8' are calculated:

Table 3: Dependent Variable Scores (Y) and predicted scores (Y') from one and two independent variables (X_1,X_2), Data of Table 1

Y	Y_1'	d_1	Y_{12}'	d_{12}
2	3.3031	-1.3031	3.0305	-1.0305
1	3.3031	-2.3031	3.0305	-2.0305
1	2.5584	-1.5584	2.3534	-1.3534
1	2.5584	-1.5584	1.9600	-0.9600
5	4.0478	0.9522	4.4944	0.5056
4	4.7925	-0.7925	5.1715	-1.1715
7	5.5372	1.4628	4.6684	2.3316
6	5.5372	0.4628	5.0618	0.9382
7	7.0266	-0.0266	6.0226	0.9774
8	6.2819	1.7181	5.3455	2.6545
3	4.7925	-1.7925	4.7781	-1.7781
3	4.0478	-1.0478	4.1010	-1.1010
6	6.2819	-0.2819	7.7059	-1.7059
6	6.2819	-0.2819	7.3125	-1.3125
10	7.7713	2.2287	7.8799	2.1201
9	8.5160	0.4840	8.9504	0.0496
6	9.2607	-3.2607	8.8407	-2.8407
6	8.5160	-2.5160	8.1636	-2.1636
9	4.7925	4.2075	5.5649	3.4351
10	7.7925	5.2075	5.5649	4.4351
Σ: 110.	110.	0	110.	0
Σ²: 770.	679.8326		688.3969	
ss: 165.	74.8326	90.1556	83.3969	81.6091

The last three rows of the table give the sums (Σ) and the sums of squares (*ss*) of the five columns. The equations for the regressions of Y on X_1 alone and Y on X_1 and X_2 are

$$Y_1' = 1.8137 + 0.7447\, X_1 \qquad \text{... (14)}$$

$$Y_{12}' = 0.1027 + 0.6771\, X_1 + 0.3934\, X_2 \qquad \text{... (15)}$$

The values of equation (14) were calculated as follows (see Table 1 for the means and Table 2 for the sums of squares and cross products):

$$b_1 = \frac{\Sigma x_1 y}{\Sigma x_1^2} = \frac{100.50}{134.95} = 0.7447$$

$$a = \overline{Y} - b_1 \overline{X}_1 = 5.50 - (.7447)(4.95) = 1.8137$$

To calculate the 20 predicted *Y* scores, simply enter the X_1 values of Table 3 in equation (14). For example, Y_1' and Y_8' are calculated:

$$Y_1' = 1.8137 + (.7447)\ (2) = 3.3031$$

$$Y_8' = 1.8137 + (.7447)\ (5) = 5.5372$$

Table 4: Sums of Squares and Reduction in Residual Sums of Squares of Regression Analyses, Addition of X_2 to X_1.

X	ss_y	ss_{reg}	ss_{res}	Reduction
1	165.0000	74.8444	90.1556	
1+2	165.0000	83.3912	81.6091	8.5465

Now, calculate the *d*'s that accompany these values:

$$d = Y - Y'$$
$$d_1 = 2 - 3.3031 = -1.3031$$
$$d_8 = 6 - 5.5372 = 0.4628$$

To calculate the predicted Y's of the regression of *Y* on X_1 and X_2 insert the values of both X_1 and X_1 of Table 1 in equation (15). [The values of equation (3.15) were calculated earlier.] For example Y_1' and Y_8', the comparable values to those just calculated for the regression of *Y* on *X*1 alone, are

$$Y_1' = 0.1027 + (0.6771)\ (2) + 0.3934)\ (4)$$
$$= 0.1027 + 1.3542 + 1.5736 = 3.0305$$
$$Y_8' = 0.1027 + (0.6771)\ (5) + (0.3934)\ (4)$$
$$= 0.1027 + 3.3855 + 1.5736 = 5.0618$$

Table 5: Analyses of Variance and R2's of the two Regressions of Y on X_1 and X_2 and Y on X_1

Source	df	ss	ms	F	p	R^2
X_1, X_2	2	83.3909	41.6955	8.686	.003	0.5054
Deviations	17	81.6091	4.8005			
X_1	1	74.8444	74.8444	14.943	.001	0.4536
Deviations	18	90.1556	5.0086			
Total	19	165.0000				

The residual scores are

$$d_1 = 2 - 3.0305 = -\ 1.0305$$
$$d_8 = 6 - 5.0618 = 0.9382$$

We should probably pause at this point to emphasize just what we are trying to do. We are trying to show, in as straightforward a way as possible, what goes into multiple regression analysis. The nonmathematical student of education and the behavioural sciences is frequently confused when confronted with regression equations, regression weights R^2's, and F ratios. Here an attempt is made to clear up at least some of this confusion by calculating many of the necessary quantities of multiple regression analysis rather directly. In actual practice they are too cumbersome. But they are good for pedagogical purposes because they approach multiple regression directly by working, as much as possible, with the original data and the sums of squares generated from the original data. Hopefully, one can "see" where the various quantities "come from".

Our main point is that the addition of X_2 to the regression reduced the residual or deviation sum of squares from 90.1556 to 81.6091 and increased the regression sum of squares from 74.8326 to 83.3969. (These last two figures, taken from the bottom line of Table 3, are slightly off due to rounding errors. The more accurate values are 74.8444 and 83.3909, as calculated by a computer.) The last line of the table, then, is the important one. It gives the sums of squares for Y, Y_1', d_1, Y_{12}', and d_{12}. Except for $\Sigma y_1'^2$, these sums of squares were calculated earlier.

The sums of squares of Table 3 are brought together for convenience in Table 4. In addition, the reduction in the sum of squares of the residuals or, conversely, the increase in the regression sum of squares – is given in the table: 8.55. In short, the table shows that the addition of $X3$ to the regression reduces the deviations from regression (the residuals) by 8.55 – or, the addition of $X2$- increases the regression sum of squares by 8.55. As we saw earlier, this is a decrease (or increase) of 5 per cent: 8.55/165.00 =.05.

Table 4 and its figures can show rather nicely just what the multiple correlation coefficient is – in sums of squares. Think of the extreme case. If we had a number of independent variables, $X_1, X_2, \ldots\ldots, X_k$, and they completely "explained" the variance of Y, the dependent variable, then $R^2_{y.12...k} = 1.00$, and the sum of squares due to the regression would be the same as the total sum of squares, namely 165, and the residual sum of squares would be zero. But we do not "know" all these independent variables; we only "know" two of them, X_1 and X_2.

'The sum of squares for the regression of Y on X_1 alone is 74.84. The proportion of the dependent variable variance is 74.84/165.00 = 0.45. The sum of squares of the regression of Y on X_1 and X_2 is 83.39. The proportion of the Y variance is 83.39/165.00 = 0.51. The quantities 0.45 and 0.1, of course, are the R^2's.

In Table 5, the analyses of variance of the two regressions are summarized. In the upper part of the table, the analysis of variance of the regression of Y on X_1 and X_2 is given. The lower part of the table gives the analysis of variance for the regression of Y on X_1 alone.

It is evident from these analyses that X_2 does not add much to X_1. It increases our predictive power by only 5 per cent. Returning to the substance of our variables and problem, verbal aptitude alone (X_1) accounts for about 45 per cent of the variance of reading achievement (Y). If achievement motivation (X_2) is added to the regression equation, the amount of variance of reading achievement accounted for by verbal aptitude and achievement motivation tighter (X_1 and X_2) is about 51 per cent, an increase of about 5 to 6 per cent.

6.4 ASSUMPTIONS BEHIND MULTIPLE REGRESSION

Like all statistical techniques, multiple regression analysis has several assumptions behind it that should be understood by researchers. Many students, overburdened by zealous instructors with admonitions on when analysis of variance, say, can and cannot be used, come to the erroneous conclusion that it can only be rarely used. Students need not turned off analysis and statistics by admonitions and cautionary precepts that usually do not matter that much. They sometimes do matter, however. Moreover, intelligent use of analytic methods requires knowledge of rationale and thus the assumptions behind the methods. Certain assumptions behind regression analysis are the following:

i) In regression analysis it is assumed that the Y scores are normally distributed at each value of *X*. (There is no assumption of normality about the *X's*). The validity of an *F* test, for instance, depends on the assumption that the dependent variable scores are normally distributed in the population. The assumption is not needed to *calculate* correlation and regression measures. There is no need to assume anything to calculate *r*'s, *b*'s, and so on. (An exception is that, if the distributions of X and Y, or the combined X's and Y, are not similar, then the range of *r* may not be from -1 through 0 to +1). It is only when we make inferences from a sample to a population that we must pause and think of assumptions.

ii) The Y scores have equal variances at each X point. The Y scores, then, are assumed to be normally distributed and to have equal variance at each X point.

Note the following equation:

$$Y = a + b_1X_1 + ... + b_k X_k e \qquad ... (16)$$

Where e = error, or residual. These errors are assumed to be random and normally distributed, with equal variances at each *X* point. The latter point can be said: the distribution of the deviations from regression (the residuals) are the same at all *X* points. These assumptions about the *e*'s are of course used in statistical estimation procedures.

In general, it is safe to say that we can ordinarily go ahead with analysis of variance and multiple regression analysis without worrying too much about assumptions. Nevertheless, researchers must be aware that serious violations of the assumptions, and especially of combinations of them, can distort results.

In much behavioural research, however, prediction, successful or not, is not enough. We want to know why; we want to "explain" the criterion performance, the phenomenon under study. This is the main goal of science. To explain a phenomenon, moreover, we must know the relations between independent variables and a dependent variable and the relations among the independent variables. This means, of course, that R^2 and its statistical significance and magnitude are not enough; our interest focuses more on the whole regression equation and the regression coefficients.

Multiple regression, while well-suited to predictive analysis, is more fundamentally oriented to explanatory analysis. We do not simply throw variables into regression equations; we enter them, wherever possible, at the dictates of theory and reasonable interpretation of empirical research findings.

6.5 MULTIPLE REGRESSION, DISCRIMINANT ANALYSIS AND CANONICAL CORRELATION

Almost all methods of numerical data analysis are the same in one respect: they identify, partition, and control variance. Multiple regression analysis and analysis of variance, for example, break down the variance of a dependent variable according to its relations to the variances of one or more independent variables. One may even go so far as to say that all methods of analysis seek to identify and quantify variance shared by variables. Multiple regression seeks to identify and estimate the magnitude and statistical significance of the variance of the dependent variable, Y, that is shared with several independent variables. If we keep this notion firmly in mind we will have little difficulty in understanding the other methods of multivariate analysis.

Discriminant Analysis

Consider a research problem that arises again and again is to classify individuals into groups on the basis of their scores on tests. The simplest case, of course, is to place individuals or any other units on which we have one or more measures into twọ groups on the basis of scores on one test. We administer a test, say, an Attitude test or Creativity test and then assign children to different groups on the basis of their attitude or creativity scores. In other words, by using test scores we are able to assign individuals to two (or more) groups.

A more interesting procedure is to assign individuals to two or more groups on the basis of their scores on two or more tests or scales. Instead of a single predict, for instance, success or lack of success in high school. By doing a discriminant analysis we can make such predictions. That is, on the basis of a least squares composite of k test scores, we predict success or lack of success in high school. This is nothing more than a multiple regression situation where the dependent variable is group membership.

Another related and perhaps more important problem is not only to discriminate maximally between two or more groups – say males and females, or successful and unsuccessful – but also to be able to specify something of the nature of the discrimination. For instance, in an example, any three behavioural measures may discriminate between the successful and unsuccessful administrators. But this may not be enough for our purposes. We may also want to "explain" the discrimination; we may want to know the relative efficacies or weights of the three tests in the discrimination.

Discriminant analysis is a way of solving such problems. The *discriminant function* is a regression equation with a dependent variable that represents groups membership. With only two groups, discriminant function analysis amounts to multiple regression analysis with the dependent variable taking the values of 1 and 0. There are several measures for each individual in a sample. Using these measures as independent variables and a vector of 1's and 0's as the dependent variable, we solve the regression in the usual manner. The resulting equation, the discriminant function, maximally discriminates the members – it tells us to which group each member probably "belongs".

The discriminant function can also be used for other groups of similar administrators without knowing whether they are successful or unsuccessful. One uses the function, in other words, for predictive purposes. It has to be born in mind, however, that if the new samples differ from the original sample, the validity of the procedure is questionable. In any case, discriminant analysis can materially aid predictive use of tests.

Research Aspects of Discriminant Analysis

Like multiple regression in general, discriminant analysis can be used in two main ways: for classification and diagnosis, and to study the relations among variables in different populations and groups. The first use will probably be more common than the second. A clinical psychologist, for example, may wish to classify youths as delinquent or nondeliquent. If he has measure that he has measures that seem to be related to delinquency – for instance, social class, values, and personal beliefs – and also knowledge of the actual delinquency of a group of youths, the measures and the knowledge of delinquency can be used in discriminant function. If the prediction is reasonably successful, the function can be used to assess the probable delinquency of other individuals. This amounts to the same procedure used in the earlier example.

The second use of the discriminant function, like one use of multiple regression analysis, is more germane to basic scientific purposes. One wishes to know, for instance, something of the relations between values and career choices.

This kind of analysis is important because it can lead to viable theory and research. The possibilities for theory development seem clear, and the use of discriminant analysis can significantly help in such development.

6.6 CANONICAL CORRELATION

Canonical correlation is the generalization of multiple regression analysis to any number of dependent variables. This is of course not a large conceptual step. It is, however, a rather large computational step. An outline of the method is sufficient for our purposes. Moreover, canonical correlation, except for the simplest problems, is so complex as to make desk calculator calculations forbidding. Here, again, intelligent and critical reliance on the computer is necessary.

Canonical correlation analysis is multiple regression analysis with *k* independent variables and *m* dependent variables. We will call the independent variables the "variables on the left" and the dependent variables the "variables on the right," or "predictor variables" and "criterion variables". The basic idea of canonical correlation is that, through least squares analysis, two linear composites are formed, one for the independent variables, X_j and one for the dependent variables, Y_n. The correlation between these two composites is the canonical correlation, R_c. the square of the canonical correlation, R_c^2, is an estimate of the variance shared by the two composites.

The parallel with multiple regression should be apparent. Like the coefficient of multiple correlation, the canonical coefficient is the maximum correlation possible between the two sets of variables. Like multiple regression, we have a least squares procedure that seeks the regression weights to be attached to each of the variables of both sets of variables. Multiple regression analysis can of course be considered a special case of canonical analysis. In view of the practical limitations on the use of canonical analysis, however, we prefer to consider it a generalization of multiple regression analysis.

As we will see, the theoretical notion of canonical correlation is an elegant and aesthetically satisfying one, even though its actual use may leave something to be desired.

Data Matrices and Canonical Correlation

It will be useful to familiarize the reader with a conceptualization and symbolism of the raw data and correlation matrices that are used in multiple regression and canonical correlation. In multiple regression analysis, one variable, the dependent variable, is partitioned from the rest of the matrix. In canonical correlation analysis, two or more variables, the dependent variables, are partitioned from the rest of the matrix.

The basic data matrix for multiple regression analysis is simple the rectangular matrix of raw scores (or z scores), X_{ij}, where i = 1, 2, ..., N, N being the number of cases or subjects, and $j = 1, 2, \ldots\ldots, k$, k being the number of variables (tests, items, scales, and so on). As usual, the first subscript of each X stands for rows (subjects, cases) and the second subscript for columns (variables, tests, items, and so on). Note the broken vertical line: it partitions the matrix into the k independent and the n − k dependent variables.

The variables are inter correlated and correlation or R matrix is formed. This matrix, too, is partitioned similarly. In the multiple regression correlation matrix the dependent variable is partitioned from the independent variables. In canonical correlation analysis the correlation matrix is partitioned as shown in Table 7. The partitioning is indicated by the broken lines, and the independent and dependent variables are labeled. It is easier to use matrix algebra and symbols than the usual statistical symbols to indicate the solution of canonical correlation problems. The four partitions of the correlation matrix are indicated in this way.

Table 7: Basic Raw Data Matrix for Canonical Correlation Analysis

Cases	Independent Variables				Dependent Variables		
1	X_{11}	X_{12}	. . .	X_{1k}	$X_{1(k+1)}$	. . .	X_{1n}
2	X_{21}	X_{22}	. . .	X_{2k}	$X_{2(k+1)}$	. . .	X_{2n}
.	.	.		.	.		.
.	.	.	. . .	.	.	. . .	.
.	.	.		.	.		.
N	X_{N1}	X_{N2}	. . .	X_{Nk}	$X_{N(k+1)}$	. . .	X_{Nn}

[a] N = Number of cases; k = number of independent variables; n = total number of variables.

$$\mathbf{R} = \begin{bmatrix} \mathbf{R}_{11} & \mathbf{R}_{12} \\ \mathbf{R}_{21} & \mathbf{R}_{22} \end{bmatrix}$$

Where R = the whole correlation matrix of the $k + (n - k)$ variables; R_{11} = the correlations of the k independent variables; R_{22} = the correlations of the $n - k$ dependent variables; R_{12} = the correlations between the independent and dependent variables; R_{21} = the transpose of R_{12}.

In computer solutions of the canonical correlation problems, the raw data matrix is read into the computer and the computer does all the basic statistics. After the Whole R matrix is calculated, the canonical correlation analysis begins by partitioning the matrix as indicated above. The user must of course "tell" the computer how to partition the matrix. Our purpose here is to give an intuitive feeling for the method. We use verbal description and provide examples so that the student can begin to interpret published research studies and computer output.

Canonical Correlation Process

The matrices of Table 9 are operated on in such a way as to produce a sort of double least squares solution. Two linear composites are formed, one of the variables on the right. In multiple regression, one linear composite of the X's is formed taking the relations among them and the relations between them and the Y vector into account. In canonical correlation analysis, the procedure is more complex because more correlations have to be taken into account and two composites formed. At any rate, the correlation between composites is the canonical correlation. Its square, R_c^2, is interpreted similarly to the squared multiple correlation coefficient: it represents the variance shared by the two composites.

Table 8: Basic Raw Data Matrix for Canonical Correlation Analysis

		Independent Variables				Dependent Variables		
		1	2	. . .	k	$k+1$	. . .	n
Independent Variables	1	r_{11}	r_{12}	. . .	r_{1k}	$r_{1(k+1)}$	. . .	r_{1n}
	2	r_{21}	r_{22}	. . .	r_{2k}	$r_{2(k+1)}$	. . .	r_{2n}
	.	.	.		.	.		.
	.	.	.	. . .	.	.	. . .	.
	.	.	.		.	.		.
	k	r_{k1}	r_{k2}	. . .	r_{kk}	$r_{k(k+1)}$	. . .	r_{kn}
Dependent Variable	$k+1$	$r_{(k+1)1}$		. . .	$r_{(k+1)k}$	$r_{(k+1)(k+1)}$	. . .	$r_{(k+1)n}$
	.				.	.		.
	.			. . .	.	.	. . .	.
	.				.	.		.
	n	r_{n1}	r_{n2}	. . .	r_{nk}	$r_{n(k+1)}$	. . .	r_{nn}

[a] k = number of independent variables; n = total number of variables.

A canonical correlation analysis also yields weights, which, theoretically at least, interpreted as regression weights. These weights appear to be the weak link in the canonical correlation analysis chain. Recall that regression weights in multiple regression analysis fluctuate from sample to sample and change when variables are added or subtracted from the regression equation.

The canonical correlation weights are more of a problem, particularly when more than one canonical correlation is calculated from the same set of data. In other words, the weights must be interpreted with great caution and circumspection.

The value of canonical correlation analysis is enhanced by another feature of the method. More than one source of common variance can be identified and analysed. In multiple regression analysis, although the dependent variable may contain more than one source of variance (for example, grade-point averages), there is only one regression equation. In canonical correlation, however, there can be more than one set of equations. In other words, the method systematically extracts the first and largest source of variance, and the canonical correlation coefficient is an index of the relation between the two sets of variables based on this source of variance.

Then the next largest source of variance, left in the data after the first source is extracted and independent of the first source, is analyzed. The second canonical correlation coefficient, which is smaller than the first, is an index of the relation between the two sets of variables due to this second source of variance.

Although factor analysis may be a better method for investigating such problems, in some cases canonical correlation can supply useful information on relations among sets of variables and also yield tests of the statistical significance of such relations. In the foregoing example, the correlation of 0.49 may not be statistically significant. Computer programmes usually do the successive analyses of canonical correlation and test the statistical significance of the successive sources of variance. If a second or third canonical *R* is not significant, of course, it and its weights are not interpreted.

EXERCISES

1. *B* and β are called regression coefficients or weights. Why are they called "weights"? Give two examples with two independent variables each.
2. Suppose the two regression equations that express the relation between age, X, and intelligence (mental age), Y, of middle-class and working-class children are:

   Middle Class: $Y' = .30 + .98X$

   Working Class: $Y' = .30 + .90X$

   The regression weights, *b*, are therefore .98 and .90.
   a) Accepting these weights at face value, what do they imply about the relation between chronological age and mental age in the two samples?
   b) Calculate *Y'* values with both equations at age 8, 10, 15, and 20. What do the *Y*"s tell us?
   c) Can the analysis between slopes (for example, the differences between slopes) sometimes be important? Why?
3. In regression analysis with one independent variable, $r_{xy} = \beta$. Suppose that a sociologist has calculated the correlation between a composite environmental variable and intelligence and $r_{xy} = 0.40$. Suppose, further, that a 3-year programme was initiated to enrich deprived children's environments. Assuming that the programme is successful (after 3 years).
   a) What should happen to the correlation between the environmental variables and intelligence, other things being equal?
   b) What should happen to the β-weight?

7

Inferential Statistics

Statistics is the study of population. It deals with the collection, classification, description and interpretation of data obtained by the conduct of surveys and experiments. Its essential purpose is to describe and draw inferences about the numerical properties of population.

In everyday language the term 'population' is used to refer to groups or aggregates of people. But to a statistician the term population refers not only to a defined group of people, but also to define groups or aggregates of animals, objects, materials, measurements and happenings of any kind.

The statistician's concern is with properties which are descriptive of the group rather than with properties of particular members. Population can be finite or infinite. When the number of a population can be counted and a finite number obtained, the population is infinite. When the number of members are not countable, it is an infinite population.

Because of the large size of many populations, it may be either impracticable or impossible for the investigator to produce statistics based on all members. So the investigator draws a sample from a population.

7.1 SAMPLING

A sample is any subgroup or sub aggregates drawn by some appropriate method from a population. The method used is important. Having drawn the sample, the investigator utilizes appropriate statistical methods to describe its property. He then proceeds to make statements about the properties of the population from his knowledge of the properties of the sample i.e., he proceeds to generalize from the sample to the population.

The fact that inferences can be made about the properties of population from a knowledge of properties of samples is basic in research thinking. Such statements are of course subject to error. The magnitude of the error involved in drawing such inferences can in most cases be estimated by appropriate procedures. Where no standard error of any kind can be made, generalization about population form sample data are worthless.

7.2 METHOD OF SAMPLING

In drawing inferences about the characteristics of population, from sample statistics, the assumption is frequently made that the sample should be drawn at random from the population. The word random is used in a theoretical sense and in operational sense. In theoretical sense, the word refer to an assumption about the equii-probability of events i.e., a random sample is one such that every member of the population has an equal probability of being included in it.

The word random in operational sense is used to describe certain operation of method (i.e., the drawing of members from a container after they have been thoroughly mixed or drawing of cards from a deck after they have been shuffled).

Mode of Selection

1. Use a table of random numbers. This is the more convenient form. Label the members of population at first. Then draw the members directly from a table of random numbers. i.e., to use the table of random numbers in getting a sample of 50 from a line of 3000 students, assign each student a number between 1 and 3000. Then go to the random number table and mentally block the table off to convenient columns. Read down the columns until you obtain 50 number that fall between 1 and 3000. The students assigned corresponding to these 50 members constitute a randomly selected sample.
2. When the members of population are listed, all the names of some odd number be entered on slips of paper. Place these in a container and mix it well. Then draw sufficient number of slips. The names of the slips identify the sample (this method is also known as lottery method).
3. If a list is arranged alphabetically or in some other systematic fashion every nth name may be chosen in the construction of the sample.

   This is sometimes known as systematic sampling. Forms of modified random sampling are sometime used.
4. Stratified Sampling: This requires prior knowledge about the strata of the population in constructing the sample the members are drawn at random from the various strata.

If the members are drawn such that the proportions in the various strata in the sample are the same as proportion in those strata in the population, the sample is proportionate stratified sample.

7.3 SAMPLING DISTRIBUTION

Even when a sample is random, it is likely to be different from the population. Samples of a population may also differ just because they are composed of different individuals.

Suppose we draw several samples from a population and statics (say, mean, s, etc.) are computed for each of these samples. Then the distribution of each of these statistics is called a sampling distribution of the statistic computed. Since mean is a statistic the distribution of the means of several samples of a population forms a sampling distribution of the mean.

Standard Error

Just as a distribution scores has certain characteristics (mean and variance) so too does a sampling distribution. The standard deviation of a sampling distribution of a statistic is called the standard error of that statistic.

Hence, the standard deviation of the sampling distribution of mean is known as the standard error of the mean. This is denoted as $\sigma_{\bar{x}}$, SE ($\bar{x}$).

Sampling Error

The statistics of one sample may not be equal to the statistics of other sample from a population.

e.g.: Mean of a sample will not be equal to the mean of other samples taken from the same population even though samples are selected randomly from the population. The fact that means differ in value from one sample to another testifies to the fact that there is variability in such a distribution of means. Since standard deviation is the most appropriate index of variability, the standard deviation of sampling distribution of means. $\sigma_{\bar{x}}$ is a numerical index of the extent to which means will vary from sample. More generally standard error is an index of the amount of sampling error with reference to a given statistic.

Standard Error of the Mean

The standard Error of the mean i.e., $\sigma_{\bar{x}}$ can be calculated by the formula.

$\sigma_{\bar{x}} = \frac{\sigma_x}{\sqrt{N}}$ where σ_x stands for the standard deviation of the population and N - sample size.

In cases when population standard deviation is unknown $\sigma\bar{x}$ is calculated by the formula, $\sigma\bar{x} = \frac{Sx}{\sqrt{N}}$

Where, S_x stands for standard deviation of the sample and N - sample size.

Problem: If the population standard deviation is as given below, what would be the standard error of sampling distribution of the mean for sample of size N?

a) $s_x = 12$ $N = 16$
b) $s_x = 10$ $N = 25$
c) $s_x = 8$ $N = 36$

Solution:

a) $\sigma_{\bar{x}} = \frac{S_x}{\sqrt{N}} = \frac{12}{\sqrt{16}} = \frac{12}{4} = \mathbf{3}$

b) $\sigma_{\bar{x}} = \frac{S_x}{\sqrt{N}} = \frac{10}{5} = \underline{2}$

c) $\sigma_{\bar{x}} = \frac{S_x}{\sqrt{N}} = \frac{8}{6} = \frac{4}{3} = \mathbf{1.33}$

7.4 APPLICATION OF THE CONCEPT OF STANDARD ERROR

Sampling Distribution and Normality

Given random sampling, the sampling distribution of the mean is a normal distribution if the population distribution of raw scores is normal and approaches a normal distribution if the size of the sample is large.

The degree to which a sample mean represents its parameter is an index of the significant or trustworthiness of the computed sample mean. Therefore, when we have calculated a statistic, we may ask ourselves a question how good an estimate is if the statistic of the parameter is based upon the entire population from which the sample was drawn. The answer to this question depends on the standard error.

Estimation of a parameter by means of a statistic can be done in two ways. (1) point estimation and (2) interval estimation. A point estimate is the value obtained by direct calculation of the sample values. e.g., If in a particular sample, $\bar{X} = 26.38$. This is a point estimate of the population.

Fixing up an interval with given degree of confidence within which the population mean may lie is the process of interval estimation.

If the sample taken is large, the sampling distribution will follow a normal distribution and hence we can say 68.26% of the statistic will be within ± 1.SE of the statistic from the parameter 95.44% of the statistic will be within ± 1.96 SE of the static from the parameter. 99.74% of the statistic will lie within ± 2.58 SE of the statistic from the parameter.

i.e., If there are 100 sample, and hence 100 sample means, then, (1) 68% sample means will not miss the population mean by ± 1 $\sigma_{\bar{x}}$ of mean. (2) 95 of 100 sample means will not miss the population mean by ± 1.96 × SE of the mean. (3) 99 of 100 sample means will not miss the population mean by ± 2.58 SE of the mean.

Stated in terms of probability, these will become (1) the probability is 0.68 that our sample mean does not miss the population mean by ± 1 S.E. of the mean. (2) the probability is 0.95 that the sample mean does not miss by ± 1.96 × SE of the mean. (3) the probability is 0.99 that our sample mean does not miss the population mean by ± 2.58 × S.E. of the mean or (1) the probability is 0.05 level, that our single mean misses the population mean by ± 1.96 × S.E. of mean. (2) the probability is 0.01 that our sample mean misses the population mean by ± 2.58 S.E. of mean.

Two confidence intervals are in general use and are accepted by most statisticians. They are the 0.95 confidence interval and 0.99 confidence interval.

We know that 95% of the cases in a normal distribution form within the limit, ± 1.96 $\sigma_{\bar{x}}$ and hence 0.95 confidence interval of the population mean is ($\bar{X}$ ± 1.96 $\sigma_{\bar{x}}$) when $\bar{X}$ is the sample mean.

Similarly, since 99% of the cases form within the limit ± 2.58 $\sigma\bar{x}$ the 0.99 confidence interval of population mean is ($\bar{X}$ ± 2.58 $\sigma_{\bar{x}}$).

The limits of the confidence interval of a parameter have been called as fiduciary limits and the confidence placed in the interval defined by the limits, or containing the parameter is called the fiduciary parameter and thus,

1) The probability is 0.95 that the population mean lies within the interval ($\bar{X}$ ± 1.96 $\sigma_{\bar{x}}$) or the probability is 0.05 that the population mean falls outside the interval ($\bar{X}$ ± 1.96 $\sigma_{\bar{x}}$).

2) The probability is 0.99 that the mean population lies within the interval ($\bar{X}$ ± 2.58 $\sigma_{\bar{x}}$) or the probability is 0.01 that the population mean fall outside the interval ($\bar{X}$ ± 2.58 $\sigma_{\bar{x}}$).

1) Given M = 26.40 σ = 5.20 N = 100

a) Compute the 0.95 confidence interval and 0.99 confidence interval of the mean.

$$\sigma_{\bar{x}} = \frac{\sigma}{\sqrt{N}} = \frac{5.2}{\sqrt{100}} = \frac{5.2}{10} = \mathbf{0.52}$$

0.95 confidence interval is, $\bar{X} \pm 1.96\,\sigma_{\bar{x}}$ i.e.,

(26.4 + 1.96 × 0.52) = 27.4192
(26.4 − 1.96 × 0.52) = 25.3808

Therefore, the 0.95 confidence interval of the mean is, 25.3808 to 27.4192

0.99 Confidence Interval $\bar{X} \pm 2.58\,\sigma_{\bar{x}}$

26.4 − 2.58 x 0.52 = 25.0584
26.4 + 2.56 x 0.52 = 27.7416

Therefore, 0.99 confidence interval is, (25.0584, 27.7416)

For a given group of 500 soldiers, the mean score is 95 and standard deviation is 25. Determine the 0.99 interval for the true mean.

0.99 confidence interval is, $\sigma_{\bar{x}} = \frac{25}{\sqrt{500}} = \mathbf{1.198}$

($\bar{X} \pm 2.58\,\sigma\bar{x}$) i.e.,
(95 − 2.58 × 1.118, 95 + 2.58 × 1.118)
i.e., (92.1156, 97.884)

Standard Error of the Mean for Small Samples

When sample is small, the sampling distribution of mean does not follow normal distribution and will follow a student's t-distribution. Standard Error of the mean is given by the formula.

$$s\bar{x} = \frac{s}{\sqrt{N}} \text{ where, } s = \sqrt{\frac{\sum x^2}{N-1}}$$

Here the degrees of freedom is N −1

Problem: 10 measures of certain observations are taken from a practised observer. The mean is 175.50 milliseconds and standard deviation is 5.82 milliseconds. Determine the 0.95 confidence interval and 0.99 confidence interval of the population mean.

N = 10 s = 5.82 $\bar{X}$ = 175.50

$$\sigma_{\bar{x}} = \frac{S}{\sqrt{N}} = \frac{5.82}{\sqrt{10}} = \underline{1.84}$$

Here degrees of freedom is 10 − 1 = **9**

From Table of t-distribution, for 9 degrees of freedom and for the probably level.

0.05, the vales is 2.262. For the probably level 0.01, value = 3.250. The 0.95 confidence interval of the population mean is

$(\overline{X} \pm 2.26\, \sigma_{\bar{x}})$

$(175.5 - 2.26 \times 1.84, \quad 175.5 + 2.26 \times 1.84)$

i.e., (171.342, 179.658)

0.99 confidence interval is,

$(\overline{X} \pm 3.25\, \sigma_{\bar{x}})$

i.e., $(1755 - 3.25 \times 1.84, \quad 175.5 + 3.25 \times 1.84)$

i.e., (169. 52, 181.48)

1) The mean of 16 independent observations of a certain sample is 100 and standard deviation is 24.

a) At the 0.05 confidence interval, what are the fiduciary limits of the true mean?
b) Taking the 0.99 confidence interval as our standard we may be assumed that the true mean is at least as large as what value?

a) $N = 16 \qquad \overline{X} = 100 \qquad s = 24$

$$\sigma_{\bar{x}} = \frac{s}{\sqrt{N}} = \frac{24}{\sqrt{10}} = \underline{6}$$

Degrees of Freedom 16 – 1 = **15**

From Table, for 15 degrees of freedom, for the probability 0.05, value is 2.131 and for 0.01 level value is, 2.947.

a) Fiduciary limits at 0.05 level are

$(\overline{X} \pm 2.131\, \sigma_{\bar{x}})$

i.e., $(100 - 2.131 \times 6, \quad 100 + 2.131 \times 6)$

i.e., (87.214, 112.786)

b) The confidence interval at 0.01 level

$(\overline{X} \pm 2.947\, \sigma_{\bar{x}})$. Here we have to calculate the large value of the mean.

i.e., $\overline{X} + 2.947 \times 6$

$= 100 + 2.947 \times 6$

$= \underline{\mathbf{117.682}}$

So the true mean can be as large as 117.682.

Standard Error of Random Sample

	Large sample	Small sample
1) $\sigma_{\bar{x}}$	$\sigma/\sqrt{N}$	$\frac{S}{\sqrt{N}}$ with N-'1df and $S = \sqrt{\frac{\sum x^2}{N-1}}$
2) σ_{Mdn}	(i) $\frac{1.253\sigma}{\sqrt{N}}$ (ii) $\frac{1.858\ Q}{\sqrt{N}}$	
3) σ_{σ}	$\frac{0.71\sigma}{\sqrt{N}}$	
4) σ_{Q}	(i) $\frac{0.786\sigma}{\sqrt{N}}$, (ii) $\frac{1.17Q}{\sqrt{N}}$	
5) $\sigma\%$	$\sqrt{\frac{PQ}{N}}$ where P is the per cent of occurrence of the behaviour and Q is 100–P	
6) σ_{r}	(i) $\frac{1-r^2}{\sqrt{N}}$ * where r is the coefficient of correlation in the population (ii) ** test against the null hypotheses (r = 0) compare the sample 'n' with the tabled value of r for N-2 df and for the required level of probability.	

Note:

1. Standard error of median $\sigma_{Mdn} = 1.25\,\sigma_{\bar{x}}$, this shows that mean is more dependable than the median.
2. When N<25 the sampling distribution of s is skewed. i.e., the distribution is normal only when N>25.
3. $\sigma_{\sigma} = 0.71\,\sigma_{\bar{x}}$
4. Sampling distribution of per cent is normal when N>50 and when p lies between 5 per cent and 95 per cent.
5. There are two serious objection to this formula
   a) The 'r' in this formula is popular r. Since this r is not known, r in the sample is to be substantiated. Therefore, if our sample is in error, sr will also be in error.
   b) The sampling distribution of r is not normal except when r =0 and N is large. When $r \geq 0.80$, (high correlation) and N is small, the sampling distribution of r is skewed. And the standard error from this formula is quite misleading. This is true also when $r \leq 0.20$.
6. The function of z has two advantages over r
   (i) Its sampling distribution is approximately normal

(ii) Its standard error depends upon the size of the sample and is independent of r. This formula is specially useful when r is very high or very low.

7. If the computed r is large enough this procedure is good. This test does not consider the size of r. This test is especially useful when N is small.

Significance of Percentage

Problem:

In a study of copying during examination, among elementary school children, 44 or 41.4% of the 348 children from homes of high economic background were found to have done copying on various tests. Assuring our sample is to be representation of children from high economic background, how much confidence can be placed in this percentage? How well does it represent the population percentage?

P = 41.4%

Q = 100 – P = 100 – 41.4 = 58.61%

$$\sigma\% = \sqrt{PQ/N} = \sqrt{\frac{41.4 \times 58.6}{348}} = 2.6\%$$

Since the sample is large, the 0.99 confidence interval of the population % is Given sample percentage $\pm$ 2.58 σ%

i.e., (41.4 $\pm$ 2.58 × 2.6)

i.e., (41.4 $\pm$ 6.708)

i.e., (34.64, 48.20)

Thus the probability is 0.99 that the population per cent lies within the limits 34.6 and 48.2, i.e., the population percentage can be at least 34.6 and as large as 48.2.

Significance of the Coefficient of Correlation

(1) Given an r of 0.45 based upon 60 cases.

a) Find the sr determine the limits of the 0.99 confidence interval for the population r.

I Method:

$$\sigma r = \frac{1-r^2}{\sqrt{N}} = \frac{1-0.45^2}{\sqrt{60}} = 0.103$$

the limits of 0.99 confidence interval is (r $\pm$ 2.58 × 0.103)

i.e., $(0.45 \pm 2.58 \times 0.103)$
i.e., $(0.185, 0.715)$
From the table of Fischer's z the equivalent of r = 0.45 is 0.48

The standard error of z is, $\frac{1}{\sqrt{N-3}}$

$\sigma_z = 0.1324$
The 0.99 confidence interval of r is $(z \pm 2.58 \times 0.132)$
i.e., $(0.48 \pm 2.58 \times 0.132)$
i.e., $(0.139, 0.820)$
0.99 confidence interval of r is
$(0.1384, 0.675)$

II Method:

(58 degrees of freedom corresponding to 0.01 level of probability)

For N – 2 df, i.e., 60 – 2 = 58df, and for 0.01 level of probability. The value of r from the table is 0.325.

(If the given statistic is less than the tabled value, it is not significant).

The given coefficient of correlation is 0.45 > 0.325 which is the tabled value of r.

i.e., ∴ the given r is significant at 0.01 level of significance.

1) Using a large sample procedure estimate for the following data the 0.95 and 0.99 per cent confidence intervals for mean.

	$\overline{X}$	N	$\sum(X-\overline{X})^2$
a	26.2	7	77
b	58.3	11	249.0
c	46.3	25	1.525
d	8.4	16	444.7

a) For the first case, $\overline{X}$ = 26.2 and N = 7 $\Sigma x^2 = 77$

for large sample
$$\sigma = \sqrt{\frac{\sum x^2}{N}} = \sqrt{\frac{77}{7}} = 3.3166$$

$$\sigma X = \frac{\sigma}{\sqrt{N}} = \frac{3.32}{\sqrt{7}} = 1.255$$

0.95 confidence interval is $(\overline{X} \pm 1.96\,\sigma_{\overline{x}})$
i.e., $(26.2 \pm 1.96 \times 1.255)$
i.e., $(23.74, 28.6598)$

0.99 confidence interval is, $(\overline{X} \pm 2.58\,\sigma_{\overline{x}})$
i.e., $(26.2 \pm 2.58 \times 1.255)$
i.e., $(22.962, 29.438)$

b) $\overline{X} = 58.3$ $N = 11$ $S(X - \overline{X})^2 = 249$

$$\sigma = \sqrt{\frac{\sum x^2}{N}} = \sqrt{\frac{249}{11}} = 4.758$$

$$\sigma_{\bar{x}} = \frac{\sigma}{\sqrt{N}} = \frac{4.758}{\sqrt{11}} = 1.435$$

0.95 confidence interval is, $(\overline{X} \pm 1.96\,\sigma_{\bar{x}})$

i.e., $(58.3 \pm 1.96 \times 1.435)$

i.e., $(55.487, 61.113)$

0.99 confidence interval is, $(\overline{X} \pm 2.58\,\sigma_{\bar{x}})$

i.e., $(58.3 \pm 2.58 \times 1.435)$

i.e., $(54.598, 62.00)$

c) $\overline{X} = 46.3$ $N = 25$ $\Sigma(X - \overline{X})^2 = 1.525$

$$\sigma = \sqrt{\frac{\sum x^2}{N}} = \sqrt{\frac{1.525}{25}} = 0.2469$$

$$\sigma \overline{x} = \frac{\sigma}{\sqrt{N}} = \frac{0.2469}{\sqrt{25}} = 0.0494$$

0.95 confidence interval is, $(\overline{X} \pm 1.96\,\sigma_{\bar{x}})$

i.e., $(46.3 \pm 1.96 \times 0.0494)$

i.e., $(46.203, 46.3968)$

0.99 confidence interval is, $(\overline{X} \pm 2.58\,\sigma_{\bar{x}})$

i.e., $(46.173, 46.427)$

d) $\overline{X} = 8.4$ $N = 16$ $\Sigma x^2 = 444.7$

$$\sigma = \sqrt{\frac{\sum x^2}{N}} = \sqrt{\frac{444.7}{16}} = 5.272$$

$$\sigma_{\bar{x}} = \frac{\sigma}{\sqrt{N}} = \frac{5.272}{\sqrt{16}} = 1.318$$

0.95 confidence interval is, $(\overline{X} \pm 1.96 \times \sigma_{\bar{x}})$

i.e., $(8.4 \pm 1.96 \times 1.318)$

i.e., $(5.817, 10.983)$

0.99 confidence interval is, $(\overline{x} \pm 2.58\,\sigma \overline{x})$

i.e., $(8.4 \pm 2.58 \times 1.318)$

i.e., $(4.999, 11.800)$

2) Using a large sample procedure obtain the 95 and 99% confidence interval for a mean of 105 were N=100 and S = 10. Obtain also the 75 and 85% confidence intervals.

$$S = 10 \quad N = 100 \therefore \sigma\bar{x} = \frac{S}{\sqrt{N}} = \frac{10}{10} = 1$$

0.95 confidence interval is, $(\bar{x} \pm 1.96\ \sigma\bar{x})$
i.e., $(105 \pm 1.96 \times 1)$
i.e., (103.04, 106.96)

0.99 confidence interval is, $(\bar{x} \pm 2.58\ \sigma\bar{x})$
i.e, $(105 \pm 2.58 \times 1)$
i.e., (102.42, 107.58)

To find 75% of the confidence interval of the mean, by theory, the cut off points of the 75% confidence interval can be found from the table of areas and ordinates under a normal curve in such a way that 37.5% of the area lies on either side of the ordinate at the mean of the sampling distribution of the mean. From the table, we can see that the limit points covering 37.5% of the career on either sides of the mean are $-1.15\,\sigma_{\bar{x}}$ and $+1.15\,\sigma_{\bar{x}}$. Hence, the 75% confidence interval of the mean is $(\bar{X} \pm 1.15\,\sigma_{\bar{x}})$.

i.e., $(105 \pm 1.15\,\sigma_{\bar{x}})$ i.e., (103.85, 106.15)

To find 85% confidence interval of the mean from the table of areas and ordinates under a normal curve, the limit points which include 85% of the area are: (i.e., 42.5% of the area on either sides of the mean) are $-1.44\,\sigma_{\bar{x}}$ and $+1.44\,\sigma_{\bar{x}}$. So the 85% confidence interval of the mean is, $(\bar{X} \pm 1.44\,\sigma_{\bar{x}})$ i.e., $(105 \pm 1.44\,\sigma_{\bar{x}})$ i.e., (103.56, 106.44).

1) A random sample of 400 observations has a mean of 50 and a standard deviation of 18. Estimate the 70%, 85%, 90%, 95% and 99% confidence interval of the mean.

$\bar{X} = 50 \quad \sigma = 18 \quad N = 400$

a) 0.70 confidence interval of the mean is, $(\bar{X} \pm 1.04\,\sigma_{\bar{x}})$ since 35% of area corresponds to the limit 1.04 from the table.
∴, the confidence interval is, $(50 \pm 1.04 \times 0.9)$

$$\sigma_{\bar{x}} = \frac{\sigma}{\sqrt{N}} = \frac{18}{\sqrt{400}} = 0.9 \quad \text{i.e., } (49.064, \quad 50.936)$$

b) 0.85 confidence interval i.e., $(\bar{X} \pm 1.44\ \sigma_{\bar{x}})$ 0.425
i.e., $(50 \pm 1.44 \times 0.9)$
i.e., (48.704, 51.296)

c) 0.90 confidence interval is , $(\bar{X} \pm 1.65\,\sigma_{\bar{x}})$
i.e., $(50 \pm 1.65 \times 0.9)$
i.e., (48.52, 51.485)

d) 0.95 confidence interval is, $(\overline{X} \pm 1.96\,\sigma_{\bar{x}})$
i.e., $(50 \pm 1.96 \times 0.9)$
i.e., (48.24, 51.76)

e) 0.99 confidence interval in $(\overline{X} \pm 2.58\,\sigma_{\bar{x}})$
i.e., $(50 \pm 2.58 \times 0.9)$
i.e., (47.68, 52.32)

EXERCISES

1. For each of the following situations calculate 95 per cent confidence interval of the mean (σ not known),
   a) N =15, Mean = 6.00, σx = 1.50
   b) N = 24, Mean = 23.40, σx = 1.73
   c) N = 13, Mean = 6.00, σx = 0.73
2. Calculate the .99 confidence interval for mean for the above cases.

8

Tests of Significance of Difference Between Statistics

A hypothesis is a tentative assumption put forward by the investigator which is to be tested and verified for its validity. Hypothesis can be stated either in declarative form or in null form.

For example, suppose there are two groups, A and B. When we are comparing their achievement levels, if we say that 'Groups A and B differ in their achievement', it is a hypothesis in the declarative form and when we say, "There is no difference between A and B with respect to achievement", then it is a hypothesis in the null form.

Sample means vary from sample to sample even though they are taken randomly from a population. i.e., there is an observed difference between means. Whether this difference is a real one i.e., a considerable one or due to sampling error only? This can be considered by the test of significance of difference between statistics.

8.1 LEVELS OF SIGNIFICANCE

The purpose of inferential statistics is to assist in making judgements about what exists on the basis of partial evidence. This is accomplished by using probability. The level of significance is the probability value that form the boundary between rejecting or not rejecting the null hypothesis.

We have seen that for large samples the sampling distribution or statistic is normal and hence 95% of the cases lie within $\pm 1.96\,\sigma_{\bar{x}}$ so also 99% of cases within $\pm 2.58\,\sigma_{\bar{x}}$; i.e., 5% of the cases lie outside the region of $\pm 1.96\,\sigma_{\bar{x}}$; 1% of cases lie $\pm 2.58\,\sigma_{\bar{x}}$

outside. These two regions are called regions of rejection and they are counted in terms of the probability, below 1.96 and 2.58 respectively. Then we may say for the 0.05 level of significance, the boundary between region of acceptance and region of rejection is 1.96 for a large sample. So, also for the 0.01 level of significance the boundary between the region of acceptance and rejection is 2.58 for a large sample.

The null hypothesis (H_0) can be stated in three ways (1) $\mu_1 = \mu_2$, i.e., $\mu_1 - \mu_2 = 0$. In this case the alternative hypothesis (H_1) will be $\mu_1 \neq \mu_2$.

1) If H_0 is $\mu_1 \geq \mu_2$ then H_1, is $\mu_1 < \mu_2$ i.e., $\mu_1 - \mu_2 < 0$
2) If H_0 is $\mu -1 \leq \mu_2$ i.e., H_1 is $\mu_1 > \mu_2$ or $\mu_1 - \mu_2 > 0$ where μ_1 and μ_2 are the parameters of two populations.

When H_0 is $\mu_1 = \mu_2$, critical region lies evenly on both sides of the normal distribution and hence test of significance in this case is called a two-tailed or two-sided test.

In the case of stating hypothesis in the form $H_0 - \mu_1 \geq \mu_2$ or $\mu_1 \leq \mu_2$. i.e., when we are indicating the direction of the difference, the critical regions falls only on the left side or right side of the distribution and hence test of significance in this case is called a one-tailed test or one-sided test.

One-tailed (directional)	Two-tailed (non-directional)
1) used for comparison of two groups	1) used for comparison of two groups
2) when H_0 is $\mu_1 \geq \mu_2$ i.e., when H_1 is $-\mu_1 < \mu_2$ or $\mu_1 > \mu_2$.	2) when H_0 is $\mu_1 = \mu_2$ i.e., when $H_1 \mu_1 \neq \mu_2$.
3) For large samples, the critical value for 0.05 level of significance is 1.65 and for 0.01 level of significance it is 2.33	3) For large samples, the critical value for 0.05 level of significance is 1.96 and for 0.01 level of significance is 2.58.
4) For small samples, refer the table of t-distribution with the degrees of freedom available for each case.	4) For small samples, refer the table of t-distribution for critical values under 0.05 and 0.01 level of significant against the df available in each case.

8.2 ERRORS IN HYPOTHESIS TESTING

In hypothesis testing it is possible to commit errors in concluding whether a hypothesized effect exists in the population. Two types of errors are possible, namely: (1) Type I error; and (2) Type II error.

Type I Error:

Hypothesis testing starts with the assumption that the null hypothesis is true, which implies that the hypothesized effect or relation does not exist in the population.

The top row in the table below indicates the situation where the null hypothesis is in fact true. Even though the null hypothesis is true, the decision may be made to reject the null hypothesis. Type I error is that error which occurs when the null hypothesis is true but the decision is made to reject the null hypothesis. Type I error may also be expressed as "concluding an effect exists when it actually does not". Type I error is rejecting Ho when Ho is true.

Probability of making a type I error is equal to α (alpha), and the probability of not making the error is 1-α.

	H_0 is true	H_1 is true
Accept H_1	α (Type I error)	Correct decision
Accept H_0	Correct decision	β (Type II error)

Type II Error:

A second type of error can be made in hypothesis testing that, not rejecting the null hypothesis when the hypothesized effect does not exist in the population. Here the alternate hypothesis will be true, meaning that the hypothesized effect does in fact exist in the population. Type II error is an error that occurs when the decision is made to not reject the null hypothesis even though the alternate hypothesis is true.

Probability of making a Type II error is equal to β (beta), and the probability of not making the error is 1-β.

Mathematically, if the probability of making a Type I error is typically 0.05 ($\alpha = 0.05$), it might seem reasonable to assume that the probability of a Type II error (β) is equal to 0.95. At the same time, β is not equal to 1-α, because Type I and Type II errors occurs under different situations.

Testing One Sample Mean

Consider a study hypothesizes a difference between a sample mean and a population mean. This difference is tested by calculating and testing an inferential statistic by stating hypotheses (H_0 and H_1) and making a decision about the hypothesis.

In testing one sample mean, the null hypothesis (H_0) states a value of the population mean μ. Depending upon the situation, whether population standard deviation is known or not, the steps for analysis may vary as follows:

When population standard deviation is known, the steps involved in decision making are:

- Set alpha (α), identify the critical values and state a decision rule
- Calculate the z value for one mean

- Make a decision whether to reject the null hypothesis and
- Determine the level of significance

The steps involved in making this decision when the population standard deviation is not known are as follows:

- calculate the degrees of freedom (*df*);
- set alpha, identify the critical values, and state a decision rule;
- calculate a statistic: t-test for one mean;
- make a decision whether to reject the null hypothesis; and
- determine the level of significance.

Calculation of the Degrees of Freedom (*df*)

The degrees of freedom (*df*) is defined as the number of values or quantities that are free to vary when a statistic is used to estimate a parameter. This step is included in this case because the standard deviation (s) is being used to estimate the population standard deviation (s). The concept of degrees of freedom will appear many places in this book, in different research situations and statistical procedures.

Let's illustrate the concept of degrees of freedom with a simple demonstration. Imagine a friend makes the following request of you: "Tell me any three numbers," to which you respond, "4, 20, and——." But your friend interrupts you before you can complete your response. "Stop!" he shouts. "I forgot to tell you this: the three numbers must add up to 80." Once this has been said, you determine that the third number can only be 56. In this example, the first two numbers you chose were free to vary and could have had any value. However, the constraint, in this case the sum of 80, meant the value of the third number was no longer free to vary but was instead fixed at 56. In this example, you had two "degrees of freedom."

The concept of degrees of freedom is relevant to inferential statistics because these statistics involve estimating population parameters from data collected from samples. In an example, from a sample of 13 participants, the standard deviation of 8.0 is an estimate of an unknown population standard deviation. As a reminder, below is the formula for the standard deviation(s).

$$s = \sqrt{\frac{\sum(X-\bar{X})^2}{N-1}}$$

We can see that the numerator of this formula involves summing deviations of scores from the mean ($X - \bar{X}$). We saw that, for any set of data, the sum of deviations $\left[\sum(X-\bar{X})\right]$ is equal to 0. In a sample of 13 participants, the first 12 deviations can be any value. However, once they are determined, the deviations of the last participant must enable the sum of the deviations to be equal to zero. Consequently, although the first 12 scores are free to vary, the 13th is not; it is predetermined by the first 12 scores.

Formula presented below calculates the degrees of freedom (*df*) for one sample:

$$df = N - 1,$$

where N is the size of the sample. In the above example

$$\begin{aligned} df &= N - 1 \\ &= 13 - 1 \\ &= 12 \end{aligned}$$

Therefore, when the sample size N is equal to 13, there are 12 degrees of freedom. Different formulas for the degrees of freedom will be used in different context.

Set Alpha (α), Identify the Critical Values, and State a Decision Rule

Traditionally, alpha (α) will be set to 0.05, meaning that the null hypothesis will be rejected if the value of the calculated statistic has less than a 0.05 probability of occurring under the assumption that the null hypothesis is true. Furthermore, because the alternative hypothesis is non-directional , alpha can be referred to as "$\alpha = 0.05$ (two-tailed)".

The next step is to identify the values of the t-statistic whose probability is low enough to lead to the decision to reject the null hypothesis. But because there are an infinite number of possible values of t and an infinite number of possible sample sizes, it would be impractical to have a table that lists the probability for every value of t for every sample size. Instead, because we are only interested in values of t that affect the decision about the null hypothesis, the only values of concern are the critical values, defined as the values of a statistic that separate the regions of rejection and non rejection.

To determine the critical values of the t-statistic, three pieces of information are needed: the degrees of freedom (*df*), alpha (α), and the directionality of the alternative hypothesis {directional (one-tailed) or non-directional (two-tailed)}. The first column of Table A, labeled *df*, lists different degrees of freedom. Because there is a different t-distribution for each sample size, each degree of freedom has its own critical values. The bottom row of this table includes the infinity (∞) symbol; this does not imply that a sample may actually contain an infinite number of degrees of freedom; rather, it provides the critical values for a population assumed to be normally distributed.

The eight columns to the right of the *df* column list different values of alpha (.10, .05, .05, .01, .001) corresponding to different levels of significance. The first four of these columns are used when the alternative hypothesis (H_1) is directional (one-tailed); the last four columns are used for a non-directional (two-tailed) alternative hypothesis.

The critical values may be identified by moving down the *df* column until we reach the appropriate row for the particular case. Next, because the alternative hypothesis is non-directional, we move to the right until we are under the heading "Level of Significance for Two-Tailed Test". Within this set of columns, assuming $\alpha = .05$, we find a critical t-value. For example, for a df = 12, $\alpha = .05$ (two-tailed) critical values = $\pm$ 2.179

The next step in hypothesis testing is to state a decision rule that uses the critical values to specify the conditions under which the null hypothesis will be rejected.

If $t < -2.179$ or > 2.179, reject H_0: otherwise, do not reject H_0

Table A: Table of Critical Values of the t-Statistic

	Level of Significance for One-Tailed Test				Level of Significance for Two-Tailed Test			
df	*.10*	*.05*	*.01*	*.001*	*.10*	*.05*	*.01*	*.001*
1	3.078	6.314	31.821	318.310	6.314	12.706	63.657	636.619
2	1.886	2.920	6.965	22.326	2.920	4.303	9.925	31.598
3	1.638	2.353	4.541	10.213	2.353	3.182	5.841	12.941
4	1.533	2.132	3.747	7.173	2.132	2.776	4.604	8.610
5	1.476	2.015	3.365	5.893	2.015	2.571	4.032	6.859
11	1.363	1.796	2.718	4.025	1.796	2.201	3.106	4.437
12	1.356	1.782	2.681	3.930	1.782	2.179	3.055	4.318
13	1.350	1.771	2.650	3.852	1.771	2.160	3.012	4.221
14	1.345	1.761	2.624	3.787	1.761	2.145	2.977	4.10
15	1.341	1.753	2.602	3.733	1.753	2.131	2.947	4.073
16	1.337	1.746	2.583	3.686	1.746	2.120	2.921	4.015
17	1.333	1.740	2.567	3.646	1.740	2.110	2.898	3.965
18	1.330	1.734	2.552	3.610	1.734	2.101	2.878	3.922
19	1.328	1.729	2.639	3.579	1.729	2.093	2.861	3.883
20	1.325	1.725	2.528	3.552	1.725	2.086	2.845	3.850
90	1.291	1.662	2.368	3.183	1.662	1.987	2.632	3.403
120	1.289	1.658	2.358	3.232	1.658	1.980	2.617	3.373
∞	1.282	1.645	2.326	3.183	1.645	1.960	2.576	3.291

This decision rule implies that if the value of t-calculated for the sample exceeds either of the critical values, it falls in the region of rejection and the null hypothesis will be rejected.

The following section details the Tests of significance for difference between different statistics.

(A) Test of Significance of difference between means for large independent samples:

In this case, the critical region CR for difference between statistics is found by the formula, $CR = \frac{D}{SE_D}$ where D = difference between statistics. In the case of difference between means, the CR is calculated by the formula,

$$CR = \frac{\overline{X}_1 - \overline{X}_2}{\sqrt{\frac{\sigma_1^2}{N_1} + \frac{\sigma_2^2}{N_2}}}$$

If the CR is greater than or equal to ± 1.96, the difference between means is said to be significant at the 5% level of significance, i.e., at 0.05 level of significance. If C.R. is greater than or equal to 2.58, the difference is said to be significant at 0.01 level. For a one-tailed test, if the CR ≥ 1.65, the difference between means is said to be significant at 5% level and if CR ≥ 2.33 the difference between means is said to be significant at 0.01 level.

Questions

1) In a study of abstract reasoning, a sample of 83 IXth standard boys and a sample of 95, IXth standard girls scored as shown below on a test of abstract reasoning.

Sex	N	Mean	S.D
Girls	95	29.21	11.56
Boys	83	30.92	7.8

Test the significance of difference between means

Let the hypothesis be, 'There is no significant difference between Boys and Girls in abstract reasoning."

.he critical ratio is $$CR = \frac{\overline{X}_1 - \overline{X}_2}{\sqrt{\frac{\sigma_1^2}{N_1} + \frac{\sigma_2^2}{N_2}}}$$

$$CR = \frac{3.92 - 29.21}{\sqrt{\frac{(7.8)^2}{83} + \frac{(11.56)^2}{95}}}$$

$$= \frac{1.71}{1.463} = 1.169$$

The CR is not significant at 0.05 level and 0.01 level since the critical ratio is less than 1.96. The difference between means is not significant. Also CR < 1.65, the difference between means is not significant at 5% level if we were making use of a one-tailed test. Thus the test is not significant for one-tailed or two-tailed.

2) On an arithmetic reasoning test, thirty one 10 year old boys and forty two 10 year old girls made the following scores. Is the mean difference of 4.58, in favour of the boys significant at the 0.05 level?

Sex	M	σ	N
Boys	40.39	8.69	31
Girls	35.81	8.33	42

$$CR = \frac{\overline{X}_1 - \overline{X}_2}{\sqrt{\frac{\sigma_1^2}{N_1} + \frac{\sigma_2^2}{N_2}}}$$

$$CR = \frac{40.39 - 35.81}{\sqrt{\frac{(8.69)^2}{31} + \frac{(8.33)^2}{42}}}$$

Let the null hypothesis (H_0) be, "there is no significant difference between the observed means of the two samples." The CR for large independent samples is

$$CR = \frac{4.58}{2.022} = 2.265$$

Since CR is greater than 1.96, the difference between means is in favour of boys and is significant at 0.05 level.

One–Tailed Test: In this case CR is greater than 1.65. So it is also significant at 0.05 level.

(B) Test of significance of difference between means for small independent samples

For small independent samples, the critical ratio can be calculated by

1) $$CR = \frac{M_1 - M_2}{\sqrt{\frac{(N_1 - 1)s_1^2 + (N_2 - 1)s_2^2}{N_1 + N_2 - 2}\left(\frac{N_1 + N_2}{N_1 N_2}\right)}}$$

Here the df is, $N_1 + N_2 - 2$

Example

1) On an arithmetic reasoning test thirty one 10 year old boys and forty two 10 year old girls made the scores below:

Gender	M	σ	N
Girls	40.39	8.69	31
Boys	35.81	8.33	42

Using a small sample test, test whether the difference between means is significant or not.

Let H_0 be "There is no significant difference between Boys and Girls on arithmetic reasoning".

$$CR = \frac{M_1 - M_2}{\sqrt{\frac{(N_1-1)^2 s_1^2 (N_2-1)s_2^2}{N_1+N_2-1}\left(\frac{N_1+N_2}{N_1N_2}\right)}}$$

df = 31 + 42 − 2 = 71

$$CR = \frac{40.39-35.81}{\sqrt{\frac{(31-1)8.69^2+(42-1)8.33^2}{71}\left(\frac{31+42}{31\times 42}\right)}}$$

$$= \frac{4.58}{\sqrt{\frac{5110.43}{71}\times 0.0561}} = \frac{4.58}{2.0088} = 2.279$$

The CR is significant at 0.05 level since it is greater than 2.00 (from table of t-distributions) for 71 degree of freedom. It is significant at 0.01 level of significance (2.65). Comparing CR, with the tabled value, the difference between means is not significant at 0.01 level of significance. So H_0 is accepted.

(C) Test of significance of difference between means for large dependent samples

Here , the formula for t-test is,
$$t = \frac{M_1 - M_2}{\sqrt{\frac{\sigma_1^2}{N_1}+\frac{\sigma_2^2}{N_2}-2r\frac{\sigma_1\sigma_2}{N_1N_2}}}$$

Example

1) Two groups of high school students are matched for Mean and σ upon a group intelligence test. There are 58 subjects in Group I and 71 in Group II. The records of these two groups upon a battery of learning tests are as follows.

	Group I	Group II
M	48.62	53.61
σ	10.60	15.35
N	58	72

The correlation of the group intelligence test and the learning battery is the entire group from which A and B were drawn is 0.50. Is the difference between groups A and B significant at 0.05 level? At the 0.01 level?

Let H_0 be "there is no significant difference between Group I and Group II in their performance"

Since matched groups are dependent, the critical ratio is given by,

$$t = \frac{M_1 - M_2}{\sqrt{\frac{\sigma_1^2}{N_1} + \frac{\sigma_2^2}{N_2} - 2r\frac{\sigma_1\sigma_2}{N_1 N_2}}}$$

Substituting the values,

$$t = \frac{48.52 - 53.61}{\sqrt{\frac{(10.60)^2}{58} + \frac{(15.35)^2}{72} - \frac{2 \times 0.5 \times 10.6 \times 15.35}{58 \times 72}}}$$

$$= \frac{-5.09}{\sqrt{\frac{(10.60)^2}{58} + \frac{(15.35)^2}{72} - 0.03896}}$$

$$= \frac{-5.09}{\sqrt{5.1708}} = -2.238$$

The t-value is −2.238

Since the CR is greater than 1.96, the difference between means is significant at 0.05 level. But the critical ratio (difference between means) is not significant at 0.01 level of significance since it is less than 2.58. Here Ho is rejected.

2) At the beginning of school year the mean score of a group of 64 children upon an educational achievement test, in reading was 45 with a σ of 6. At the end of the school year the mean score on an equivalent form of the same test was 50 with a σ of 5. The correlation between scores made on the initial and final testing was 0.60. Have the children made significant progress in reading during the year?

Given that, $N_1 = N_2 = 64$

$M_1 = 45 \quad \sigma_1 = 6 \quad r = 0.60$

$M_2 = 50 \quad \sigma_2 = 5$

Let the hypothesis be "Mean scores at the end of the class is significantly higher than the mean scores at the beginning of the class" (Therefore we have to make use of a one-tailed test).

Critical Ratio is given by

$$t = \frac{M_1 - M_2}{\sqrt{\frac{\sigma_1^2}{N_1} + \frac{\sigma_2^2}{N_2} - 2r\frac{\sigma_1\sigma_2}{N_1N_2}}}$$

Substitute the values

$$t = \frac{45 - 50}{\sqrt{\frac{6^2}{64} + \frac{5^2}{64} - 2\times\frac{0.6\times6\times5}{64\times64}}}$$

$$= \frac{-5}{\sqrt{0.5625 + 0.3906 - 0.008789}}$$

$$= \frac{-5}{\sqrt{0.9443}}$$

$$= -5.1453$$

The difference between means is significant beyond 0.01 level of significance because the critical ratio is greater than 2.53 or 1.65.

Therefore, the progress in mean scores is significant at 0.05 level and at 0.01 level.

D) Test of significance of difference between means for small dependent samples (Garrett, 1979)

Example

12 students are given 5 successive trials upon a non verbal intelligence test of which only the scores for trials 1 and 5 are shown. Is the mean gain from initial to final trial significant?

Trial 1	Trial 5	D
50	62	12
42	40	–2
51	61	10
26	35	9
35	30	–5
42	52	10
60	68	8
41	51	10
70	84	14
55	63	8
62	72	10
38	50	12

Let the hypothesis be, "there is no difference between the mean scores of trial 1 (initial trial) and trial 5 (final trial)

$$\bar{D} = \frac{96}{12} = 8$$

The standard error of a mean = $\frac{\sigma}{\sqrt{N}}$ where σ stands for the standard deviation of the given set of scores. Therefore, $SE_{\bar{D}} = \frac{\text{S.D. of D's}}{\sqrt{N}}$

When X is the given variable, $\sigma x = \sqrt{\frac{\sum(X-\bar{X})^2}{N}}$

when the sample is small. In this techniques X = D, and $\bar{X} = \bar{D}$

$$\therefore \text{S.D. of D's} = \sqrt{\frac{\sum(D-\bar{D})^2}{N}}$$

$D-\bar{D}$	$(D-\bar{D})^2$
4	16
–10	100
2	4
1	1
–13	169
2	4
0	0
2	4
6	36
0	0
2	4
4	16
	Σ = 354

$$\text{S.D. of D's} = \sqrt{\frac{354}{12}} = \underline{5.43}$$

$$\text{S.E. of } \bar{D} = \frac{\text{S.D. of D's}}{\sqrt{N}}$$

$$= \frac{5.43}{\sqrt{12}}$$

$$= \underline{1.567}$$

The critical ratio, $t = \frac{\bar{D}}{S.E_{\bar{D}}}$

$$= \frac{8}{1.56}$$

$$= 5.12$$

Since the sample is small and N = 12 the CR follows students t-distribution with 11 (i.e., 12–1) degrees of freedom. Therefore, to find the t values for 11 df, we have to refer the table of t-distribution. From the table of t, for 11 degrees of freedom and for 0.05 level of significance, the value of t is 2.20.

The obtained CR is greater than the tabled value of t at 0.05 level of significance and hence, we may say the difference between means of trial 1 and trial 5 is significant at 0.05 level of significance.

The tabled value of t for 11df and for 0.01 level of significance is, 3.11. Here also the obtained CR is greater than the tabled value of t, and hence we may say the difference between mean scores of initial trial and final trial is significant at 0.01 level of significance.

3) Two groups X and Y of VIIIth standard students, with 72 in each group are paired for age and score in Creativity test. Three weeks later, both groups are given parallel form of the same test. Before the second test, group X i.e., experimental group is praised for its performance on the first test and urged to try to better its score group Y, the controlled group is given the second test without comment. Will the incentive (praise) cause the final scores of group X and group Y to differ significantly. The relevant data are given below.

	Group X	**Group Y**
Number of students	72	72
Mean scores on form A	80.42	80.51
Standard deviation on form A	23.61	23.46
Mean scores on form B	88.63	83.24
Standard deviation on form B	24.36	21.62
correlation between final scores	0.65	

Let the hypothesis be, "there is no significant difference in the mean scores on second form of the creativity test." Since the second form of the creativity test is given, after the incentive between the experimental group (group x) and the control group (Y).

Since the samples are matched pairs,

$$CR = \frac{M_1 - M_2}{\sqrt{\frac{\sigma_1^2}{N_1} + \frac{\sigma_2^2}{N_2} - 2r\frac{\sigma_1\sigma_2}{N_1N_2}}}$$

Here $M_1 = 88.63$
$M_2 = 83.24$
$\sigma_1 = 24.36$
$\sigma_2 = 21.62$
$r = 0.65$

Submitting these values, the CR is,

$$t = \frac{88.63 - 83.24}{\sqrt{\frac{(24.36)^2}{72} + \frac{(21.62)^2}{72} - \frac{2 \times 0.65 \times 24.36 \times 21.62}{72 \times 72}}}$$

$$= \frac{5.39}{\sqrt{8.2418 + 6.492 - 0.1321}}$$

$$= \frac{5.39}{\sqrt{14.734 - 0.1321}}$$

$$= \frac{5.39}{\sqrt{14.602}}$$

$$= 1.411$$

The CR, 1.411 is less than 1.96 or 2.58. The incentive will not cause any significant change on the final scores. Between group X and group Y, since t value is not significant at 0.05 level. It is not significant at form B of intelligence scores on X and Y at 0.01 level. Thus, we can infer that the incentive given to the that experimental group does not cause a significant change in mean scores of group X than of Group Y.

Test of Significance of Difference between Percentages

When P_1 and P_2 are the percentages of occurrence of certain behaviour, than critical ratio for the test of significance of difference between two percentages is calculated by the formula,

$$CR = \frac{P_1 - P_2}{\sqrt{PQ\left(\frac{1}{N_1} + \frac{1}{N_2}\right)}}$$

Where, P – the combined percentage for the population is calculated as

$$P = \frac{N_1P_1 + N_2P_2}{N_1 + N_2} \text{ and}$$

Q = 100 – P (q = 1–p, when p is in proportion)

Example

In a study of examination anxiety among elementary school children 144 or 41.4% of 348 children from homes of poor S.E.S. were found to show anxiety on various examinations. In the same study, 133 or 50.2% of 265 children from homes of good S.E.S also expressed anxiety on the same test. Is there a true difference in anxiety between these two groups?

Here, $P_1 = 41.4\%$
$P_2 = 50.2\%$

$$P = \frac{N_1P_1 + N_2P_2}{N_1 + N_2}$$

$$= \frac{348 \times 41.4 + 265 \times 50.2}{348 + 265}$$

$$= \frac{27710.2}{613}$$

$$P = 45.20\%$$

$\therefore Q = 100 - P = 54.8\%$

$$\text{Critical ratio} = \frac{P_1 - P_2}{\sqrt{PQ\left(\frac{1}{N_1} + \frac{1}{N_2}\right)}}$$

$$= \frac{41.4 - 50.2}{\sqrt{45.2 \times 54.8\left(\frac{1}{348} + \frac{1}{265}\right)}}$$

$$= \frac{-8.8}{\sqrt{2476.96 \times 6.64714 \times 10^{-3}}}$$

$$= \frac{-8.8}{4.058}$$

$$CR = -2.17$$

Here, the critical ratio is –2.17. The value exceeds 1.96. So, the difference between percentage is significant at 5% level. Since CR is less than 2.58; it is not significant at 1% level.

Exercise

1) In a school of 500 pupils, 52.3% are girls and in a second school of 300 pupils 47.7% are girls. Is there a significant difference between the percentage of girls enrolled in two schools.

N1 = 500 N2 = 300

P1 = 52.3% P2 = 47.7%

$$P = \frac{P_1N_1 + P_2N_2}{N_1 + N_2}$$

$$= \frac{52.3 \times 500 + 47.7 \times 300}{500 + 300}$$

$$= 50.58$$

$Q = 100\text{-}50.58 = 49.42$

$$\text{Critical Ratio} = \frac{P_1 - P_2}{\sqrt{PQ\left(\frac{1}{N_1} + \frac{1}{N_2}\right)}}$$

$$= \frac{52.3 - 47.7}{\sqrt{50.58 \text{x} 49.42\left(\frac{1}{500} + \frac{1}{300}\right)}}$$

$$= \frac{4.6}{3.65}$$

$$CR = 1.26$$

The CR = 1.26. The value is less than both 1.96 and 2.58. So, it is not significant at 5% and 1% levels of significance. There is not a significant difference between the percentage of girls enrolled in the two-schools. The two groups are almost equal.

Test of Significance of Difference between Two Correlations

Let the given correlation coefficients be r_1 and r_2. To test the significance of the difference between r_1 and r_2, convert r_1 and r_2 to Fischer's z-functions. Let them be z_1 and z_2 respectively. Then the CR is calculated by

$$CR = \frac{z_1 - z_2}{\sqrt{\frac{1}{N_1 - 3} + \frac{1}{N_2 - 3}}}$$

(1) The correlation between intelligence and achievement in a class of college A is 0.40. for N = 147 and r between intelligence and achievement in the class of the same subject of college B is 0.60 for N = 125. Is the relationship between intelligence and achievement higher in college B than in College A?

$r_1 = 0.4$ $N_1 = 147$ $z_1 = 0.42$

$r_2 = 0.6$ $N_2 = 15$ $z_2 = 0.69$

Ho : "Let there is no significant difference between the two groups."

$$CR = \frac{z_1 - z_2}{\frac{1}{N_1 - 3} + \frac{1}{N_2 - 3}}$$

$$= \frac{0.42 - 0.69}{\sqrt{\frac{1}{144} + \frac{1}{122}}}$$

$$= -2.194$$

Since the value exceeds 1.96, it is significant at 0.05 level. Thus, the correlation differ significantly.

EXERCISES

1. Two researchers separately tested the same research hypothesis on a sample size of N = 12 and standard deviations for the two groups are $s_1 = 0.50$ and $s_2 = 0.75$. The experimental manipulation is more effective for the second researcher. The means of the two groups are $M_1 = 2.50$ and $M_2 = 2.70$, for the first experiment, as well as $M_1 = 2.70$ and $M_2 = 1.95$ for the second experiment.
   Calculate the t-value for the difference between independent means
   (**Ans:** First study, t=1.25; For the second study, t=2.88)
2. The correlation between psychological-test scores and academic achievement for a sample of 150 boys is 0.50. The corresponding correlation for a sample of 125 girls is 0.60. Do these correlations differ significantly?
   (**Ans:** 2.064)

REFERENCES

1. Ferguson, G.A (1971). *Statistical Analysis in Psychology and Education*(3rd Edn.). Tokyo: Mc Graw Hill.
2. Hays, W.L (1988). *Statistics* (4th Ed). New York: Holt, Rinehart & Winston.
3. Garrett, H. E & Woodworth, R. S. (1961). *Statistics in Psychology and Education.* New York: Vakils, Feffer and Simon Ltd.
4. Springer, K (2010). *Educational Research – A contextual approach*. Chennai: John Wiley & Sons, Inc.
5. Tokunaga, H.T (2016). *Fundamental Statistics for the Social and Behavioural Sciences*. New Delhi: Sage.

9

Analysis of Variance (ANOVA)

This is one of the most powerful and most common tests employed in the social sciences and is suitable for interval/ratio level distributions. It is known either as ANOVA or as F-test, these tests are also known as single or one-way (when one criterion is used), as two-way (when two criteria are used), or as N-way (factorial) analysis when more criteria are used. It is called F-test after its creator, Sir R.D. Fischer.

ANOVA is similar to the t-test. The main characteristics and the advantage of the F-test over other tests is that it is employed when more than two variables are studied. It is a parsimonious test i.e., a single test that produces results which would otherwise have required several tests.

9.1 CONDITIONS/BASIC ASSUMPTION OF ANOVA

ANOVA can be employed if certain conditions are met. Three such conditions are:

1. Independence: that scores are independent from each other
2. Normality: that scores are normally distributed
3. Homogeneity: the variances are equal.

There are several types of ANOVA. The most common are one-way and two-way ANOVA. One way is employed when there is one independent variable (factor) and one dependent. We are looking at whether the sample groups vary systematically in one way, or with regard to one aspect only.

		Independent	Dependent
e.g.: 1)	Factor	: Marital status ---- affect----	overall happiness
	Levels	: Single, married, divorced	very happy, happy, unhappy, very unhappy
2)	Factor	: Gender ------affect------	Scholastic Achievement
		Male, female	Very high, High, Moderate, Low, Very Low

i.e., Effect of marital status on overall happiness,

Effect of gender on scholastic achievement.

A two way-ANOVA includes two criteria of classification as well as two independent variables and one dependent variable.

For example: Effect of Gender and Experience on Teaching Competence
Effect of Social Class and Marital Status on Overall Happiness

Certain common terms related to ANOVA are explained below:

The difference between means of two samples can be calculated using the t-test for independent means.

$$t = \frac{\overline{X}_1 - \overline{X}_2}{SE_D}$$

The calculated value of t-statistic is a function of two factors that correspond to the numerator and denominator of the above formula. The numerator, the difference between means of the two groups was referred to as between -group variability. Between group variability was defined as difference among the means of the different groups that comprise an independent variable. The denominator, the standard error of the difference represents within group variability, defined as the variability of the dependent variable within the groups comprising an independent variable.

Increasing between group variability and / or decreasing within group variability results in a larger calculated value of the t-statistic, which in turn increases the likelihood of rejecting the null hypothesis.

Between Group and Within Group Variances

The numerator of the formula for the t-test, the difference between the means of the two groups ($\overline{X}_1 - \overline{X}_2$) represents between -group variability. We can refer the variability which cannot be explained or accounted for, as "error". Taking this into consideration, we may state that between group variability comprises two parts: the hypothesized "effect" and "error".

The denominator of the formula for the t-test, within group variability is represented by the standard error of the difference, SE_D. Within group variability can be defined as an error. In summary, testing the difference between group means involves relating two types of variability to each other: Between group variability and Within group variability. Between group variability (differences between groups) consists of the hypothesized effect and error, whereas within group variability (differences within groups) is error.

i.e., t = Difference between groups / Difference within groups
t = (effect+error) / error

The "Analysis of variance" (ANOVA) involves a family of statistical procedures used to test differences between two or more group means. It is called the Analysis of Variance because it involves analyzing different types of variances, such as between group variances and within group variances.

The one way ANOVA is a statistical procedure used to test differences between the means of three or more groups that comprises a single independent variable. It is a simple extension of the t-test, in that both statistical procedures involves dividing between group variances by within group variances. Therefore, F-ratio is given by,

$$F = \frac{\text{Between group variance}}{\text{Within group variance}}$$

9.2 COMPUTING ANOVA

ANOVA works on the following assumptions:

1) The total variation (TV) can split into two components – each of which has a certain source of variation: small components are the within sample variation (WV) and between sample variation (BV) i.e., TV = WV + BV.
2) The samples are randomly selected.
3) The population is normally distributed.
4) The samples are independent.
5) The samples have a common variance.

F-test is computed by the formula,

$$F = \frac{\frac{BV}{k-1}}{\frac{WV}{N-k}} \qquad \ldots (1)$$

(Total sample N – 1 = N – k + k – 1)
Where k is the number of categories (groups) and N is the total sample

Steps in Computation

1) A table is set up with scores and squared scores for each group

Effect of Seating Position in the Classroom on Achievement

Group A		Group B		Group C		Group D		Group E	
X_1	X_1^2	X_2	X_2^2	X_3	X_3^2	X_4	X_4^2	X_5	X_5^2
7	49	4	16	6	36	7	49	8	64
4	16	9	81	5	25	9	81	6	36
5	25	3	9	4	16	8	64	7	49
4	16	5	25	6	36	7	49	7	49
6	36	5	25	6	36	7	49	9	81
$\Sigma x_1=26$	$\Sigma x_1^2=142$	$\Sigma x_2=26$	$\Sigma x_2^2=156$	$\Sigma x_3=27$	$\Sigma x_3^2=149$	$\Sigma x_4=38$	$\Sigma x_4^2=292$	$\Sigma x_5=39$	$\Sigma x_5^2=311$

2) The sums for all columns (for scores and squared scores) are computed. i.e., the means of scores and squared scores are computed

3) The total variation (TV) is computed by the formula

$$TV = \sum x^2 - \frac{\left(\sum x\right)^2}{N} \quad \ldots (3)$$

Where, $\sum x^2$ – is obtained by adding the squared scores of each group.

$\left(\sum x\right)^2$ – is obtained by squaring the sum of the scores of each group.

in the example, $TV = 1050 - \frac{24336}{25} = 76.56$

4) The values of WV are computed for the five groups by employing the above formula for each group separately and adding up the scores for each group.

$$WV = \sum x^2 - \frac{\left(\sum x\right)^2}{n}$$

Where n – the number of respondents in the group for which WV is computed.

For A: $WV = 142 - \frac{(26)^2}{5} = 6.8$

B: $WV = 156 - \frac{26^2}{5} = 20.8$

Thus, WV = 6.8 + 20.8 + 3.2 + 6.8 = 40.8

5) The between-samples variation (BV) is computed by the formula

$$BV = TV - WV$$

i.e., BV = 76.56 – 40.8= 35.76

6) k-1 which is the df for BV and N-k; the df for WV, are computed k is the no. of groups, N is the total sample.

i.e., $k - 1 = 5 - 1 = 4$

$N - k = 25 - 5 = 20$

$\frac{BV}{k-1}$ = mean square for Between groups

$\frac{WV}{N-k}$ = mean square for Within groups

7) The values obtained above are substituted in formula (1) to obtain F-score.

$$F = \frac{BV/_{k-1}}{WV/_{N-k}} = \frac{35.76/_{4}}{40.8/_{20}} = 4.3824$$

The values obtained from the above computation are usually represented in a summary table, known as ANOVA summary table

The ANOVA Summary Table

Source of Variation	Sum of Squares	df	Mean Square	F
Between groups (BV)	35.76	4	8.94	4.3824
Within groups (WV)	40.80	20	2.04	
Total	**76.56**	**24**		

8) Interpretation of F: Critical value of F is located from Table of F. df of BV is across the table and df for WV is down the left-hand column. If the F value is greater than critical value of F, the null hypothesis is rejected.

In our example, df for BV and WV are 4 and 20 respectively. Critical Value for F at 0.05 level is 2.87. Since our F value is greater than CVF, null hypothesis is rejected.

Exercise

I. An ANOVA summary table is given below: Fill the missing material and continue with the following questions.

Source of Variance	Sum of Squares	df	Mean Square	F
Between groups (BV)	39.636	3	13.212	6.25
Within groups (WV)	33.824	16	2.114	
Total	**73.460**	**19**		

1) How many levels of the independent variable are there?
2) Assuming equal sample sizes, how many subjects were there in each treatment condition?
3) What are the degrees of freedom for the F-ratio?
4) Assuming a = 0.05, what is the CVF required to reject the null hypothesis?

5) Can the null hypothesis be rejected in this case?
6) How should the F-ratio be reported according to APA style?

Ans: 1) Four levels
2) 5
3) 3, 16
4) 3.63
5) Yes, since 6.25>3.63
6) Publication manual of American Psychological Association (1994) recommended for reporting the results of an F-test as,
F (dfB, dfW) = F
$F(3, 16) = 6.25$ $P < 0.05$

II. Fill in the blanks

Source of Variations	Sum of Squares	df	Mean Square	F
Between groups (BV)	12.450	—	6.225	
Within groups (WV)	—	27	—	—
Total	**60.609**	**29**		

9.3 ONE-WAY ANOVA—THEORETICAL EXPLANATION

Consider an experiment involving k experimental treatments. Let the number of members in the k groups be N_1, N_2, ... Nk. Total number of members in all groups combined is, $N_1 + N_2 + \ldots Nk = N$.

Sum of Measurements

Group I : $X_{11}, X_{21}, X_{31} \ldots\ldots X_{N1}$ i.e., $\sum_{i=1}^{N} X_{i1}$

Group II: $X_{12}, X_{22}, X_{32} \ldots\ldots\ldots X_{N2}$ ie., $\sum_{i=1}^{N} X_{i2}$

i.e., $\sum_{i=1}^{N} X_{ik}$

Group Means: $\overline{X}_1, \overline{X}_2, \ldots\ldots\ldots \overline{X}_k$ Grand mean = $\overline{X}$

Total variation in the data is represented by the sum of squares of deviations of all the observations from the grand man.

For the first group observations, sum of squares (SS) is,

$$\sum_{i=1}^{N} \left(X_{i1} - \overline{X}\right)^2$$

Total sum of squares may be divided into two parts:

1) Within groups.
2) Between groups.

Components of Variance: The variance of all scores in the data set regardless of experimental group is called the total variance. We can partition the total variance into two smaller components.

1) *Between group variance:* estimate of variance based upon variability between groups (index of the degree to which the independent is associated with differences among the subjects as well as some chance differences between the groups due to sampling error).
2) *Within group variance:* Estimate of variance based upon the variability within groups.

Mean Squares

Each sum of squares has an associated number of df.

1) Total sum of squares has N-1 df (one df is lost by taking deviation about the grand mean)

2) df associated with the within-groups, sum of squares is, $(N_1-1)+(N_2-1) + \ldots (N_k-1) = N - k$.

3) df associated with the between groups sum of squares is, k – 1, (we have k means)

$$\underset{\text{Total}}{N-1} = \underset{\text{within}}{(N-k)} + \underset{\text{between}}{(k-1)}$$

Sum of squares within group is, $s_w^2 = \dfrac{\sum_{j=1}^{k}\sum_{i=1}^{Nj}\left(Xij-\overline{X}_j\right)^2}{N-k}$

Sum of squares between group is, $s_b^2 = \sum_{j=1}^{k}\dfrac{N_j\left(\overline{X}_j-\overline{X}\right)^2}{k-1}$

To test the hypothesis, Ho: $\mu_1 = \mu_2$,

Find F – ratio $F = \dfrac{s_b^2}{s_w^2}$ Test significance F ratio from the Table,

$$F = \frac{\text{Between group variance}}{\text{Within group variance}}$$

9.4 SUMMARY OF ANOVA

To test the significant difference between k means using the analysis of variance, the following steps are involved

(1) Partition the total sum of squares into two components - a within groups and a between-groups sum of squares, using the appropriate computation formulae.
(2) Divide these sum of squares by the associated number of degrees of freedom to obtain s_w^2 and s_b^2 the within - and between - group mean squares.
(3) Calculate F ratio $\frac{s_b^2}{s_w^2}$ and refer this to the Table of F.

    Consult the Table F associated with the numerator and with (k-1) df and with the denominator with N - k df.
(4) If the probability of obtaining the observed F value is small, say, less than 0.05 or 0.01, under the null hypothesis rejected the hypothesis

ANOVA for the Two Factor Research Design (Two way ANOVA)

The one way ANOVA was used to test the differences between the means of three or more groups that comprise a single independent variable. Conducting the one way ANOVA involves calculating a statistic known as F-ratio, which is the ratio of the two types of variance: between group variance and within group variance.

Effect is statistically significant by calculating the F ratio statistic, a statistic that contains between group and within group variance, before implementing the two-factor research design we must first redefine the term group. In the two-factor research design, a "group" represents a *combination of two independent variables.*

We can assert that between group variance in the two-factor research design comprise three elements: the *Main effect of factor A, the Main effect of factor B* and the *A x B Interaction effect.*

This may be also expressed using the following formula:

Between group variance = Main effect of Factor A + Main effect of Factor B + A x B Interaction effect

There are two important aspects of the relationship between main effects and interaction effects. First, the presence or absence of main effects provides no indication of whether an interaction effect is present or absent and vice versa. Second, whether and how one interprets main effects depends on the presence or absence of interaction effects. If an interaction effect is present, the effects of both independent variables must be considered simultaneously rather than in isolation of each other. If an interaction effect is not present, the two factor design may be treated as if it were two separate single factor designs, one for each main effect.

A significant A × B interaction effect implies that the effect of one independent variable changes at different levels of the other independent variable. To more precisely determine the source of a significant interaction effect, additional analyses must be conducted that break down a larger factorial research design into a number of smaller designs.

Since the calculation of F- value under Two Way ANOVA is a complex process, it can be done using statistical softwares and hence the procedure is not described in this section.

10

Non-Parametric Tests

10.1 WHY NONPARAMETRIC STATISTICAL TESTS?

There are two primary reasons why nonparametric statistical tests may be used in a research study – these reasons relate to how variables have been measured as well as concerns regarding the shape of the distribution of scores in the sample. First, nonparametric statistical tests are used in research situations in which the dependent variable is measured at *a level of measurement other than interval or ratio*. For example, the Chi-square statistic is used for categorical variables, which are variables measured at the nominal level of measurement. Spearman correlation is used to measure the relationship between two variables measured at the ordinal level of measurement.

A second reason for using nonparametric statistical tests is when data have been collected on variables measured at the interval or ratio level of measurement, but there is concern that the sample data are *not normally distributed*. Parametric statistical tests such as the t-test, F-ratio, and Pearson r assume scores are normally distributed. If this assumption is not met, incorrect conclusions may be drawn from statistical analyses conducted on the data. For example, if one or both of the variables used to calculate a Pearson correlation are severely asymmetrical (skewed) rather than symmetrical, the relationship between the two variables may not be linear. As a result, the Pearson correlation does not provide an accurate indication of the relationship between the variables in this sample. In such a situation, a nonparametric statistical test rather than a parametric test may be used to analyze the data.

10.2 EXAMPLES OF NONPARAMETRIC STATISTICAL TESTS

Several parametric statistical tests have a non-parametric alternative. Although these nonparametric tests are designed for use with variables measured at the ordinal or nominal levels of measurement, they can also analyze variables measured at the interval or ratio level of measurement. Researchers may choose to use a nonparametric test if they are concerned about the shape of the distribution of data in their samples, particularly when their sample is small or the sample sizes of the groups differ greatly from one another. In this situation, nonparametric tests are used to lower the possibility of drawing inappropriate conclusions from statistical analyses.

Table: Parametric and Corresponding Nonparametric Statistical Tests

Parametric Test	Corresponding Non-parametric Test
t-test for two independent means	Mann-Whitney test
t-test for dependent means	Wilcoxon matched-paired signed-rank test
One-way ANOVA	Kruskal-Wallis test
Pearson correlation, r	Spearman rank-order correlation

When a continuous variable is in fact normally distributed, the nonparametric test has less statistical power than its parametric counterpart. Stated differently, this means that the nonparametric test is more likely to make a Type II error, which was defined as concluding an effect does not exist when it in fact does. Therefore, using nonparametric tests may be an overly conservative strategy that makes it difficult to detect effects.

10.3 ADVANTAGES OF NON-PARAMETRIC STATISTICS

1) If the sample size is very small, there may be no alternative to using a nonparametric statistical test unless the nature of the population distribution is known exactly.
2) Nonparametric tests typically make fewer assumptions about the data and may be more relevant to a particular situation. In addition, the hypothesis tested by the nonparametric test may be more appropriate for the research investigation.
3) Nonparametric tests are available to treat data which are simply classificatory or categorical i.e., are measured in a nominal scale. No parametric techniques apply to such data
4) Nonparametric tests are available to analyse data which are inherently in ranks as well as data whose seemingly numerical scores have the strength of ranks.
5) Nonparametric tests are typically much easier to learn and apply than parametric tests. Also, their interpretation is more direct than the interpretation of parametric tests.

6) Nonparametric tests are intuitive and are simple to carry out by hand, for small samples at least.
7) Non parametric tests require no or very limited assumptions to be made about the format of the data and they may therefore be preferable when the assumptions required for parametric tests are not valid.

10.4 DISADVANTAGES OF NON-PARAMETRIC TESTS

1) Nonparametric methods may lack power as compared to more traditional approaches. This is a particular concern if the sample size is small or if the assumptions for the corresponding parametric method hold.
2) Nonparametric methods are geared toward hypothesis testing rather than estimation of effects.
3) Tied values can be problematic, when these are common, and adjustments to the test statistic may be necessary.
4) Appropriate computer software for nonparametric methods are limited.
5) Nonparametric tests are less powerful because parametric tests use more of the information available in a set of numbers. Parametric tests make use of information consistent with interval scale measurement, whereas parametric tests typically make use of ordinal information only.
6) Parametric tests are much more flexible comparing to nonparametric tests. There are nonparametric tests to use for certain kinds of interaction comparing with ANOVA, but these are much more limited than the corresponding parametric tests.

In this chapter, some of the nonparametric tests are described such as Chi square test, Mann Whitney test and Sign test.

10.5 CHI-SQUARE (χ^2)TEST

In the chi-square statistic tests the difference between observed frequencies, which is the frequency of a group in the sample of data and expected frequencies, which is the frequency of a group expected to occur in a sample of data.

When the data comprises a single categorical variable, the appropriate statistical procedure is the Chi-square Goodness of fit test, which tests the "fit" between observed frequencies in a set of data and expected frequencies derived from theory of research.

There are two important assumptions of the chi-square statistic: independence of observations and minimum expected frequencies. Independence of observations implies that each observation is independent of all other observations in the set of data. Minimum expected frequencies means that none of the expected frequencies should be equal to zero, and most if not all of the expected frequencies should be greater than 5. When one or more of the expected frequencies are smaller than 5,

Fischer's exact test may be used to analyse the data. If any of the expected frequencies falls between 5 and 10, ***Yates's correction for continuity*** may be used.

When there are two categorical variables, a ***Contingency table*** is created, which is a table whose rows and columns represent the values of categorical variables and whose cells contain observed frequencies for combination of the variables. In this situation, the appropriate statistical test is the ***Chi square test of Independence,*** which tests whether the distribution of frequencies for one variable is either independent or dependent on another variable.

Characteristics of the Distribution of Chi-square Statistics

In order for the probability of any particular value of the chi-square statistic to be determined, it must be located within a distribution of chi-square statistics.

Several aspects of this distribution are important to understand. First, like the t-statistic, F-ratio, and Pearson correlation, there is not just one chi-square statistic distribution; instead, there are different distributions depending on the number of groups that comprise the variable of interest.

Second, because calculating the chi-square statistic involves squared differences between observed and expected frequencies $[(f_0 - fe)^2]$, the value for the chi-square statistic is always a positive number. Consequently, like the F-ratio, the distribution of chi-square statistics is positively skewed rather than symmetrical; as the number of groups comprising the variable of interest increases, the degree of skewness decreases such that the chi-square distribution approaches a normal distribution.

Assumptions underlying the Chi-square Statistic

In addition to the shape of the distribution of chi-square statistics, it is important to discuss two important assumptions on which this statistic is based: the independence of observations and minimum expected frequencies. Each of these two assumptions is discussed below.

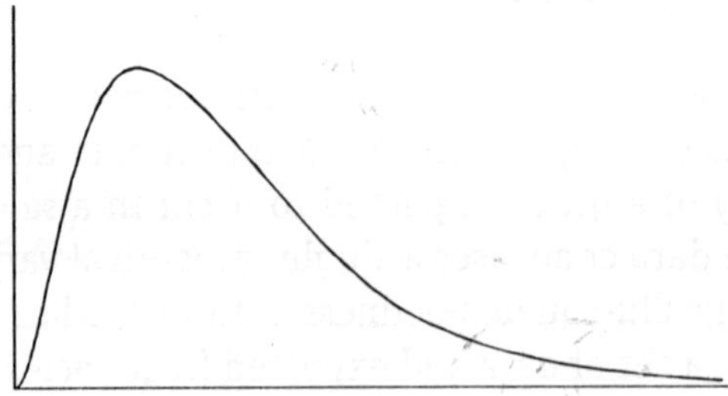

Example Distribution of a Chi-Square Statistic

Independence of Observations

In using the chi-square statistic, it is assumed that each observation in a set of data is independent of all other observations. In other words, an observation cannot be related to any other observation. This assumption, known as the assumption of independence of observations, is typically met by assigning each research participant to only one group; a violation of this assumption would occur if a student could somehow be classified as belonging to more than one type at the same time.

Minimum Expected Frequencies

The size of the sample on which the statistic is based plays a critical role. The smaller the sample size, the less confidence we have that the sample is representative of the population from which the sample was drawn. In using the chi-square statistic, two rules of thumb have been developed to address the effect of small sample sizes on expected frequencies: (1) None of the expected frequencies should be equal to zero, and (2) most if not all of the expected frequencies should be greater than 5. Failure to follow either or both of these two rules of thumb may limit the ability of the chi-square statistic to resemble or approximate the population from which the sample was drawn.

Differential statistics have been developed to use samples with small expected frequencies. For example, when any of the expected frequencies in a sample of data are less than 5, it has been recommended that the Fisher's exact test be used rather than the chi-square statistic (Hays, 1988). On the other hand, if any of the expected frequencies are between 5 and 10, Yates's correction for continuity may be used to test the differences between the observed and expected frequencies.

Chi-Square Goodness-of-Fit Test

To test the differences between the observed and expected frequencies in a set of data, a chi-square statistic is calculated. When the data comprise a single variable, the appropriate statistical procedure is known as the chi-square goodness-of-fit test. It has been given this name because it tests the "fit" between observed frequencies in a set of data and expected frequencies derived from theory or research.

Chi-Square Test of Independence

To test difference between observed and expected frequencies in a set of data, a chi-square statistic is calculated. When the data comprise a single variable, the chi-square goodness-of-fit is conducted. However, when the data consist of two categorical variables, the appropriate statistical procedure is the chi-square test of independence. As its name suggests, the chi-square test of independence allows us to determine whether the distribution of frequencies for one variable is independent of another variable.

Variables are not independent when the distribution of frequencies for one variable changes as a function of a second variable, which implies the two variables are related.

The steps involved in conducting the chi-square test of independence are the same as the other inferential statistical procedures state the null and alternative hypotheses (H_0 and H_1).

- make a decision about the null hypothesis,
- draw a conclusion from the analysis, and
- relate the result of the analysis to the research hypothesis.

As you will see, adding a second categorical variable makes completing the steps for the chi-square test of independence slightly more complicated than the goodness-of-fit test.

Calculation of Chi-square (χ^2)

Calculating the chi-square statistic for the chi-square test of independence involves the same two steps as for the goodness-of-fit test: calculating expected frequencies (f_e) and calculating the chi-square statistics (χ^2). However, the addition a second variable changes how the expected frequencies are calculated.

Calculate Expected Frequencies (f_e)

When there is one categorical variable, the expected frequency for a group is based on a hypothesized proportion based on theory or research. However, when there are two categorical variables, each expected frequency is based on the number participants in the sample. More specifically, because each observed frequency represents a combination of the two variables in a sample of data, the formula for an expected frequency (*fe*) in the chi-square test of independence is based on these combinations:

$$f_e = \frac{(\text{row total})\ (\text{column total})}{\text{N}}$$

where "row total" and "column total" refer to the different rows and columns in a contingency table, and N is equal to the total sample size.

Calculate the Chi-square Statistics (χ^2). Once the expected frequencies have been determined the chi-square statistics is calculated using the same formula as for the goodness-of-fit test. Using the observed and expected frequencies, chi-square statistic is calculated as follows:

$$\chi^2 = \Sigma \frac{(f_0 - f_e)^2}{f_e}$$

Table of observed frequencies (f_0) and Expected Frequencies (f_e) for a Colour Preference Study

		Skin Colour: Black	Skin Colour: White	Raw Total
Hair Colour	Red	$f_0 = 15$ $f_e = \frac{(21)\ (20)}{40} = 10.50$	$f_0 = 6$ $f_e = \frac{(21)\ (20)}{40} = 10.50$	21
	Green	$f_0 = 2$ $f_e = \frac{(9)\ (20)}{40} = 4.50$	$f_0 = 7$ $f_e = \frac{(9)\ (20)}{40} = 4.50$	9
	Gray	$f_0 = 3$ $f_e = \frac{(10)\ (20)}{40} = 5.00$	$f_0 = 7$ $f_e = \frac{(10)\ (20)}{40} = 5.00$	10
	Column Total	20	20	N = 40

$$\chi^2 = \Sigma\frac{(f_0 - f_e)^2}{f_e}$$

$$= \frac{20.25}{10.50} + \frac{6.25}{4.50} + \frac{4.00}{5.00} + \frac{20.25}{10.50} + \frac{6.25}{4.50} + \frac{4.00}{5.00}$$

$$= 1.93 + 1.39 + .80 + 1.93 + 1.39 + .80$$

$$= 8.24$$

In calculating the chi-square value, it is important to be sure to divide each squared difference between an observed and expected frequency ($(f_0 - f_e)^2$ by the expected frequency (*fe*).

For the above study, do you reject the null hypothesis that the two variables are independent of each other? Comparing the value of the chi-square statistic calculated from the sample with the identified critical value,

$\chi^2 = 8.24 > 5.99 \therefore$ reject H_0 ($p<.05$)

In this example, the decision to reject the null hypothesis implies that hair colour and skin colour are related to each other such that a person's preference for the red, green or gray hair colour depends on the type of skin colour as shown.

Determine the Level of Significance

Because in this example the null hypothesis has been rejected, it is appropriate to determine whether the probability of the chi-square statistic is less than 0 .01 (1%). Looking at Table of χ^2, for $df = 2$ and $\alpha = 0.01$, the critical value for the chi-square statistic is 9.21. Comparing the colour preference study chi-square value with this critical value, the following conclusion is drawn:

$$\chi^2 = 8.24 < 9.21 \therefore p < .05 \text{ (but not } <.01)$$

Because the value of the chi-square statistic falls between the 0.05 and0 .01 critical values, its probability is less than 0.05 but not less than 0.01. Consequently, the level of significance for this chi-square statistic would be reported as "$p< .05$".

χ^2 Test as a Test of Goodness-of-Fit

χ^2 test enables us to ascertain how well the theoretical distributions such as Binomial, Poisson or Normal etc. fit empirical distributions, i.e., distributions obtained from sample data. If the calculated value of χ^2 is less than the tabled value at a specified level (generally 5%) of significance, the fit is considered to be good i.e., the divergence between actual and expected frequencies is attributed to fluctuations of simple sampling. If the calculated value of χ^2 is greater than the table value, the fit is considered to be poor.

Examples

Example 1: The following table gives the number of accidents that took place in an industry during various days of the week. Test if accidents are uniformly distributed over the week.

Day	Mon	Tue	Wed	Thu	Fri	Sat	Total
No. of accidents	14	18	12	11	15	14	84

Let the Null Hypothesis H_0. is, "The accidents are uniformly distributed over the week." Under this H_0, the expected frequencies of the accidents on each of these days $= \frac{84}{6} = 14$.

Observed frequency fo	*14*	*18*	*12*	*11*	*15*	*14*
Expected frequency *fe*	14	14	14	14	14	14
(fo–fe)^2	0	16	4	9	1	0

$$\chi^2 = \sum_{i-1}^{n}\left(\frac{(fo - fe)^2}{fe}\right) = \frac{30}{14} = 2.1428$$

Conclusion. Table value of χ^2 at 5% level for (6 – 1 = 5df) is 11.09.

Since the calculated value of χ^2 is less than the tabulated value, H_0 is accepted i.e., the accidents are uniformly distributed over the week.

Example 2. A die is thrown 270 times and the results of these throws are given below:

No. appeared on the die	1	2	3	4	5	6	Total
Frequency	40	32	29	59	57	59	276

Test whether the die is biased or not. **The Null hypothesis H_0.** is "Die is unbiased".

Under this H_0, the expected frequencies for each digit is $\frac{276}{6} = 46$

To find the value of χ^2

fo	40	32	29	59	57	59
fe	46	46	46	46	46	46
$(fo–fe)^2$	36	196	289	169	121	169

$$c^2 = \sum_{i-1}^{n}\left(\frac{(fo-fe)^2}{fe}\right) = \frac{980}{46} = 21.30$$

Conclusion. Tabulated value of χ^2 at 5% level of significance for (6–1 = 5) df is 11.09. Since the calculated value of $\chi^2 = 21.30 > 11.07$ the tabulated value, H_0 is rejected i.e., die is biased.

Example 3. The following table shows the distribution of digits in numbers chosen at random from a telephone directory:

Digits	0	1	2	3	4	5	6	7	8	9
Frequency	1026	1107	997	966	1075	933	1107	972	964	853

Test whether the digits may be taken to occur equally frequently in the directory.

Null hypothesis H_0. The digits taken in the directory occur equally frequency. i.e., there is no significant difference between the observed and unexpected frequency. i.e., there is no significant difference between the observed and expected frequency.

Under H_0, the expected frequency is given by = $\frac{10,000}{10}$ = 1000 to find the value of χ^2

fo	1026	1107	997	996	1075	1107	933	972	964	853
fe	1000	1000	1000	1000	1000	1000	1000	1000	1000	1000
$(fo-fe)^2$	676	11449	9	1156	5625	11449	4489	784	1296	21609

$$\chi^2 = \sum_{i-1}^{n}\left(\frac{(fo-fe)^2}{fe}\right) = \frac{58542}{1000} = 58.542$$

Conclusion. The tabulated value of χ^2 at 5% level of significance for 9 df is 16.919. Since the calculated value of χ^2 is greater than the tabulated value, H_0 is rejected.

i.e., there is significant difference between the observed and theoretical frequency.

Example 6: Let theory predicts the proportion of students in the four groups as per their achievement is, G_1, G_2, G_3, G_4 should be in the ratio 9: 3: 3: 1. In an experiment with 1600 students, the numbers in the four groups were 882, 313, 287 and 118. Does the experimental result support the theory?

The experimental result supports the theory. i.e., there is no significant difference between the observed and theoretical frequency under H_0, the theoretical frequency can be calculated as follows:

$$f_e(G_1) = \frac{1600 \times 9}{16} = 900; \; f_e(G_2) = \frac{1600 \times 3}{16} = 300;$$

$$f_e(G_4) = \frac{1600 \times 3}{16} = 300; \; f_e(G_4) = \frac{1600 \times 1}{16} = 100$$

To calculate the value of χ^2.

Observed frequency f_o	882	313	287	118
Expected frequency f_e	900	300	300	100
$\frac{(fo-fe)^2}{fe}$	0.36	0.5633	0.5633	3.24

$\chi^2 = 4.7266$

Conclusion: Table value of χ^2 at 5% level of significance for 3 df is 7.815. Since the calculated value of χ^2 is less than that of the tabulated value. Hence, H_0 is accepted. i.e., the experimental result supports the theory.

For example, consider four group of students who showed favourable attitude towards a social issue. The observed frequencies are recorded below. As per equal probability hypothesis, the expected frequencies can be calculated as in the third column.

Group	Observed Frequency (f_o)	Expected Frequency (f_e)
A	251	0.25*588 = 147
B	65	0.25*588 = 147
C	194	0.25*588 = 147
D	78	0.25*588 = 147
Total	**588**	**588**

Based on the above calculations, in a sample of 588 students, it is expected that 147 students belong to each of the four types.

Once the observed and expected frequencies have been determined, the next step is to calculate the difference between these two frequencies for each group:

Group	Observed Frequency (f_o)	Expected Frequency (f_e)	Observed – Expected ($f_o - f_e$)
A	251	147	251 – 147 = 104
B	65	147	65 – 147 = – 82
C	194	147	194 – 147 = 47
D	78	147	78 – 147 = – 69
Total	**588**	**588**	**0 (sum of the differences)**

To evaluate the data for the entire sample, we must combine the differences between the observed and expected frequencies across all of the groups. The last column shows us that the differences sum to 0. (104+ –82 + 47 + –69 = 0).

Similar to the differences between group means and the mean of the total sample in the one-way and two-way analysis of variance (ANOVA), the differences between observed and expected frequencies in any set of data will always sum to 0.

These squared differences between observed and expected frequencies are the basis of the chi-square statistic (χ^2). The chi-square statistic tests the difference between the distribution of observed frequencies in a sample and a proposed distribution of expected frequencies. The chi-square statistic calculated in this chapter is some-times called the *Pearson's chi-square statistic*. It is named after Karl Pearson, who also developed the Pearson correlation coefficient.

Group	Observed Frequency (f_o)	Expected Frequency (f_e)	(Observed – Expected)^2 $(f_o - f_e)^2$	$\frac{(f_o - f_e)^2}{f_e}$
A	251	147	$(104)^2 = 10816$	73.58
B	65	147	$(-82)^2 = 6724$	45.74
C	194	147	$(47)^2 = 2209$	15.03
D	78	147	$(-69)^2 = 4761$	32.39
Total	**588**	**588**		**Σ = 166.74**

$$\chi^2 = \Sigma \frac{(f_0 - f_e)^2}{f_e}$$

From the Table of Chi-square, for (c–1)(r–1) = 3×1 = 3df, and for 0.01 level of significance, the critical value for Chi-square is found to be 11.34. Since the obtained value is much higher than the tabled value, chi-square is significant at 0.01 level.

10.6 MANN–WHITNEY U-TEST

This nonparametric test is included under rank sum tests. This is a method based on ranks. It is known as Mann Whitney test, named after the two statisticians who first described in 1947. The test, like other nonparametric tests, does not require rigid assumptions about the populations from which samples are taken. The only assumption needed is that the values of the random variable on which two groups are to be compared are continuously distributed.

The null hypothesis to be tested is that two samples independently taken come from populations having the same mean. The test may be either one or two tailed. It is referred to as U test since the test statistics U is computed from the sample data for testing the null hypothesis. The U test is usually employed when the two independent samples are involved. It can be seen that as the sample size increases, the distribution of U rapidly approaches normal distribution.

Step by Step Procedure

We can take the given samples as an example.

Observed frequency f_o	882	313	287	118
Expected frequency f_e	900	300	300	100
$\frac{(fo-fe)^2}{fe}$	0.36	0.5633	0.5633	3.24

Here, n_1, is the number of individuals in experimental group and n_2 that of control group. For the samples, the U test can be employed as follows:

i) Group n_1 and n_2 are independently selected and $n_1 + n_2$ scores are arranged in an array of descending or ascending order. A rank is assigned to each score according to the magnitude.
ii) Then one of the two samples, say Experimental group is selected which has n_1 observations, and the sum of its ranks is computed. Let it be R_1. The test statistic U can be defined as

$$U = n_1 n_2 + \frac{n_2 (n_2 + 1)}{2} - R_1$$

iii) Similarly, U can be obtained by using the formula

$$U = n_1 n_2 + \frac{n_2 (n_2 + 1)}{2} - R_2$$

Where, R_2 is the sum of the ranks in control group with n_2 observations.

iv) The two formulae may yield two different values of U. What will be actually used is the smaller of the two U values.

v) The larger values is designed as U'. Before employing the test, we should check whether we have found U or U' by comparing it with $\frac{n_1 n_2}{2}$. If the resulting value is larger than $\frac{n_1 n_2}{2}$, it is then U', and the value of U can be obtained by the equation

$$U = n_1 n_2 - U'$$

In our example, $n_1 = 4$, $n_2 = 5$

Let the hypothesis be Ho, "There is no significant difference between experimental and control groups."

Rank all of the values for both samples ***from smallest to the largest.***

Experimental	Rank (E)	Control	Rank (c)
16	8	12	6.5
5	1	7	2
9	3	10	4.5
10	4.5	12	6.5
		17	9
	R_1 = 16.5		**R_2 = 28.5**

Calculate U value for both the samples

$$U_E = n_1 n_2 + \frac{n_1 (n_1 + 1)}{2} - R_1$$

$= 4 \times 5 + 4\,(4+1)/2 - 16.5$

$= \mathbf{13.5}$

$$U_c = n_1 n_2 + \frac{n_1 (n_1 + 1)}{2} - R_2$$

$= 4 \times 5 + 5\,(5+1)/2 - 28.5$

$= \mathbf{6.5}$

From the U Table, find the critical value for the U at 5% level for samples $n_1 = 4$ and $n_2 = 5$

$$U_{critical} = 1$$

Here, the smaller value of U, i.e., 6.5 is greater than U critical. We can reject the null hypothesis. It implies that the experimental group and control group differ significantly.

10.7 SIGN-RANK TEST

The sign test is used to test the null hypothesis that the median of a distribution is equal to some value. It can be used

i) In place of a one-sample test
ii) In place of a paired t-test
iii) For ordered categorical data where numerical scale is inappropriate but where it is possible to rank the observations

The observations in a sample of size n are $p_1, p_2, p_3 \dots p_n$. The null hypothesis is that the population median is equal to some value, Median. Suppose r+ observations are greater than median, Mdn and r– observations are less than Mdn. Values of p which are exactly equal to Mdn are ignored; the sum r+ + r– may therefore be less than n then we will denote it as n′.

Under the null hypothesis we can expect that half the p's to be above the median and half below. Therefore, under the null hypothesis both r+ and r- follow a binomial distribution with probability equal to half and n=n′.

Example

The following are the data for two groups of experimental animals:

Group I:	2	3.6	2.6	2.6	7.3	3.4	14.9	6.6	2.3	2.0	6.8	8.5
Group II:	3.5	5.7	2.9	2.4	9.9	3.3	16.7	6.0	3.8	4.0	9.1	20.9

Apply a Sign test to test the hypothesis that the two samples come from populations with the same median.

In this case the null hypothesis is that the median difference is zero. Actual differences are:

+1.5, +2.1, +0.3, -0.2, +2.6 , -0.1, +1.8 , -0.6, +1.5 , +2.0 . +2.3 , +12.4

Actual median difference is 1.65 hours. We have r+ =9 r_ = 3 , n = 12 , r = max (r, r+) = 9

The two tailed p-value from binomial tables is p = 0.146

We would conclude that there is no evidence for a difference between the two treatments. Note that the Wilcoxon Signed Rank Sum Test would also be appropriate in this case and is a more powerful test because it takes account of the magnitude of the differences as well as the sign.

EXERCISES

1. The following data relate to students in a school of visually challenged:

	Boys	Girls	Total
Method A	16	28	44
Method B	9	37	46
Total	25	65	90

Test the hypothesis that a new teaching method is independent of the gender of the students.

REFERENCES

1. Ferguson, G.A. (1971). *Statistical Analysis in Psychology and Education* (3rd Edn.). Tokyo: Mc Graw Hill.
2. Hays, W.L. (1988). *Statistics* (4th Ed). New York: Holt, Rinehart & Winston.
3. Garrett, H.E. & Woodworth, R.S. (1961). *Statistics in Psychology and Education.* New York: Vakils, Feffer and Simon Ltd.
4. Springer, K. (2010). *Educational Research—A contextual approach*. Chennai: John Wiley & Sons, Inc.
5. Tokunaga, H.T. (2016).*Fundamental Statistics for the Social and Behavioural Sciences*. New Delhi: Sage

11

Introduction to Statistical Package for Social Sciences

Statistical Package for the Social Sciences (SPSS) is a very powerful and user friendly software package for statistical analyses. Anyone with a basic knowledge of statistics

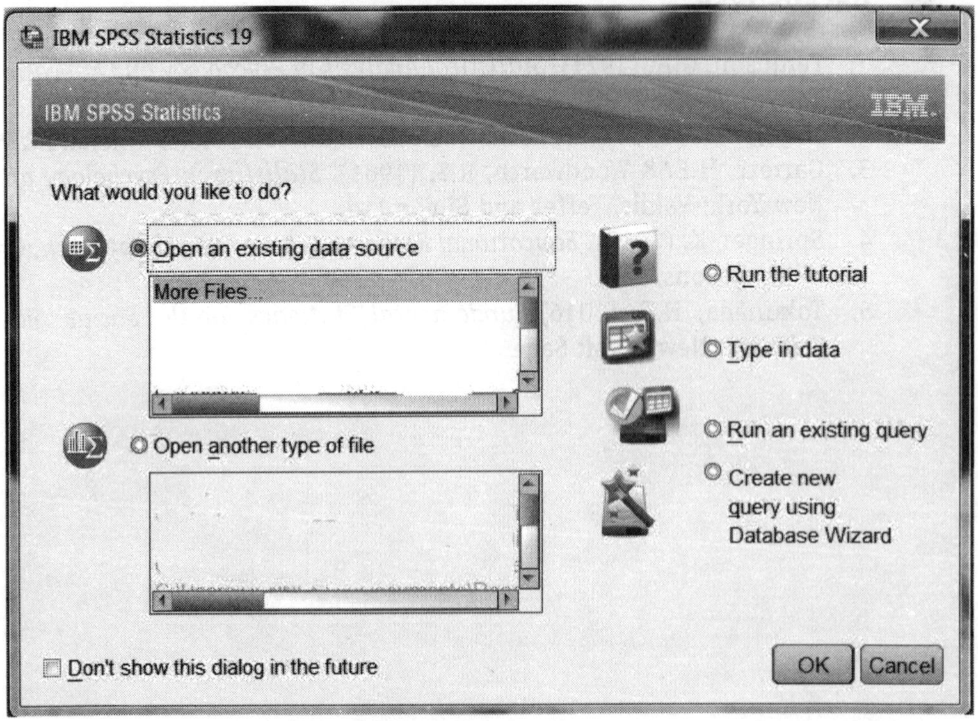

who is familiar with *Microsoft Office* can easily learn how to run very complicated analyses in SPSS with a simple click of the mouse.

The SPSS package can be installed in a computer using a CD or from the network. Once installed, SPSS can be opened like any other Windows-based application by clicking on the *Start* menu at the bottom left hand corner of the screen and clicking on *SPSS for Windows* from the list of programmes.

Above is an illustration of how the first page should appear.

The three most common options at this point are:

a. Run a tutorial – this will take you through a tour of how to use SPSS 10
b. Type in data – this is used to begin entering a new data set
c. Open an existing data source – this is used to work with an existing data set

Each little box is called a Cell. To access a cell, simply move the mouse pointer to the cell and click the left mouse button.

Once you have entered data in a cell, you can either hit ENTER, or one of the direction arrows.

To modify information in a cell, you can also use the **data view "window".** Click on the cell you want to modify and then click the mouse pointer in the data view window (the data presently in the cell should appear once you click on the window). Now you move around in the data by using the direction arrows to delete all or some of the information (by using the DELETE button) or add new information.

Along the side and bottom of SPSS, you will find **"scroll bars"** that allow you to move the view up/down or left/right (by clicking the appropriate arrows at the ends of the scroll bars).

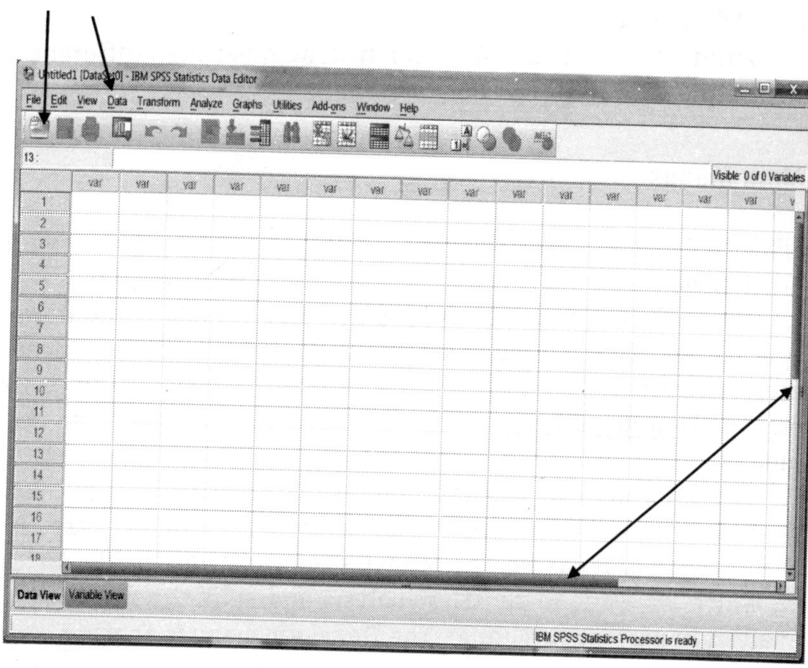

Then, the main data editor window will open where all the data is entered, much like an Excel spreadsheet. A quick look at this screen reveals that it is quite similar to most of the other Windows-based applications such as MS Excel.

At the top of the screen there are different menus, which give access to various function of SPSS. Below this, there is a toolbar, which has buttons for quick access to various functions. The same functions can be performed by choosing relevant options from the menu. At the bottom of the screen we have a status bar. At the bottom of the figure, we can see "SPSS Processor is ready" in the status bar. It implies that SPSS has been installed properly and the license is valid. If the analysis is being run by the process, status bar shows a message to that effect. The programme can be closed by clicking on the close button at the top right hand corner, just like in any other Windows application software.

11.1 SPSS MENU AND TOOLBARS

The main menu is as follows:

File, Edit, View, Window and Help. This is similar to most windows applications.

File – Standard options for opening, saving, printing and exiting

Edit – Standard commands to undo, redo, cut, copy and paste

View – Options for showing/hiding toolbars, displaying values or their labels in Data Editor

Window – Provides option for switching between different SPSS windows

Help – Contains SPSS help system

Main Menus

SPSS 14.0 has 11 main menus, which provide access to every tool of the SPSS programme.

The *File, Edit* and *View* menus are very similar to what we get on opening a spreadsheet. The *File* menu lets us open, save, print and close files and provides access to recently used files. The *Edit* menu lets us do things like cut, copy, paste etc. The *View* menu lets us customize the SPSS desktop. Using the *View* menu we can hide or show the toolbar, status bar, gridlines, etc.

The *Data* menu is an important tool in SPSS. It allow to manipulate the data in various ways. We can define variables, go to a particular case, sort cases, transpose them, merge cases as well as variables from some other file. We can also select cases on which we want to run the analysis and split the file to arrange the output of analysis in particular manner. The *Transform* menu is another very useful tool, which lets us compute new variables and make changes to existing ones.

The *Analyze* menu is the function which lets us perform all the statistical analyses. This have various statistical tools grouped under different categories. The *Graph* menu help to make various types of plots from our data. The *Utilities* menu gives us information about variables and files. It is more of an advertising option for other programmes, as it only briefs us about the additional programmes. Finally, the *Windows* and *Help* menu are very similar to other Windows application menus.

Toolbars

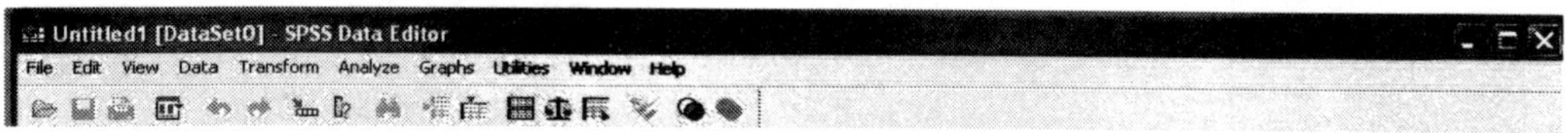

Data – Used to manipulate the data; sort, merge, etc.

Transform – Creation of new variables.

Analyze – Heart of SPSS. This menu provides access to the statistical procedures for analysing your data set. All the items on the analyze menu have sub menus.

Graphs – Provide options to create high quality plots and charts.

Utilities – Used to display information on individual variables

Getting Help

There are Various ways to get help through the SPSS Help system.

i) ***Select Help-Topics.*** Very useful in giving information about how to carry out particular tasks.
ii) ***Select Help-Case Studies.*** Provides hands-on examples of how to create various types of statistical analyses and how to interpret the results.
iii) ***Select Help-Statistics Coach.*** Designed to assist in data analysis by leading you through a series of questions about your data and what you want to do with your data.

11.2 DATA VIEW

There are two different views within the data editor in SPSS. They are data view and Variable view. In SPSS 13.0 and earlier versions, one could open only one data editor window at a time, however in SPSS 14.0, multiple data editor windows can be opened simultaneously, much like Microsoft Excel. At the bottom of the data editor there are two tabs – *Data View* and *Variable View*. When in *Data View*, the data editor works pretty much in the same manner as an Excel spreadsheet. One can enter values in different cells, modify them and even cut and paste to and from an excel spreadsheet.

When in *Variable View*, the data editor window looks as shown in Figure. In addition to entering the values of the variables, we have to provide information about them in SPSS. This can be done when the data editor in *Variable View*. Notice that there are 10 columns in the data editor window.

a) Data View: The data view is used for entering, editing and modifying data. The appearance is very much like an excel spreadsheet.

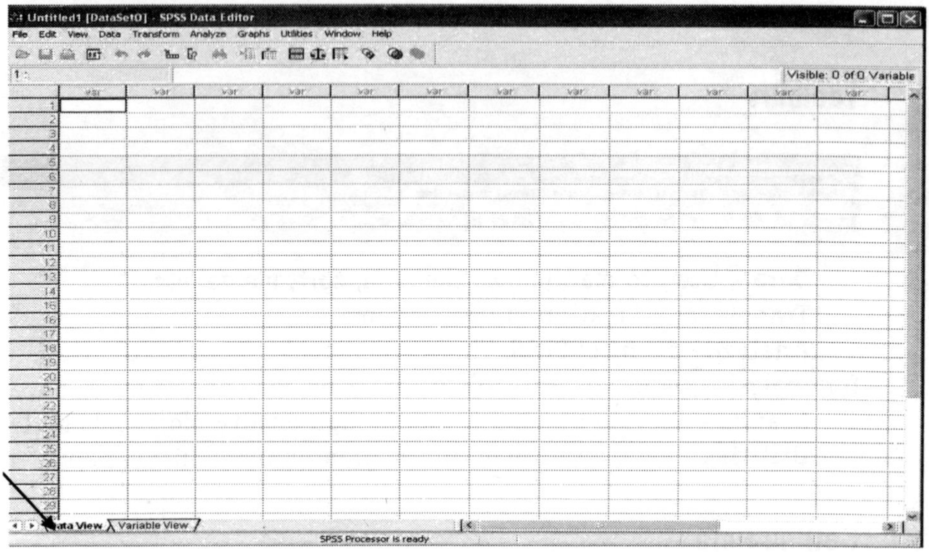

b) Variable View: It is used to define the type of information that is entered in to each column in data view.

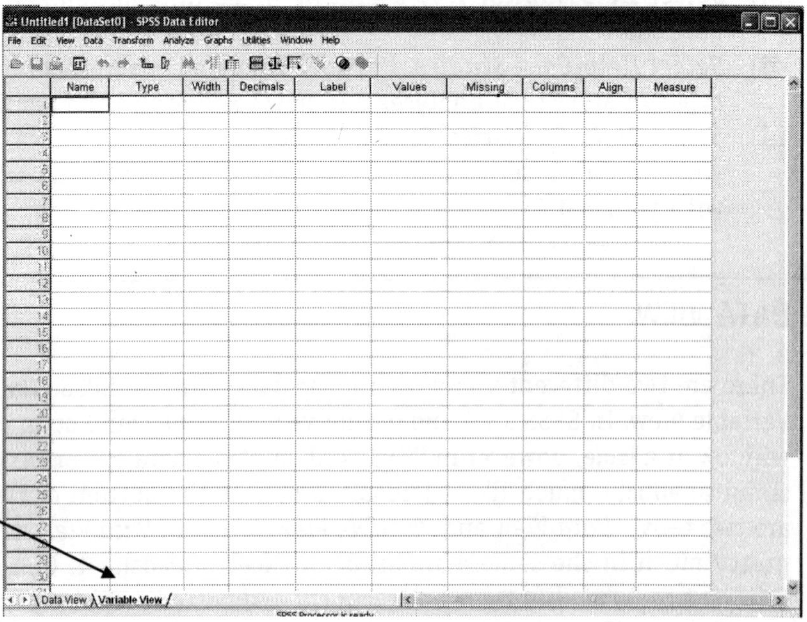

It is used to define the type of information that is entered in to each column in data view.

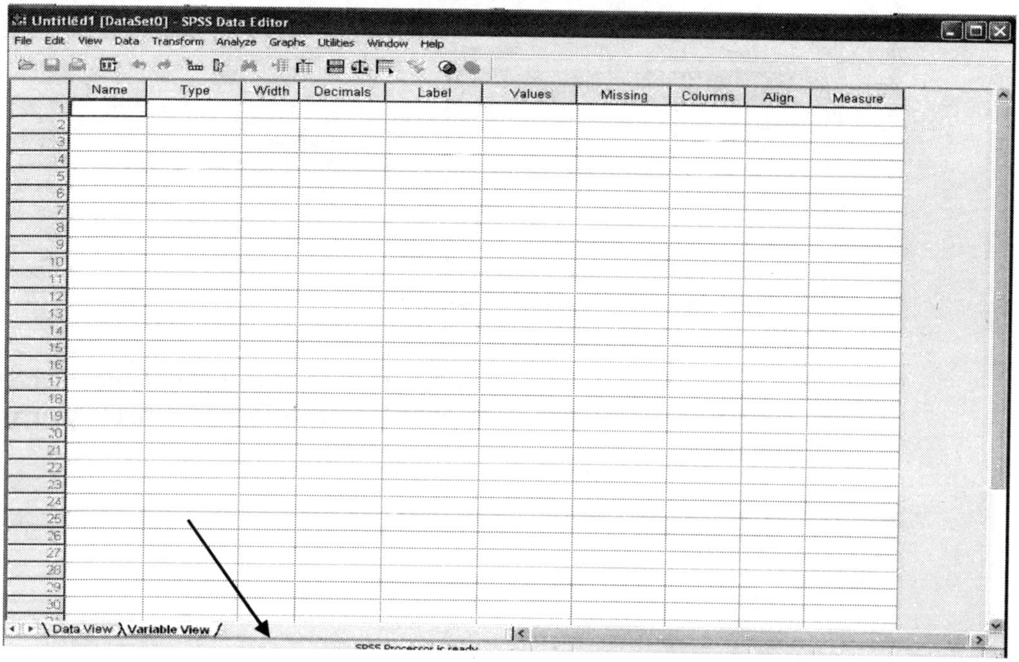

Entering Data:

For entering data in the format we can use either of the two following procedure:

i) **File** – Open an existing SPSS data document (. sav)

Or

ii) **Manually Enter Data:**

1. Define Variables in Variable View
2. Enter data in Data view

Or

ii) **Read Data in** – from Excel

Manually Entering Data – Defining Variables

- In Variable View first name your variable in the Name column
- In the Type column click on the button to reveal the Variable type dialogue box and select the appropriate variable type.

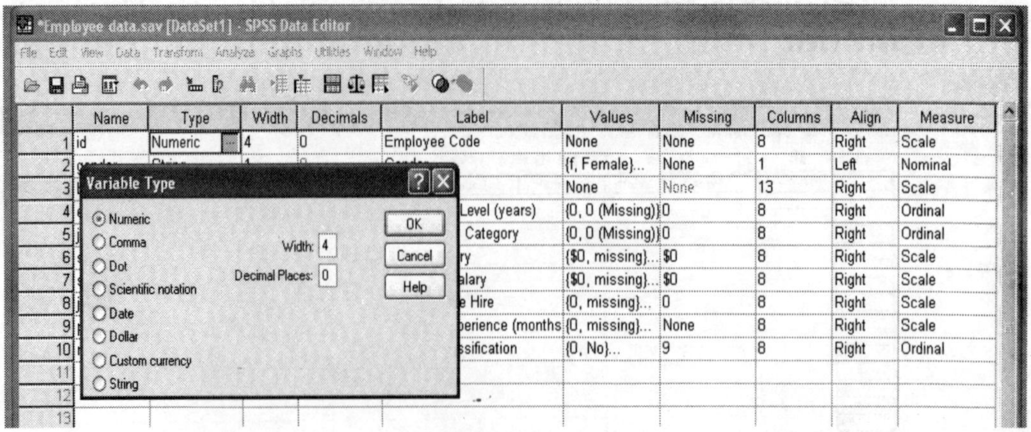

- In the Values column Click on the button to reveal the Values Labels dialogue box. Enter your values and corresponding labels for the variable you are defining if appropriate.

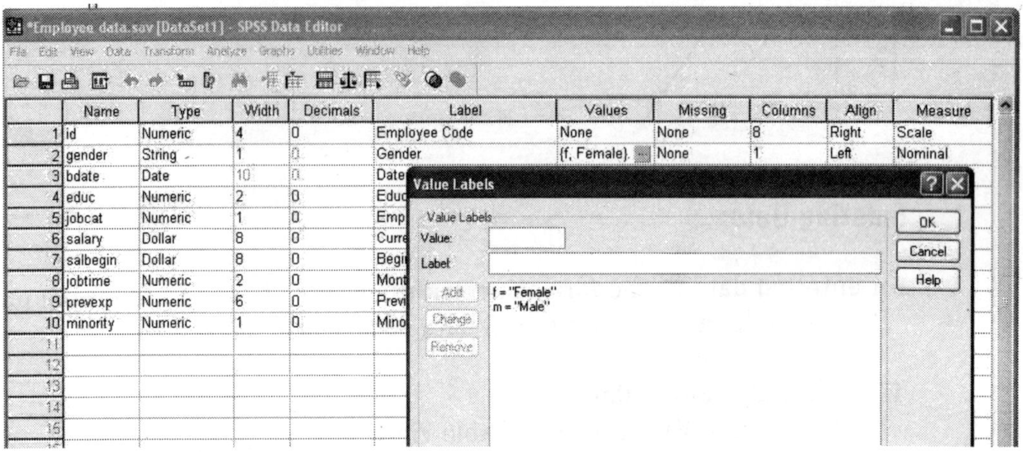

Define "Measure" (specific variable type e.g. nominal/ordinal/scale). Directly enter the data values in **Data View.**

Reading in Data from Excel to SPSS

There are Two options in reading data from Excel to SPSS

1. Copy data in excel and paste directly into the Data View screen
2. Read in an excel file (.xls)

Manually Entering Data – Defining Variables

In Variable View first name your variable in the Name column.

In the Type column click on the button to reveal the Variable type dialogue box and select the appropriate variable type.

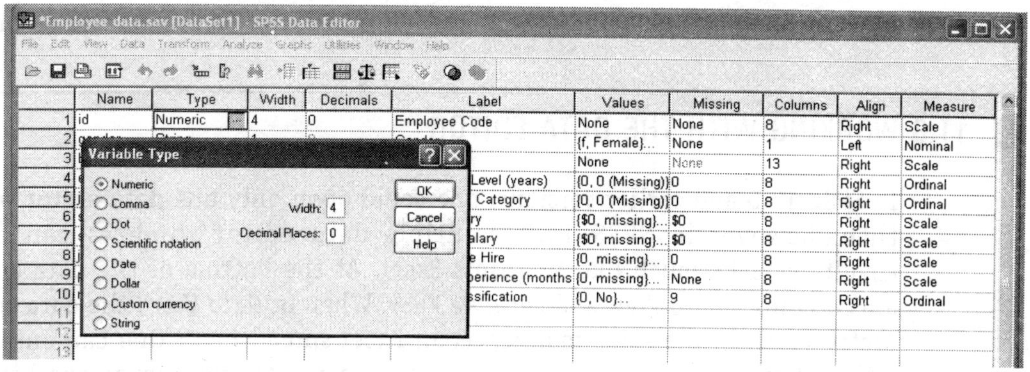

In the Values column Click on the button to reveal the Values Labels dialogue box. Enter your values and corresponding labels for the variable you are defining if appropriate.

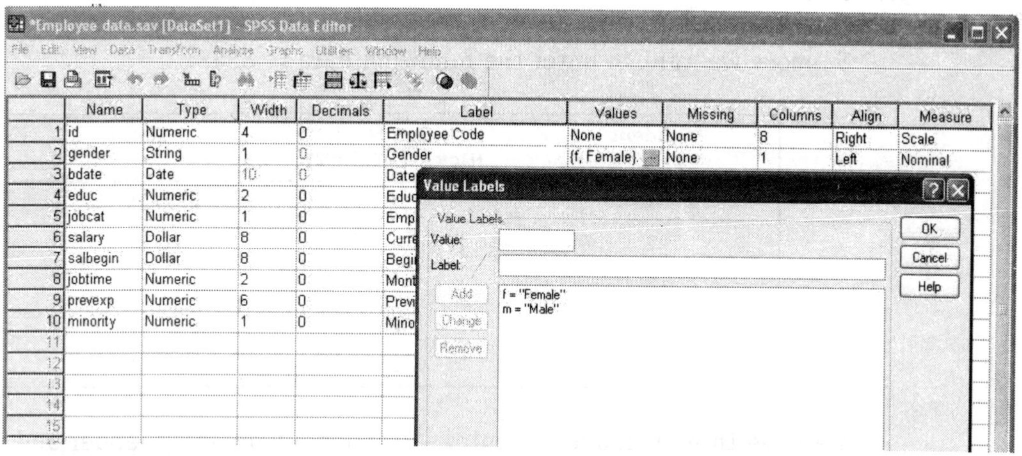

Define "Measure" (specific variable type e.g. nominal/ordinal/scale)
Directly enter the data values in Data View.

Reading in Data from Excel to SPSS

- **Two options:**
  1. Copy data in excel and paste directly into the Data View screen
  2. Read in an excel file (.xls)

  But you must remember that,
- SPSS is much better at handling numeric variables than string variables (categorical data entered as text).

- Therefore, if you want to transfer data from Excel to SPSS it is a good idea to ensure that any categorical data (e.g. yes/no/don't know, male/female, etc.) are entered in Excel as numeric data (codes) rather than text.
- For example, you could always code 'No' as 0 and 'Yes' as 1, and so on.

11.3 WORKING WITH THE DATA EDITOR

In SPSS 13.0 and earlier versions, one could open only one data editor window at a time, however in SPSS 14.0, multiple data editor windows can be opened simultaneously, much like Microsoft Excel. At the bottom of the data editor, there are two tabs – *Data View* and *Variable View*. When in *Data View*, the data editor works pretty much in the same manner as an Excel spreadsheet. One can enter values in different cells, modify them and even cut and paste to and from an excel spreadsheet. When in *Variable View*, the data editor window looks as shown in Figure. In addition to entering the values of the variables, we have to provide information about them in SPSS. This can be done when the data editor in *Variable View*. Notice that there are 10 columns in the data editor window. We will explain the usage of each of them with the help of following small exercise of data entry:

Suppose we want to enter the following data in SPSS:

Student	Gender (Boy = 1, Girl = 2)	Marks
1	1	25
2	1	22
3	2	20
4	2	27
5	2	28

We have three variables to enter – respondent number, gender and marks. The first column in the variable view is *Name*. Earlier versions of SPSS (SPSS 12.0 and earlier) could take a maximum of eight characters starting with a letter to identify a variable. There is no limit for the length of variable name in SPSS 13.0 and SPSS 14.0. In this example, we will name student number as stdnt_id; gender and marks can be named as they are. The next column titled *Type* lets us define the variable type.

Data can be of several types, including numeric, date, text, etc. An incorrect type-definition may not always cause problems, but sometimes does, and should therefore be avoided. The most common type used is "numeric", which means that the variable has a numeric value. The other common choice is "string", which means that the variable is in text format. We cannot perform any statistical analysis on a numeric variable if it is specified as a string variable. Below is a table showing the data types:

Type	Example
Numeric	1,000.01
Comma	1,000.01
String	IIT Mumbai

Since all our three variables are of the numeric type, we select numeric. We can also specify the width of the variable column and decimal places. It only affect the way variables are shown when the data editor is on data view. Click on *OK* to return to the data editor. Next two columns titled *Width* and *Decimals* also allow us to specify these factors for the data view. Please note that these have no impact on the actual values we enter in the data editor, they only affect the display of the data.

Once the variables are specified, you can switch to *Data View* and enter the data. The data editor on entering the data will look as shown in Figure above This data file can be saved just as an MS Word or MS Excel file and reopened by double clicking on the file from its saved location.

11.4 SPSS VIEWER

Whenever we run any command in SPSS, the output is shown in the SPSS Viewer which opens as a separate window. We can also specify the commands to be displayed in log in the Viewer window. This option can be activated by selecting *Display commands in log* option on the dialogue box, obtained by clicking Edit Options Viewer. If this option is selected, a Viewer window will open displaying the save command once we save the file.

The SPSS Viewer window has two panels. The right hand panel shown the actual output and log of commands (if the same is activated), the left hand panel shows an outline of the output shown in the right hand panel. One can quickly navigate through the output by selecting the same from the outline provided in the left hand panel.

The menu items are quite similar to what we find on the Data Editor. However, here we have to additional menus – *Insert and Format*. The *Insert* command can be used to insert headings, comments, page breaks, etc. to organize the output if the output file is very large. The *Format* command has a similar role of arranging the output in a user friendly manner. The *Format* command is rarely used as the output can be copied and pasted onto a MS Word or MS Excel file. The output can also be exported to a variety of other formats. The export option can be accessed under the *File* menu. Clicking on *Export* will produce a dialogue box. On this window we can specify the part of the output we want to export from the drop down menu against *Export*. We can also specify the format of the exported file by selecting a particular file type from the drop down menu below *File Type*. SPSS provides four formats in which the output can be exported-HTML file, Text file, Excel file, and Word/RTF file.

11.5 IMPORTING AND EXPORTING DATA

SPSS gives users a variety of options to open a data file. Click on File Open Data. This will produce a dialogue box.

Here we can choose the types of wile we want to open in SPSS. The file type can be chosen from the drop down menu against *Files of Type* as shown in Figure. SPSS 14.0 can open data files from programmes like Excel, Systat, Lotus, dBase, SAS, STATA in addition to text and ASCII formats. SPSS 14.0 is an improvement as it can support more file types such as STATA files. Which was not possible in earlier versions.

If we want to open data from an Excel file, we select the file and click on *Open*. This will produce a dialogue box as shown in Figue above In this dialogue box, we can specify the specific work sheet from which we want to import the data. We can also read the variable names if the same have been specified in the Excel sheet by clicking on a small box against *Read variable names from the first row of data*. Please note that if the variable namscified in Excel have more than eight characters, SPSS 12.0 and earlier versions would assign a name to them automatically as they do not support variable names bigger than eight characters.

Just as we can import data into SPSS from many formats, we can also save a SPSS data file into different formats. This can be done by clicking on *File Save as* and selecting the required format in the resulting dialogue box.

11.6 GUIDELINES FOR CREATING DATA SETS

A savvy information guru once remarked that data are no more information than 50 tons of cement is a skyscraper. Like a builder that transforms raw materials into a functional skyscraper, statistical data analysis transforms raw data into meaningful and useful information. However, before you can begin to perform your data analysis, you must get that raw data into the software programme.

Decide What Variables You Need and Document them

Your research question determines which variables are needed for your analysis. Researchers should document their variables in a "data dictionary" that contains the important information defining the variables. (Some texts refer to this as a data codebook.)

The table is a document you create during your planning stage. It can be created using a spreadsheet or a word processor. Creating this sample "dictionary" before you collect your data not only forces you to consider which variables you will need in your data set, their types, and how they will be named, but it also provides documentation that can be a valuable tool in performing and interpreting your analyses later on.

Variables may contain values that are either string (such as M and F or A, B, and C) or numbers (such as 0 and 1) whose meaning may not be completely clear. For example, if you coded a *gender* variable as 1 and 2 and *race* as AA, C, H, O, and X, you will want to define those codes in your data dictionary, as illustrated for the *sex* variable.

Note that when you create a categorical variable, you should include an "other" designation when the list does not include an exhaustive collection of possibilities. For example, if you have a variable for "What magazine do you enjoy the most?" and you include a list of 10 magazines. You should also include an "Other" category since the answer for the person filling out the questionnaire may not be in your list. You might also include "None" as an answer for those people who don't read magazines at all.

Design Your Data Set with One Subject (or Observation) Per Line

The vast majority of data analyses require your data set to contain one subject (or entity) per row.

Notice how this data set is designed. Each row contains data from a single subject. Each column contains the data from a single variable. You may be tempted to have multiple rows per subject or to design your data set with subjects as columns, but if you enter your data in that manner, you are only asking for problems later on in most cases. If your data are already in a data set where the subjects are in columns and your variables are in rows.

Each Variable Must Have a Properly Designated Name

Variables names are often short designations such as ID for subject identification number, SSBP (supine systolic blood pressure), and so on. Each statistical package has a set of restrictions for naming variables. The guidelines given here will help you design your data dictionary with variable names that are acceptable to most statistical programmes:

- Variable names should begin with a letter but may also include numbers.
- Keep variable names short. Some programmes require variable names of 8 or fewer characters, although many allow names upto 64 characters in length.
- Do not use blanks or special characters (e.g., !, ?, ', and *).
- Variable names must be unique; no duplicate names are allowed.
- Case usually does not matter. Use any mixture of uppercase and lowercase characters when naming or referring to your variables.

Select Descriptive Labels for Each Variable

Creating a variable label allows you to associate a descriptive label with each variable name. Variable labels are important because they help you more clearly to understand and interpret statistical output, particularly if the variable names are ambiguous, similar, or difficult decipher. Typical names and labels might be the following:

Age	:	Age on January 1, 2005
SBP	:	Systolic blood pressure
S1 to S50	:	Answers to a satisfaction survey
Gender	:	Male or female

Select a Type for Each Variable

Each variable designates a particular type of information. The most commonly used variable types are numeric (a quantitative value) and character (also called string or text and often used for categorical-type data). A good rule of thumb is to designate as numeric only those variables that could be used in a calculation or that are factor or grouping codes for categorical variables. For example, a Social Security number, an ID number, and a telephone number are not really "numbers" that are used in calculations, and they can be designated as character values. This prevents the programme from accidentally using that number in a calculation.

However, it is common to designate dichotomous or grouping variables using numeric codes such as 0 and 1 or 1, 2, and 3, but care must be taken if you use these numbers in calculations. Also, never use codes such as "NA", "Missing", ">100", or "10 to 20" as entries in numeric fields (which may occur if you first enter your data into a spreadsheet such as Excel and then import the data into your statistics programme).

Additional Tips for Categorical (Character) Variables

Keep Case Consistent. For coded variables that are of the character (string or text) type, it is always good advice to maintain consistent case in data values. For example, use all uppercase ('M' and 'F') or all the lowercase ('m' and 'f') for a character-type gender variable. Even when case does not matter for variable names, it does matter for the data contents of the variables. The computer recognizes uppercase *M* as a different character than lowercase *m*. Therefore, if you haphazardly use *M, m, F,* and *f* as data entries, your programme may recognize the data as having four categories instead of two.

Avoid Long Data Codes. Avoid long (and easy to misspell) string variables such as Influenza or Timer Clock Malfunction. Use shortened codes such as FLU and TCM instead. The Label field (see item number 4) can be used for a more complete description of the variable if needed.

Consider Binary Coding. If your data are binary (having only two levels such as male and female), creating a numeric variable that uses the values 0 and 1 may save time later since some analyses (such as regression) require numeric data.

Define Missing Value Codes

Sometimes data are lost or never collected. For example, a test tube is broken, a subject refuses to answer, or a patient fails to show up for an appointment. This type of data should be coded using a missing value code. Always select a missing value code that is an "impossible value" for the particular variable. For example, a – 99 (negative 99) is an appropriate missing value code *for age, weight,* or *height,* since, that value would never be observed for those variables. Specifically, avoid using a blank or a 0 as a missing value code since that may cause confusion as to whether the data value was ever recorded and may cause an incorrect number to be used in a calculation. For a date variable, you can use a "highly unlikely" date such as 11/11/1111 as a missing value code (assuming your data do not include observations from the 12th century!). Once you specify a missing value code in your statistics programmes, the programme will take that missing value into account when performing an analysis.

Consider the Need for a Grouping Variable

A grouping variable is a code that tells the statistical programme how to separate records into groups – such as control group and experimental group. Therefore, if your data set contains information on two or more groups, you should include a variable that specifies the group membership of each observation. A grouping specification could be a single character (A, B, C), numeric (1, 2, 3), or names (CONTROL, TRT1, TRT2).

Preparing Excel Data for Import

A number of researchers choose to first enter data using the Microsoft Excel programme and then subsequently import that data set into a statistical programme. This section describes how you should prepare your data in Excel (or any other spreadsheet or database programme) for importation into a statistics programme. Using the guidelines in the previous section, here are several additional items you should keep in mind.

Row 1 of your Excel spreadsheet should contain only variable names. Do not extend names to row 2.

- Each subsequent row (line) in the Excel spreadsheet should contain data for a single subject or observed entity (in almost all cases).
- Avoid blank rows – it will complicate your import and analysis.
- If you have missing data in your data set, define a missing value code and place that code in any cell that contains missing data.
- Always use date variables with four-digit year formats in Excel. That is, enter the date in Excel using the format 01/01/2005 and not 01/01/05.

- Use your data dictionary (previously discussed), making sure to include all of the variables you will need. Use the specifications in the data dictionary such as codes, formats, and data ranges to determine how you will enter your data into Excel.
- If you have the time or resources, enter your data twice (preferably using two different data entry people) and compare the two files.
- Avoid putting any extraneous text into your spreadsheet. Instead, put explanatory information in other sheets in the same spreadsheet file. Extraneous data in your primary spreadsheet can make importing the data more difficult.

11.7 GUIDELINES FOR REPORTING RESULTS

All the statistics in the world will not get your point across unless you properly report your results. Most journals and publications have guidelines that you must follow when submitting your results. Since a number of guidelines are commonly adopted when reporting statistics results, we present these general rules:

- Computer programmes tend to report statistics to more digits than are necessary or meaningful. A generally accepted practice is to report statistics to one decimal place more than the resolution of the original measurements. For example, if age is measured as integer, report the average age using one decimal place. Occasionally, if precision is important, you may report more decimals. APA guidelines state that two or three significant digits (e.g., digits that convey information and are not merely place holders) are usually sufficient for reporting any statistic.
- For very large numbers, you have to limit the number of significant digits depending on the nature of the measure. For example, if you are reporting the average salary of corporate presidents, you might report a mean of Rs. 723,000 and a standard deviation of Rs. 59,000 rather than Rs. 723,471.20 and Rs. 59,356.10
- Whenever a number is less than 0, place a zero before the decimal. For example, use 0.003 instead of .003.
- When reporting percentages, include the counts as well. For example, "There were 19% males (12 to 64) represented in the sample." Note also that the percentage was rounded. In general, give percentages as whole numbers if the sample size is less than 100 and to one decimal place if the sample size is larger than 100 .
- When using the APA for reporting statistics, use the appropriate abbreviations for common statistical measures. Examples are the following:

  Mean : $M = 1.34$
  Standard deviation : $SD = 3.21$
  Sample size : $N = 203$

p- value	: $p = 0.03$ or $p < 0.001$
t-statistic with degrees of freedom	: $t(13) = 2.12$
Chi-square results	: χ^2 (2, N = 97) = 7.6, $p = 0.02$
F-test	: F (2, 21) = 3.33, p = 0.04

11.8 Guidelines for Creating and Using Graphs

The old adage about a picture being worth a thousand words may be altered slightly when dealing with data. Our revised adage states, "A graph is worth a thousand numbers."

Graphs can be useful for identifying problems or interesting data points in your data set. When reporting your results, graphs are useful in clarifying findings. In general, graphs should be used as an alternative to tables when the table would contain too many entries to be easily understood or when the graph more clearly illustrates your results. Any number of text-books and journal specifications contain guidelines relating to the use of graphs. Here are a few general guidelines for using and reporting graphs:

- Use simple graphs when possible. Avoid three-dimensional graphs since they often distort your message and contain spurious and distracting information.
- Label all plots and axes clearly.
- When creating two or more graphs that will be compared in some way, the range of values for each axis on every graph should be the same. Axes should generally begin with zero if that is the natural minimum. Otherwise, use the minimum value of the measurement as the minimum value for the axis.
- Axis intervals on plots should be equal.
- Use bar charts instead of pie charts.
- Stick with standard charts when possible. Avoid custom complex charts that attempt to display several messages at once.

Opening Data Files for Examples

Once you have downloaded the sample data onto your hard drive, you can open these data files in the SPSS programme using the following steps:

- Begin SPSS. From the main menu select File/Open/Data.
- In the "Look In" option on the open dialog box.
- Select the file to open and click OK. (Or simply double-click on the file name). The data will be opened into the SPSS data grid.
- You are now ready to use that data in an analysis.

You should use the above steps to open designated data files to perform the analyses.

REFERENCES

1. Hays, W.L. (1988). *Statistics* (4th Ed). New York: Holt, Rinehart & Winston.
2. Garrett, H .E. & Woodworth, R. S. (1961). *Statistics in Psychology and Education*. New York: Vakils, Feffer and Simon Ltd.
3. Springer, K (2010). *Educational Research – A contextual approach*. Chennai: John Wiley & Sons, Inc.
4. Tokunaga, H.T. (2016). *Fundamental Statistics for the Social and Behavioural Sciences*. New Delhi: Sage.

Appendix IA
Areas and Ordinates of the Normal Curve

$\frac{x-\mu}{\delta}$	Area under the Curve between m and x	Ordinate (y) of the curve at x
(1)	(2)	(3)
.00	.00000	.39894
.01	.00399	.39892
.02	.00798	.39886
.03	.01197	.39876
.04	.01595	.39862
.05	.01994	.39844
.06	.02392	.39822
.07	.02790	.39797
.08	.03188	.39767
.09	.03586	.39733
.10	.03983	.39695
.11	.04380	.39654
.12	.04776	.39608
.13	.01572	.39559
.14	.05567	.39505
.15	.05962	.39448
.16	.06356	.39387
.17	.06749	.39322
.18	.07142	.39253
.19	.07535	.39181
.20	.07926	.39104
.21	.08317	.39024
.22	.08706	.38940
.23	.09095	.38853
.24	.09483	.38762
.25	.09871	.38667
.26	.10257	.38568
.27	.10642	.38466
.28	.11026	.38361
.29	.11409	.38251
.30	.11791	.38139
.31	.12172	.38023
.32	.12552	.37903
.33	.12930	.37780
.34	.13307	.37654
.35	.13683	.37524
.36	.14058	.37391
.37	.14431	.37255
.38	.14803	.37115
.39	.15173	.36973

(1)	(2)	(3)
.40	.15542	.36827
.41	.15910	.36678
.42	.16276	.36526
.43	.16640	.36371
.44	.17003	.36213
.45	.17364	.36053
.46	.17724	.35889
.47	.18082	.35723
.48	.18439	.35553
.49	.18793	.35381
.50	.19146	.35207
.51	.19497	.35029
.52	.19847	.34849
.53	.20194	.34667
.54	.20540	.34486
.55	.20884	.34294
.56	.21226	.34105
.57	.21566	.33912
.58	.21904	.33718
.59	.22240	.33521
.60	.22575	.33322
.61	.22907	.33121
.62	.23237	.32918
.63	.23565	.32713
.64	.23891	.32506
.65	.24215	.32297
.66	.24537	.32086
.67	.24857	.31874
.68	.25175	.31659
.69	.25490	.31447
.70	.25804	.31225
.71	.26115	.31006
.72	.26424	.30785
.73	.26730	.30563
.74	.27035	.30339
.75	.27337	.30114
.76	.27637	.29887
.77	.27935	.29659
.78	.28230	.29431
.79	.28524	.29200
.80	.28814	.28969

(1)	(2)	(3)
.81	.29103	.28737
.82	.29389	.28504
.83	.29673	.28269
.84	.29955	.28034
.85	.30234	.27798
.86	.30511	.27562
.87	.30785	.27324
.88	.31057	.27086
.89	.31327	.26848
.90	.31594	.26609
.91	.31859	.26369
.92	.32121	.26129
.93	.32381	.25888
.94	.32639	.25647
.95	.32894	.25406
.96	.33147	.25164
.97	.33398	.24923
.98	.33646	.24681
.99	.33891	.24239
1.00	.34134	.24197
1.01	.34375	.23955
1.02	.34614	.23713
1.03	.34850	.23471
1.04	.35083	.23230
1.05	.35314	.22988
1.06	.35543	.22747
1.07	.35769	.22506
1.08	.35993	.22265
1.09	.36214	.22025
1.10	.36433	.21785
1.11	.36650	.21546
1.12	.36864	.21307
1.13	.37076	.21069
1.14	.37286	.20831
1.15	.37493	.20594
1.16	.37698	.20357
1.17	.37900	.20121
1.18	.38100	.19886
1.19	.32298	.19652
1.20	.38493	.19419
1.21	.38686	.19186

(Contd.)

(1)	(2)	(3)
1.22	.38877	.18954
1.23	.39065	.18754
1.24	.39251	.18494
1.25	.39435	.18265
1.26	.39617	.18037
1.27	.39796	.17810
1.28	.39973	.17585
1.29	.10147	.17360
1.30	.40320	.17137
1.31	.40490	.16915
1.32	.40658	.16694
1.33	.40824	.16474
1.34	.40988	.16256
1.35	.41149	.16038
1.36	.41309	.15822
1.37	.41466	.15608
1.38	.41621	.15395
1.39	.41774	.15183
1.40	.41924	.14973
1.41	.42073	.14764
1.42	.42220	.14556
1.43	.42364	.14350
1.44	.42507	.14146
1.45	.42647	.13943
1.46	.42786	.13742
1.47	.42922	.13542
1.48	.43056	.13344
1.49	.43187	.13147
1.50	.43319	.12952
1.51	.43448	.12758
1.52	.43574	.12566
1.53	.43699	.12376
1.54	.43822	.12188
1.55	.43943	.12001
1.56	.44062	.11816
1.57	.44179	.11632
1.58	.44295	.11450
1.59	.44408	.11270
1.60	.44520	.11092
1.61	.44630	.10915
1.62	.44738	.10741
1.63	.44845	.10567
1.64	.44950	.10396
1.65	.45053	.10226
1.66	.45154	.10059
1.67	.45254	.09893
1.68	.45352	.09728
1.69	.45449	.09566
1.70	.45543	.09405

(1)	(2)	(3)
1.71	.45637	.09246
1.72	.45728	.09089
1.73	.45818	.08933
1.74	.45907	.08780
1.75	.45994	.08628
1.76	.46080	.08478
1.77	.46164	.08329
1.78	.46246	.08183
1.79	.46327	.08083
1.80	.46407	.07895
1.81	.46485	.07754
1.82	.46562	.07614
1.83	.46638	.07477
1.84	.46712	.07341
1.85	.46784	.07206
1.86	.46856	.07074
1.87	.46926	.06943
1.88	.46995	.06814
1.89	.47062	.06687
1.90	.47128	.06562
1.91	.47193	.06438
1.92	.47257	.06316
1.93	.47320	.06195
1.94	.47381	.06077
1.95	.47441	.05959
1.96	.47500	.05844
1.97	.47558	.05730
1.98	.47615	.05618
1.99	.47670	.05508
2.00	.47725	.05399
2.01	.47778	.05292
2.02	.47831	.05186
2.03	.47882	.05082
2.04	.47932	.04980
2.05	.47982	.04879
2.06	.48030	.04780
2.07	.48077	.04682
2.08	.48124	.04586
2.09	.48169	.04491
2.10	.48214	.04398
2.11	.48257	.04307
2.12	.48300	.04217
2.13	.48341	.04128
2.14	.48382	.04041
2.15	.48422	.03955
2.16	.48461	.03871
2.17	.48500	.03788
2.18	.48537	.03706

(1)	(2)	(3)
2.19	.48574	.03626
2.20	.48610	.03457
2.21	.48645	.03470
2.22	.48679	.03394
2.23	.48713	.03319
2.24	.48745	.03246
2.25	.48778	.03174
2.26	.48809	.03103
2.27	.48840	.03034
2.28	.48870	.02965
2.29	.48899	.02898
2.30	.48928	.02833
2.31	.48956	.02768
2.32	.48983	.02705
2.33	.49010	.02643
2.34	.49036	.02582
2.35	.49064	.02522
2.36	.49086	.02463
2.37	.49111	.02406
2.38	.49134	.02349
2.39	.49158	.02294
2.40	.49180	.02239
2.41	.49202	.02186
2.42	.49224	.02134
2.43	.49245	.02083
2.44	.49266	.02033
2.45	.49286	.01984
2.46	.49305	.01936
2.47	.49324	.01889
2.48	.49343	.01842
2.49	.49361	.01797
2.50	.49379	.01753
2.51	.49396	.01709
2.52	.49413	.01667
2.53	.49430	.01625
2.54	.49446	.01585
2.55	.49461	.01545
2.56	.49477	.01506
2.57	.49492	.01468
2.58	.49506	.01431
2.59	.49520	.01394
2.60	.49534	.01358
2.61	.49547	.01358
2.62	.49560	.01289
2.63	.49573	.01256
2.64	.49858	.01223
2.65	.49598	.01191

(Contd.)

(1)	(2)	(3)
2.66	.49609	.01160
2.67	.49621	.01130
2.68	.49632	.01100
2.69	.49643	.01071
2.70	.49653	.01042
2.71	.49664	.01014
2.72	.49674	.00987
2.73	.49683	.00961
2.74	.49693	.00935
2.75	.49702	.00909
2.76	.49711	.00885
2.77	.49720	.00961
2.78	.48728	.00837
2.79	.49736	.00814
2.80	.49744	.00792
2.81	.49752	.00770
2.82	.49760	.00748
2.83	.49767	.00727
2.84	.49774	.00707
2.85	.49781	.00687
2.86	.49788	.00668
2.87	.49795	.00649
2.88	.49801	.00631
2.89	.49807	.00613
2.90	.49813	.00595
2.91	.49819	.00578
2.92	.49825	.00562
2.93	.49831	.00545
2.94	.49836	.00530
2.95	.49841	.00514
2.96	.49846	.00499
2.97	.49851	.00485
2.98	.49856	.00471
2.99	.49861	.00457
3.00	.49865	.00443
3.01	.49869	.00430
3.02	.49874	.00417
3.03	.49878	.00405
3.04	.49882	.00393
3.05	.49886	.00381
3.06	.49889	.00370
3.07	.49893	.00358
3.08	.49897	.00348
3.09	.49900	.00337
3.10	.49903	00327

(1)	(2)	(3)
3.11	.49906	.00317
3.12	.49910	.00307
3.13	.49913	.00298
3.14	.49916	.00288
3.15	.49918	.00279
3.16	.49921	.00271
3.17	.49924	.00262
3.18	.49926	.00254
3.19	.49929	.00246
3.20	.49931	.00238
3.21	.49934	.00231
3.22	.49936	.00224
3.23	.49938	.00216
3.24	.49940	.00210
3.25	.49942	.00203
3.26	.49944	.00196
3.27	.49946	.00190
3.28	.49948	.00184
3.29	.49950	.00178
3.30	.49952	.00172
3.31	.49953	.00167
3.32	.49955	.00161
3.33	.49957	.00156
3.34	.49958	.00151
3.35	.49960	.00146
3.36	.49961	.00141
3.37	.49962	.00136
3.38	.49964	.00132
3.39	.49965	.00127
3.40	.49966	.00123
3.41	.49968	.00119
3.42	.49969	.00115
3.43	.49970	.00111
3.44	.49971	.00107
3.45	.49972	.00104
3.46	.49973	.00100
3.47	.49974	.00097
3.48	.49975	.00094
3.49	.49976	.00090
3.50	.49977	.00087
3.51	.49978	.00084
3.52	.49978	.00081
3.53	.49979	.00079
3.54	.49980	.00076
3.55	.49981	.00073

(1)	(2)	(3)
3.56	.49981	.00071
3.57	.49982	.00068
3.58	.49983	.00066
3.59	.49983	.00063
3.60	.49984	.00061
3.61	.49985	.00059
3.62	.49985	.00057
3.63	.49986	.00055
3.64	.49986	.00053
3.65	.49987	.00051
3.66	.49987	.00049
3.67	.49988	.00047
3.68	.49988	.00046
3.69	.49989	.00044
3.70	.49989	.00042
3.71	.49990	.00041
3.72	.49990	.00039
3.73	.49990	.00038
3.74	.49991	.00037
3.75	.49991	.00035
3.76	.49992	.00034
3.77	.49992	.00033
3.78	.49992	.00031
3.79	.49992	.00030
3.80	.49993	.00029
3.81	.49993	.00028
3.82	.49993	.00027
3.83	.49993	.00026
3.84	.49994	.00025
3.85	.49994	.00024
3.86	.49994	.00023
3.87	.49995	.00022
3.88	.49995	.00021
3.89	.49995	.00021
3.90	.49995	.00020
3.91	.49995	.00019
3.92	.49996	.00018
3.93	.49996	.00018
3.94	.49996	.00017
3.95	.49996	.00016
3.96	.49996	.00016
3.97	.49996	.00015
3.98	.49997	.00014
3.99	.49997	.00014

Appendix I(i)
Standard Normal (z) Table

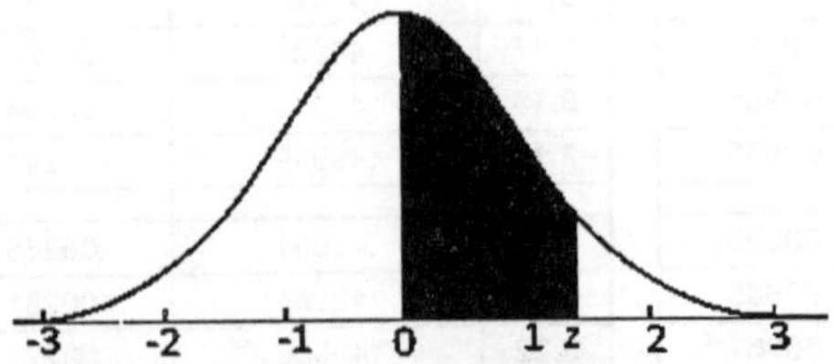

	0.00	0.01	0.02	0.03	0.04	0.05	0.06	0.07	0.08	0.09
0.0	0.0000	0.0040	0.0080	0.0120	0.0160	0.0199	0.0239	0.0279	0.0319	0.0359
0.1	0.0398	0.0438	0.0478	0.0517	0.0557	0.0596	0.0636	0.0675	0.0714	0.0753
0.2	0.0793	0.0832	0.0871	0.0910	0.0948	0.0987	0.1026	0.1064	0.1103	0.1141
0.3	0.1179	0.1217	0.1255	0.1293	0.1331	0.1368	0.1406	0.1443	0.1480	0.1517
0.4	0.1554	0.1591	0.1628	0.1664	0.1700	0.1736	0.1772	0.1808	0.1844	0.1879
0.5	0.1915	0.1950	0.1985	0.2019	0.2054	0.2088	0.2123	0.2157	0.2190	0.2224
0.6	0.2257	0.2291	0.2324	0.2357	0.2389	0.2422	0.2454	0.2486	0.2517	0.2549
0.7	0.2580	0.2611	0.2642	0.2673	0.2704	0.2734	0.2764	0.2794	0.2823	0.2852
0.8	0.2881	0.2910	0.2939	0.2967	0.2995	0.3023	0.3051	0.3078	0.3106	0.3133
0.9	0.3159	0.3186	0.3212	0.3238	0.3264	0.3289	0.3315	0.3340	0.3365	0.3389
1.0	0.3413	0.3438	0.3461	0.3485	0.3508	0.3531	0.3554	0.3577	0.3599	0.3621
1.1	0.3643	0.3665	0.3686	0.3708	0.3729	0.3749	0.3770	0.3790	0.3810	0.3830
1.2	0.3849	0.3869	0.3888	0.3907	0.3925	0.3944	0.3962	0.3980	0.3997	0.4015
1.3	0.4032	0.4049	0.4066	0.4082	0.4099	0.4115	0.4131	0.4147	0.4162	0.4177
1.4	0.4192	0.4207	0.4222	0.4236	0.4251	0.4265	0.4279	0.4292	0.4306	0.4319
1.5	0.4332	0.4345	0.4357	0.4370	0.4382	0.4394	0.4406	0.4418	0.4429	0.4441
1.6	0.4452	0.4463	0.4474	0.4484	0.4495	0.4505	0.4515	0.4525	0.4535	0.4545
1.7	0.4554	0.4564	0.4573	0.4582	0.4591	0.4599	0.4608	0.4616	0.4625	0.4633
1.8	0.4641	0.4649	0.4656	0.4664	0.4671	0.4678	0.4686	0.4693	0.4699	0.4706
1.9	0.4713	0.4719	0.4726	0.4732	0.4738	0.4744	0.4750	0.4756	0.4761	0.4767
2.0	0.4772	0.4778	0.4783	0.4788	0.4793	0.4798	0.4803	0.4808	0.4812	0.4817
2.1	0.4821	0.4826	0.4830	0.4834	0.4838	0.4842	0.4846	0.4850	0.4854	0.4857
2.2	0.4861	0.4864	0.4868	0.4871	0.4875	0.4878	0.4881	0.4884	0.4887	0.4890
2.3	0.4893	0.4896	0.4898	0.4901	0.4904	0.4906	0.4909	0.4911	0.4913	0.4916
2.4	0.4918	0.4920	0.4922	0.4925	0.4927	0.4929	0.4931	0.4932	0.4934	0.4936
2.5	0.4938	0.4940	0.4941	0.4943	0.4945	0.4946	0.4948	0.4949	0.4951	0.4952
2.6	0.4953	0.4955	0.4956	0.4957	0.4959	0.4960	0.4961	0.4962	0.4963	0.4964
2.7	0.4965	0.4966	0.4967	0.4968	0.4969	0.4970	0.4971	0.4972	0.4973	0.4974
2.8	0.4974	0.4975	0.4976	0.4977	0.4977	0.4978	0.4979	0.4979	0.4980	0.4981
2.9	0.4981	0.4982	0.4982	0.4983	0.4984	0.4984	0.4985	0.4985	0.4986	0.4986
3.0	0.4987	0.4987	0.4987	0.4988	0.4988	0.4989	0.4989	0.4989	0.4990	0.4990

Appendix II
t Table with Right Tail Probabilities

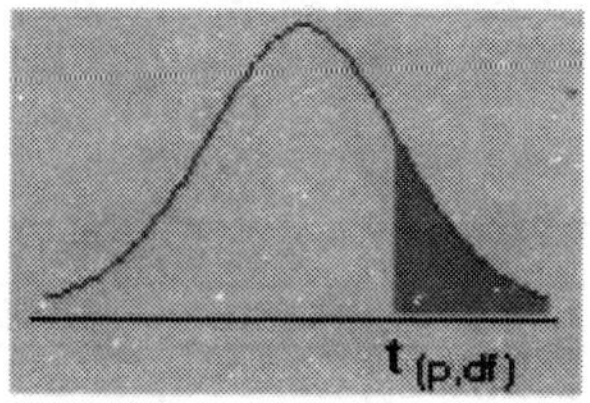

df\p	0.40	0.25	0.10	0.05	0.025	0.01	0.005	0.0005
1	0.324920	1.000000	3.077684	6.313752	12.70620	31.82052	63.65674	636.6192
2	0.288675	0.816497	1.885618	2.919986	4.30265	6.96456	9.92484	31.5991
3	0.276671	0.764892	1.637744	2.353363	3.18245	4.54070	5.84091	12.9240
4	0.270722	0.740697	1.533206	2.131847	2.77645	3.74695	4.60409	8.6103
5	0.267181	0.726687	1.475884	2.015048	2.57058	3.36493	4.03214	6.8688
6	0.264835	0.717558	1.439756	1.943180	2.44691	3.14267	3.70743	5.9588
7	0.263167	0.711142	1.414924	1.894579	2.36462	2.99795	3.49948	5.4079
8	0.261921	0.706387	1.396815	1.859548	2.30600	2.89646	3.35539	5.0413
9	0.260955	0.702722	1.383029	1.833113	2.26216	2.82144	3.24984	4.7809
10	0.260185	0.699812	1.372184	1.812461	2.22814	2.76377	3.16927	4.5869
11	0.259556	0.697445	1.363430	1.795885	2.20099	2.71808	3.10581	4.4370
12	0.259033	0.695483	1.356217	1.782288	2.17881	2.68100	3.05454	4.3178
13	0.258591	0.693829	1.350171	1.770933	2.16037	2.65031	3.01228	4.2208
14	0.258213	0.692417	1.345030	1.761310	2.14479	2.62449	2.97684	4.1405
15	0.257885	0.691197	1.340606	1.753050	2.13145	2.60248	2.94671	4.0728
16	0.257599	0.690132	1.336757	1.745884	2.11991	2.58349	2.92078	4.0150
17	0.257347	0.689195	1.333379	1.739607	2.10982	2.56693	2.89823	3.9651
18	0.257123	0.688364	1.330391	1.734064	2.10092	2.55238	2.87844	3.9216
19	0.256923	0.687621	1.327728	1.729133	2.09302	2.53948	2.86093	3.8834
20	0.256743	0.686954	1.325341	1.724718	2.08596	2.52798	2.84534	3.8495
21	0.256580	0.686352	1.323188	1.720743	2.07961	2.51765	2.83136	3.8193
22	0.256432	0.685805	1.321237	1.717144	2.07387	2.50832	2.81876	3.7921
23	0.256297	0.685306	1.319460	1.713872	2.06866	2.49987	2.80734	3.7676
24	0.256173	0.684850	1.317836	1.710882	2.06390	2.49216	2.79694	3.7454
25	0.256060	0.684430	1.316345	1.708141	2.05954	2.48511	2.78744	3.7251
26	0.255955	0.684043	1.314972	1.705618	2.05553	2.47863	2.77871	3.7066
27	0.255858	0.683685	1.313703	1.703288	2.05183	2.47266	2.77068	3.6896
28	0.255768	0.683353	1.312527	1.701131	2.04841	2.46714	2.76326	3.6739
29	0.255684	0.683044	1.311434	1.699127	2.04523	2.46202	2.75639	3.6594
30	0.255605	0.682756	1.310415	1.697261	2.04227	2.45726	2.75000	3.6460
□	0.253347	0.674490	1.281552	1.644854	1.95996	2.32635	2.57583	3.2905

Appendix III
Table: Chi-Square Probabilities

The areas given across the top are the areas to the right of the critical value. To look up an area on the left, subtract it from one, and then look it up (i.e.: 0.05 on the left is 0.95 on the right)

df	0.995	0.99	0.975	0.95	0.90	0.10	0.05	0.025	0.01	0.005
1	---	---	0.001	0.004	0.016	2.706	3.841	5.024	6.635	7.879
2	0.010	0.020	0.051	0.103	0.211	4.605	5.991	7.378	9.210	10.597
3	0.072	0.115	0.216	0.352	0.584	6.251	7.815	9.348	11.345	12.838
4	0.207	0.297	0.484	0.711	1.064	7.779	9.488	11.143	13.277	14.860
5	0.412	0.554	0.831	1.145	1.610	9.236	11.070	12.833	15.086	16.750
6	0.676	0.872	1.237	1.635	2.204	10.645	12.592	14.449	16.812	18.548
7	0.989	1.239	1.690	2.167	2.833	12.017	14.067	16.013	18.475	20.278
8	1.344	1.646	2.180	2.733	3.490	13.362	15.507	17.535	20.090	21.955
9	1.735	2.088	2.700	3.325	4.168	14.684	16.919	19.023	21.666	23.589
10	2.156	2.558	3.247	3.940	4.865	15.987	18.307	20.483	23.209	25.188
11	2.603	3.053	3.816	4.575	5.578	17.275	19.675	21.920	24.725	26.757
12	3.074	3.571	4.404	5.226	6.304	18.549	21.026	23.337	26.217	28.300
13	3.565	4.107	5.009	5.892	7.042	19.812	22.362	24.736	27.688	29.819
14	4.075	4.660	5.629	6.571	7.790	21.064	23.685	26.119	29.141	31.319
15	4.601	5.229	6.262	7.261	8.547	22.307	24.996	27.488	30.578	32.801
16	5.142	5.812	6.908	7.962	9.312	23.542	26.296	28.845	32.000	34.267
17	5.697	6.408	7.564	8.672	10.085	24.769	27.587	30.191	33.409	35.718
18	6.265	7.015	8.231	9.390	10.865	25.989	28.869	31.526	34.805	37.156
19	6.844	7.633	8.907	10.117	11.651	27.204	30.144	32.852	36.191	38.582
20	7.434	8.260	9.591	10.851	12.443	28.412	31.410	34.170	37.566	39.997
21	8.034	8.897	10.283	11.591	13.240	29.615	32.671	35.479	38.932	41.401
22	8.643	9.542	10.982	12.338	14.041	30.813	33.924	36.781	40.289	42.796
23	9.260	10.196	11.689	13.091	14.848	32.007	35.172	38.076	41.638	44.181
24	9.886	10.856	12.401	13.848	15.659	33.196	36.415	39.364	42.980	45.559
25	10.520	11.524	13.120	14.611	16.473	34.382	37.652	40.646	44.314	46.928
26	11.160	12.198	13.844	15.379	17.292	35.563	38.885	41.923	45.642	48.290
27	11.808	12.879	14.573	16.151	18.114	36.741	40.113	43.195	46.963	49.645
28	12.461	13.565	15.308	16.928	18.939	37.916	41.337	44.461	48.278	50.993
29	13.121	14.256	16.047	17.708	19.768	39.087	42.557	45.722	49.588	52.336
30	13.787	14.953	16.791	18.493	20.599	40.256	43.773	46.979	50.892	53.672
40	20.707	22.164	24.433	26.509	29.051	51.805	55.758	59.342	63.691	66.766
50	27.991	29.707	32.357	34.764	37.689	63.167	67.505	71.420	76.154	79.490
60	35.534	37.485	40.482	43.188	46.459	74.397	79.082	83.298	88.379	91.952
70	43.275	45.442	48.758	51.739	55.329	85.527	90.531	95.023	100.425	104.215
80	51.172	53.540	57.153	60.391	64.278	96.578	101.879	106.629	112.329	116.321
90	59.196	61.754	65.647	69.126	73.291	107.565	113.145	118.136	124.116	128.299
100	67.328	70.065	74.222	77.929	82.358	118.498	124.342	129.561	135.807	140.169

Appendix IV
F Distribution Critical Values

F Distribution critical values for P = 0.05

↓ Denominator														
	Numerator DF													
DF	1	2	3	4	5	7	10	15	20	30	60	120	500	1000
1	161.45	199.50	215.71	224.58	230.16	236.77	241.88	245.95	248.01	250.10	252.20	253.25	254.06	254.19
2	18.513	19.000	19.164	19.247	19.296	19.353	19.396	19.429	19.446	19.462	19.479	19.487	19.494	19.495
3	10.128	9.5522	9.2766	9.1172	9.0135	8.8867	8.7855	8.7028	8.6602	8.6165	8.5720	8.5493	8.5320	8.5292
4	7.7086	6.9443	6.5915	6.3882	6.2560	6.0942	5.9644	5.8579	5.8026	5.7458	5.6877	5.6580	5.6352	5.6317
5	6.6078	5.7862	5.4095	5.1922	5.0504	4.8759	4.7351	4.6187	4.5582	4.4958	4.4314	4.3985	4.3731	4.3691
7	5.5914	4.7375	4.3469	4.1202	3.9715	3.7871	3.6366	3.5108	3.4445	3.3758	3.3043	3.2675	3.2388	3.2344
10	4.9645	4.1028	3.7082	3.4780	3.3259	3.1354	2.9782	2.8450	2.7741	2.6996	2.6210	2.5801	2.5482	2.5430
15	4.5431	3.6823	3.2874	3.0556	2.9013	2.7066	2.5437	2.4035	2.3275	2.2467	2.1601	2.1141	2.0776	2.0718
20	4.3512	3.4928	3.0983	2.8660	2.7109	2.5140	2.3479	2.2032	2.1241	2.0391	1.9463	1.8962	1.8563	1.8498
30	4.1709	3.3159	2.9223	2.6896	2.5336	2.3343	2.1646	2.0149	1.9317	1.8408	1.7396	1.6835	1.6376	1.6300
60	4.0012	3.1505	2.7581	2.5252	2.3683	2.1666	1.9927	1.8365	1.7480	1.6492	1.5343	1.4672	1.4093	1.3994
120	3.9201	3.0718	2.6802	2.4473	2.2898	2.0868	1.9104	1.7505	1.6587	1.5544	1.4289	1.3519	1.2804	1.2674
500	3.8601	3.0137	2.6227	2.3898	2.2320	2.0278	1.8496	1.6864	1.5917	1.4820	1.3455	1.2552	1.1586	1.1378
1000	3.8508	3.0047	2.6137	2.3808	2.2230	2.0187	1.8402	1.6765	1.5811	1.4705	1.3318	1.2385	1.1342	1.1096

Appendix VI
Conversion of 'r' into Fischer's z

r	z'
0.00	0.0000
0.01	0.0100
0.02	0.0200
0.03	0.0300
0.04	0.0400
0.05	0.0500
0.06	0.0601
0.07	0.0701
0.08	0.0802
0.09	0.0902
0.10	0.1003
0.11	0.1104
0.12	0.1206
0.13	0.1307
0.14	0.1409
0.15	0.1511
0.16	0.1614
0.17	0.1717
0.18	0.1820
0.19	0.1923
0.20	0.2027
0.21	0.2132
0.22	0.2237
0.23	0.2342
0.24	0.2448
0.25	0.2554

r	z'
0.26	0.2661
0.27	0.2769
0.28	0.2877
0.29	0.2986
0.30	0.3095
0.31	0.3205
0.32	0.3316
0.33	0.3428
0.34	0.3541
0.35	0.3654
0.36	0.3769
0.37	0.3884
0.38	0.4001
0.39	0.4118
0.40	0.4236
0.41	0.4356
0.42	0.4477
0.43	0.4599
0.44	0.4722
0.45	0.4847
0.46	0.4973
0.47	0.5101
0.48	0.5230
0.49	0.5361
0.50	0.5493
0.51	0.5627

r	z'
0.52	0.5763
0.53	0.5901
0.54	0.6042
0.55	0.6184
0.56	0.6328
0.57	0.6475
0.58	0.6625
0.59	0.6777
0.60	0.6931
0.61	0.7089
0.62	0.7250
0.63	0.7414
0.64	0.7582
0.65	0.7753
0.66	0.7928
0.67	0.8107
0.68	0.8291
0.69	0.8480
0.70	0.8673
0.71	0.8872
0.72	0.9076
0.73	0.9287
0.74	0.9505
0.75	0.9730
0.76	0.9962
0.77	1.0203

r	z'
0.78	1.0454
0.79	1.0714
0.80	1.0986
0.81	1.1270
0.82	1.1568
0.83	1.1881
0.84	1.2212
0.85	1.2562
0.86	1.2933
0.87	1.3331
0.88	1.3758
0.89	1.4219
0.90	1.4722
0.91	1.5275
0.92	1.5890
0.93	1.6584
0.94	1.7380
0.95	1.8318
0.96	1.9459
0.97	2.0923
0.98	2.2976
0.99	2.6467

Appendix VII
Mann-Whitney U table

n1\n2	2	3	4	5	6	7	8	9	10	11	12	13	14	15	16	17	18	19	20
2							0	0	0	0	1	1	1	1	1	2	2	2	2
3				0	1	1	2	2	3	3	4	4	5	5	6	6	7	7	8
4			0	1	2	3	4	4	5	6	7	8	9	10	11	11	12	13	14
5		0	1	2	3	5	6	7	8	9	11	12	13	14	15	17	18	19	20
6		1	2	3	5	6	7	10	11	13	14	16	17	19	21	22	24	25	27
7		1	3	5	6	8	10	12	14	16	18	20	22	24	26	28	30	32	34
8	0	2	4	6	7	10	13	15	17	19	22	24	26	29	31	34	36	38	41
9	0	2	4	7	10	12	15	17	20	23	26	28	31	34	37	39	42	45	48
10	0	3	5	8	11	14	17	20	23	26	29	33	36	39	42	45	48	52	55
11	0	3	6	9	13	16	19	23	26	30	33	37	40	44	47	51	55	58	62
12	1	4	7	11	14	18	22	26	29	33	37	41	45	49	53	57	61	65	69
13	1	4	8	12	16	20	24	28	33	37	41	45	50	54	59	63	67	72	76
14	1	5	9	13	17	22	26	31	36	40	45	50	55	59	64	67	74	78	83
13	1	5	10	14	19	24	29	34	39	44	49	54	59	64	70	75	80	85	90
16	1	6	11	15	21	26	31	37	42	47	53	59	64	70	75	81	86	92	98
17	2	6	11	17	22	28	34	39	45	51	57	63	67	75	81	87	93	99	185
18	2	7	12	18	24	30	36	42	48	55	61	67	74	80	86	93	99	106	112
IS	2	7	13	19	25	32	38	45	52	58	65	72	78	85	92	99	106	113	119
20	2	8	13	20	27	34	41	48	55	62	69	76	83	90	98	105	112	119	127